Migrating from Novell NetWare to Windows NT Server 4

Migrating from Novell NetWare to Windows NT Server 4

Sue Plumley

WILEY COMPUTER PUBLISHING

JOHN WILEY & SONS, INC.
New York • Chichester • Weinheim • Brisbane • Singapore • Toronto

Executive Publisher: Katherine Schowalter

Editor: Marjorie Spencer

Managing Editor: Mark Hayden

Text Design & Composition: SunCliff Graphic Productions

Designations used by companies to distinguish their products are often claimed as trademarks. In all instances where John Wiley & Sons, Inc. is aware of a claim, the product names appear in initial capital or all capital letters. Readers, however, should contact the appropriate companies for more complete information regarding trademarks and registration.

This text is printed on acid-free paper.

Copyright © 1997 by John Wiley & Sons, Inc.

All rights reserved. Published simultaneously in Canada.

This publication is designed to provide accurate and authoritative information in regard to the subject matter covered. It is sold with the understanding that the publisher is not engaged in rendering legal, accounting, or other professional service. If legal advice or other expert assistance is required, the services of a competent professional person should be sought.

Reproduction or translation of any part of this work beyond that permitted by section 107 or 108 of the 1976 United States Copyright Act without the permission of the copyright owner is unlawful. Requests for permission or further information should be addressed to the Permission Department, John Wiley & Sons, Inc.

Library of Congress Cataloging-in-Publication Data

ISBN: 0-471-17563-3

Printed in the United States of America
10 9 8 7 6 5 4 3 2 1

To Geneva and Carlos:
I'm thankful for your patience, support, advice, and for your love.

About the Author

Sue Plumley and her husband, Carlos, have owned and operated Humble Opinions since 1988. Humble Opinions is a consulting firm that specializes in installing, maintaining, and troubleshooting both NetWare and Microsoft networks in southern West Virginia for both small businesses and large corporations; some of the larger corporations include Georgia-Pacific Corporation, Bank One, Columbia/HCA Healthcare Corporation, and the National Mine Health and Safety Academy.

In addition to her business, Sue has written 27 books about operating systems; word processing, spreadsheet, illustration, and e-mail applications; and office suites. She has also co-authored 37 books about networking, operating systems, and software. You can reach Sue via the Internet at splumley@citynet.net.

Contents

Preface	xix
Acknowledgments	xxi
Introduction	xxiii

Part One: Getting Started   1

CHAPTER 1
Commonly Asked Questions   3

NetWare Directory Services (NDS)	4
Administration	4
Client Software	5
Domains	6
Files and File Systems	7
Gateway Services	8
Hardware	9
Login Scripts	9
Migrating from NetWare to NT	10
Networking	11
Printing	12
Protocols	13
The Registry	13
Replication	13
Security	14
Server	14

Users and Groups	17
Utilities and Applications	18
Workstations	19

CHAPTER 2
Concepts Comparison — 21

Basic Operating System Information	21
NT Overview	22
Network Components	24
Directory Services	24
Domains	25
Domain Controllers	26
File System	27
Workstations	28
Protocols	28
Security Issues	29
Users	30
Groups	31
Permissions	31
Accessing the Network	32
Viewing and Accessing Network Resources	33
Mapping Drives	35
Printing Issues	36

Part Two: Understanding NT Networks — 39

CHAPTER 3
Working with Users and Groups — 41

User Manager for Domains	41
Editing Users	44
Groups	46
Profile	47
Hours	49
Logon To	50
Account	50
Dialin	52
Adding and Deleting Users	53
Adding Users	53

    Adding Multiple Users   54
    Deleting Users   54
  Managing Groups   54
    Groups Description   54
    Local Groups   55
    Global Groups   57

CHAPTER 4

Managing Security Policies   63

  Using Rights, Abilities, and Permissions   64
  NT Server Rights and Abilities   65
    Describing Rights and Abilities   65
    Assigning Rights to Users and Groups   68
  Setting Account Policies   71
  Setting Audit Policies   72
  Sharing Resources   74
    Sharing Resources Guidelines   75
    Sharing NT Server Resources   77
    Stopping Sharing   78
    Printer Sharing and Permissions   79
  Granting Permissions   83
    File Systems and Sharing   83
    Directory and File Permissions Described   84
    Setting Permissions   85
    Taking Ownership   87
    Auditing Security Events   88

CHAPTER 5

Managing Print Services   91

  Advantages of the NT Print Server   91
  Planning Your Printing   92
    Print Devices   92
    Print Servers   93
    Access to Printers   93
  Creating Printers   94
  Configuring a Printer   99
    General Tab   100
    Ports Tab   101
    Scheduling Tab   102

Sharing Tab	103
Security Tab	103
Device Settings	104
Configuring Server Properties	106
Forms Tab	106
Ports Tab	107
Advanced Tab	107
Using the Print Queue	108
Font Management	111

Part Three: Planning and Preparing for Migration   113

CHAPTER 6
Preparing for the Migration   115

Server Considerations	115
NT Server Hardware Requirements	115
Protocols and Gateway Service for NetWare	116
Choosing One or Multiple Domains	117
Domain Controllers	117
Single Domain Model	118
Multiple Domain Models	118
Other Elements	121
Workstation Issues	121
Peripheral Factors	123
Application Considerations	124
Backing Up before Migration	124
Preparing for Migrating a NetWare 4.x Server	125

CHAPTER 7
Planning the Migration   127

User Account Comparisons	127
Rights Transferred by Individual User Account	129
Rights Transferred by Policy for Entire Domain	130
Rights Not Transferred	132
Administrative Account Comparisons	132
Supervisors/Admin	132
Workgroup Managers and User Account Managers	134

File Server Console Operator	134
Print Server Operator and Print Queue Operator	135
File and Directory Permissions	135
File Rights	136
Directory Rights	137
File Attributes	139
Next Steps	140

Part Four: Gateway Service for NetWare — 141

CHAPTER 8

Considerations for Using a Gateway Service — 143

Understanding the Gateway Service	143
Core Protocols	144
Network Redirector	144
Sharing Resources	144
Why Use a Gateway?	145
Client Issues	146
Security Considerations	147
Printing through the Gateway	149
NetWare Version Issues	150
Understanding Bindery Context	150
Using the Bindery Context Path	151
Problems with the Gateway Service	152

CHAPTER 9

Using the Gateway Service for NetWare — 155

Installing the Gateway Service	155
Removing Unnecessary Redirectors	156
Creating the NT User	156
Adding the Gateway Service	157
Creating the NetWare User	158
Completing the Gateway Installation	159
Enabling and Configuring the Gateway Service	161
Enabling the Service	161
Setting Permissions	163
Installing NetWare Printers for use with the Gateway Service	167
Installing the NetWare Printer	168

       Sharing a Printer   172
       Setting Permissions   173

Part Five: Migrating the Network   177

CHAPTER 10
Using the Migration Tool with NetWare   179

Last-Minute Checklist   179
Starting the Migration Tool   180
Selecting User and Group Options   184
    Transferring Users and Groups   184
    Methods of Transferring Accounts   185
    Setting Options in the Default Tab   190
    Advanced Option   191
Setting File Options   192
    Transferring Files   192
    Setting the Destination of the Volumes   193
    Selecting Files to Transfer   194
Recording the Migration in a Log   196

CHAPTER 11
Running a Migration   199

Why Run a Trial Migration?   199
Running a Trial Migration   200
Using the LogView Utility   201
Trial Migration Log Files   202
    LogFile.log   203
    Error.log   209
    Summary.log   209
Problem-Solving the Trials   210
    Checklist for General Problems   211
    NetWare Versions and Migration   212
Performing the Migration   212
    Migration Log Files   213
    Viewing User Transfers   214
    Viewing Group Transfers   216
    Viewing Transferred File and Directories   217

Chapter 12
Client Considerations — 221

- Client Software Overview — 221
  - Starting the Network Client Administrator — 222
  - Copying the Installation Files — 223
- Creating the DOS Client — 225
  - Creating a Startup Disk — 225
  - Creating an Installation Disk Set — 228
- Installing the DOS Client — 229
  - Using Installation Disks — 229
  - Using the Startup Disk — 230
  - Attaching to the Network — 230
- Creating a Windows for Workgroups Client — 231
  - Creating the Client Disks — 231
  - Installing the Client to Windows for Workgroups — 232
  - Accessing the Network — 235
- Using Windows 95 Clients — 235
  - Creating the Windows 95 Client Installation Startup Disk — 236
  - Configuring Windows 95 Network Components — 237
  - Connecting to the Network — 240
- Using Windows NT Workstation Clients — 242
  - Configuring the Network — 243
  - Connecting to the Network — 246

Part Six: Migrating the Network — 247

Chapter 13
Tying Up Loose Ends — 249

- Client Clean-Up — 249
  - Logon Scripts — 249
  - Mapping Drives — 250
  - Applications — 251
- Configuring Peripherals — 251
  - Control Panel Overview — 251
  - Setting Up Devices — 253
  - SCSI Adapters — 254
  - Services — 255
  - Tape Devices — 256
  - UPS — 256

Backing Up and Restoring Files ... 257
Macintosh Considerations ... 260

CHAPTER 14
Advanced Network Management — 263

Managing User Profiles ... 264
   Default User Profile Folder ... 264
   Roaming User Profiles ... 266
Using the Server Manager ... 269
   Starting and Exiting the Server Manager ... 271
   Viewing Connections and Resource Usage on the Server ... 272
   Viewing User Sessions ... 273
   Viewing Shared Resources ... 275
   Viewing Resources in Use ... 276
   Alerts ... 276
   Viewing Resources and Users of Selected Computers ... 277
   Sending a Message to a Computer ... 281
Directory Replication ... 281
   Requirements for Replication ... 282
   Configuring the Export Server ... 284
   Configuring the Import Computer ... 286
Diagnosing and Viewing Configuration Information ... 288
   Version ... 288
   System ... 289
   Display ... 290
   Drives ... 290
   Memory ... 291
   Services ... 292
   Resources ... 292
   Environment ... 292
   Network ... 293

CHAPTER 15
Managing Multiple Domains — 297

Working in a Single Domain ... 298
   Single Domain Components ... 298
   Security Considerations ... 298
Multiple Domain Considerations ... 299
   Trust Relationships ... 299

Multiple Domain Models	300
Logging On Multiple Domains	301
Administering Multiple Domains in the User Manager	302
Setting Up Trust Relationships	303
Removing Trust Relationships	306
Administering Users in Multiple Domains	307
Managing the User Rights Policy	308
Using Domain Resources	310
Browsing the Domains	312
Mapping Drives to Domains	312
Sharing Printers	314
Managing Servers and Domains	314
Adding Computers to the Domain	315
Promoting a Domain Controller	317
Synchronizing Controllers	318

Part Seven: Reference 319

APPENDIX A
Installing Windows NT Server and Configuring the Network 321

Preparing to Install	321
Installing NT Server	323
Beginning Setup	323
Configuring a Mass Storage Device	323
Configuring Disk Partitions	324
Directory Considerations	325
Setup Type	325
Licensing	326
Server Type	326
Optional Components	327
Networking Components	327
Starting and Shutting Down NT Server	328
Configuring Network Components after Setup	329
Identification	330
Services	330
Protocols	331
Adapters	332
Bindings	335

APPENDIX B
NetWare to NT Server Terms   337

APPENDIX C
Glossary   341

APPENDIX D   355
Common Problems and Solutions   355

- Installation Problems — 356
  - Floppy Disk Problems — 356
  - CD-ROM Recognition — 356
  - Partitioning the Drive — 357
  - Disk Compression — 357
- Server Crashes and Boot Failure — 357
  - Memory Dump — 358
  - Boot Failure — 358
- Client Software Problems — 359
  - MS-DOS Client — 359
  - Windows for Workgroups — 360
- Problems with Users and Groups — 360
  - Re-creating a User Account — 361
  - Unavailable Features in the User Manager for Domains — 361
  - Deleting a Group — 361
  - Home Directories — 361
  - User Profiles — 362
- Sharing Resources, Rights, and Permissions — 362
  - Sharing Problems — 362
  - Default Permissions — 362
- Printing Problems — 362
  - Parallel Port Problems — 363
  - Serial Port Problems — 363
  - Unsupported Printer — 363
  - Printing from DOS-Based Applications — 364
- Gateway Services — 364
  - Access Denied — 364
  - Gateway Service Unavailable — 364
  - Service Startup Problems — 364
  - Can't See NetWare Server — 365
  - File Attribute Problems — 365

Contents   xvii

Migration Problems	365
Migration Tool Won't Start	365
Can't Select NetWare Server	365
Can't Select NT Server	366
Application Problems	366
Windows 3.x Application Problems	366
Windows for Workgroups Password Problem	366
Memory Allocation Error When Using the MAP Utility	366
NetWare-Aware Application Problems	367
AUTOEXEC.BAT and CONFIG.SYS	367
PIFs	367
TSRs	368
Replication Problems	368
Access Denied	368
Exporting and Importing to All Computers	369
Lost Permissions	369
Domain Problems	369
Multiple Domain Sharing	369
Access Is Denied	370
TCP/IP Configuration	370
Client Problems with IP Addresses and Related Data	370
DHCP Functionality	370
WINS Problems	370
Workstation Disk Space Problems	371
The Registry	371

APPENDIX E
TCP/IP Issues   373

TCP/IP Structure	373
Common TCP/IP Protocols	375
TCP/IP Utilities	375
Installing and Configuring TCP/IP	376
Adding TCP/IP	377
Configuring TCP/IP	378
DHCP Configuration	378
WINS Configuration	381
Domain Name System (DNS) Server	382
TCP/IP Utilities and Services	384

Index   385

Preface

Migrating from Novell NetWare to Windows NT Server 4.0 is a comprehensive, step-by-step guide to migrating your NetWare network to an NT network with skill, efficiency, and confidence. In addition to actual migration instructions, this book includes a detailed checklist that helps you prepare your system and your users for the migration, a handy table listing NetWare terms with the corresponding NT nomenclature, and essential how-to information about using NT Server to manage your network after the migration.

It's perfectly natural to have questions and concerns about the migration. What happens to the Novell file system? What about network security? How will Windows NT Server handle organization of users and groups? NetWare administrators are sure to feel comfortable with their existing network but will be wary of Windows NT Server.

To ease your concerns and answer your questions, I've included information about managing and administering an NT network. In each chapter about NT Server, I've offered comparisons and translations to NetWare for you, as the network administrator, to use as a reference point. Following are some of the NT Server management issues addressed in the book:

- Domain models and multiple domain management
- Client and protocol issues for the server and clients
- User and group creation and management
- Management of security policies, including rights, permissions, and file attributes
- Print services creation, management, and customization
- Creating user profiles and monitoring resource use

Planning for the migration involves many considerations and preparations. I've outlined system requirements for NT Server, the steps to preparing both the server and the clients, including installation instructions for the Windows NT Server operating system and installation of client software.

I've also included information about migrating both NetWare 3.1x or 4.x, discovering and solving problems before the actual migration, and creating and installing client software for MS-DOS machines, and Windows for Workgroups, Windows 95, and NT Workstation computers.

You might think that's a lot of information (it is), and you might think that's all there is to this book. But I also show you how to configure a UPS service, install print drivers, check on the clients, and create user profiles and monitor resource usage.

This book is a comprehensive guide for the network administrator who's considering migration to NT. It answers many of your questions, addresses problems and considerations of a migration, helps you plan for the migration, and guides you in managing your network after the migration.

Acknowledgments

I'd like to thank everyone at John Wiley & Sons for their contribution to this project. I've enjoyed working with Marjorie Spencer and I appreciate her resourceful ideas and unwavering support. I'm also grateful to Frank Grazioli for his guidance. Thanks, too to Margaret Hendrey, who took care of the details and kept me "in touch."

Janice Borzendowski did a great job checking the text for clarity and sense and I also appreciate Jeff Bankston for his help ensuring the technical accuracy of the text. I also want to thank my husband Carlos, who is not only a knowledgeable and experienced Novell CNE, but a remarkable hardware man, as well.

And a special thanks to my agents, Lisa Swayne and Bill Adler, for their inner strength, common sense, and good humor.

Introduction

You might ask: "Why a book about migrating from a NetWare network to NT?" Perhaps you don't think too much of changing networks, especially if you're comfortable with Novell NetWare. The prospect of such a change may be intimidating, even frightening.

So why migrate to Microsoft Windows NT? Because NT is easier to use, performs many of the same functions as NetWare, while offering some additional advantages; has an architecture that adapts well to faster and multiple processors, supports small networks and large enterprises, and provides for a variety of operating systems on the client; the list goes on and on. Further, NT is quickly gaining on NetWare in the market, which means more applications are being developed for NT, and more people are using NT. Windows NT is the smart choice, the choice of the future.

Who Should Use This Book?

This book is written for administrators of small business networks using Novell's NetWare 3.1x or 4.x. Small business networks are those using one or two servers in a single facility as opposed to an enterprise or campus network that may use as many as 50 or more servers between buildings, cities, and even countries. The number of users on a small network, however, might be as many as 1,000 to 2,000; although more likely, the number is nearer to 500. Migrating a huge enterprise would take thousands of hours in planning and preparation; whereas migrating the small business office is a less formidable task.

The network administrator who should use this book may be considering migration, or may be ready to change over to NT. Also, the administrator may be knowledgeable in both NetWare and NT, in only NetWare, or relatively new to both systems. Although this book assumes knowledge of NetWare, you do not need to be a CNA (Certified NetWare Administrator) or a CNE (Certified NetWare Engineer) to understand the terms, procedures, and theories outlined in this book. In short, anyone in charge of a NetWare network who wants migrate to a Windows NT network can do so using this book and the NT Server software.

How to Use This Book

This book is written to help the NetWare network administrator decide whether to migrate to NT and how to migrate to NT most efficiently and effectively. *Migrating from Novell NetWare to Windows NT Server 4.0* is designed to answer your questions, prepare you for migration, help you use NT Server after a migration, and to alleviate your fears.

You may want to read the book from the beginning so you can see how NT compares to NetWare before you perform the actual migration. There are several tasks and procedures you'll need to know before you can perform the migration; Chapters 3 through 5 present those skills.

On the other hand, most administrators probably will read the questions chapter and the concepts chapter (Chapters 1 and 2), then skip to Chapters 7, 8, 9, 10, 11, and 12 to begin the migration immediately. After the migration, you can easily come back to the NT chapters at the beginning of the book to learn how to administer your new network.

What's in This Book?

Specifically, this book is organized in seven parts, which are described briefly here.

Part One: Getting Started

The first part of this book addresses common questions a NetWare administrator may ask about networking with NT and about the actual migration. Answers to questions about domains, file systems, login scripts, printing, protocols, the registry, and so on give an idea of what the rest of the book covers in detail.

Part One also includes a chapter that offers a comparison of fundamental concepts between the two network operating systems. Using NetWare terminology, the text translates theory and procedures to NT Server terms.

Part Two: Understanding NT Networks

Part Two of the book covers network administration with Windows NT, including working with users and groups, managing security, and controlling printing services. These chapters present NT information so that the network administrator can, first, get an idea of how NT works; second, the text gives the administrator the knowledge he or she needs to configure and run the NT network after the migration.

Part Three: Planning and Preparing for the Migration

The third part of the book details information about the hardware requirements needed for the NT server, domain models, workstation issues, application and peripheral considerations, and ideas for backing up before you choose to migrate the server.

Part three compares NetWare's user accounts to NT's; you learn exactly which rights and restrictions transfer during the migration and which don't. Chapter 7 also covers group accounts that transfer and those that don't, and lists the file and directory permissions that move with the migration as well.

Part Four: Gateway Service for NetWare

Part Four of *Migrating from Novell NetWare to Windows NT Server 4.0* describes Microsoft's Gateway Service for NetWare, a method of connecting the NetWare and NT networks before migration. Installing the Gateway Service is both an integral part of the migration and can be an alternative to migration.

You'll see how the Gateway works and why you might want to use it. This part also introduces some problems with the Gateway Service so you can make an intelligent decision about the change.

Also in this part are the step-by-step instructions for installing the Gateway Service, enabling the Service, and even connecting and accessing NetWare printers through the Service.

Part Five: Migrating the Network

"Migrating the Network," Part Five of the book, leads the administrator step by step through the migration. With considerations for both NetWare version 3.1x and 4.x, the chapters include options for migrating, options for file and folder treatment, and information about working with logon scripts. Additionally, one chapter leads the user through a trial migration before the actual procedure and discusses potential problems and their solutions.

Part five also instructs the administrator in creating and installing client software—including MS-DOS, Windows for Workgroups 3.11, Windows 95, and Windows NT Workstation—and connecting to the server.

Part Six: Follow-Up to Migration

You might think the book's conclusion comes with the end of the migration, but this book takes the process a step further. Part Six offers information the administrator can use after migration. The first chapter in this part discusses installation of software, peripheral configuration, cleaning up client machines, and other issues.

The second chapter in this part covers advanced administration, including creating mandatory and roaming user profiles, replicating directories, and using the Server Manager to view connections and resource usage.

The final part chapter covers the use of Windows NT Server with multiple domains and larger networks, for the eventual growth of the network.

Part Seven: Reference

The appendices present reference information for the administrator. Appendix A discusses installation of the NT Server operating system, as well as information about configuring the network components on the server.

Appendix B offers a table of NetWare terms translated to NT terminology so you can quickly interpret NT terms that come up on-screen or in the text.

Appendix C is a glossary that defines many of the terms used in the book. A quick reference to the glossary can save you time and possible misunderstandings.

Appendix D includes many common problems an administrator may run into and some solutions to those problems, including installation problems, server crashes, printing problems, trouble with the Gateway Service and Migration, application troubles, and more.

Appendix E introduces TCP/IP in the NT environment, covering the common TCP/IP protocols, installation of TCP/IP, and configuration of the protocol.

Migrating from Novell NetWare to Windows NT Server 4.0 offers the small business network administrator not only a complete, comprehensive guide to planning and performing a migration, but enough background and post-migration information to make the task attainable.

Introduction

Conventions Used in This Book

Preferably, you will use a mouse with Windows NT; however, to assist those using the keyboard, I've boldfaced the letters in menus, commands, dialog boxes, and so on that you use in combination with the Alt key to access those items. For example, if you want to open the **F**ile menu, you press Alt+F; I've boldfaced the F in File within the instructions.

You'll notice tips and notes scattered throughout the text. These specially formatted elements offer important additions related to the current topic.

Migrating from Novell NetWare to Windows NT Server 4

PART I

Getting Started

1 Commonly Asked Questions

If you're a NetWare network administrator who's considering migrating to Windows NT Server 4.0, you probably have hundreds of questions. How will your files transfer? How do you set up a print server? What kinds of adjustments will your users need to make? What happens to NDS?

This book attempts to answer all of those questions and more. You'll find comparisons of NetWare and NT Server; information about how to perform common network management tasks in NT; facts about NT protocols, clients, and server services, and more.

This chapter initiates the process by anticipating some of the more common questions you may have about the migration, NT procedures, solutions to problems, and more. The questions are presented in boldfaced type and organized under alphabetized topics. Additionally, for your convenience, I've referenced chapters in this book that contain more detailed information on the subject. The chapter name is listed the first time the chapter appears; only the chapter number is listed thereafter.

In this chapter, you find answers to many questions about various subjects, including:

- NDS considerations
- Client software
- Domains
- Hardware
- Migration
- Networking
- Printing

- Security
- Servers
- Workstations

NetWare Directory Services (NDS)

What about my NDS structure? Will I lose my containers?

You can keep your NDS structure, organizing your NT network along the same organizational hierarchy as you use in NetWare 4.x. In NetWare 4.x, you have multiple containers on perhaps an arbitrary number of levels. Each container may include its own set of users and groups. If a name is repeated in multiple file directories or containers, it doesn't cause a problem because the path leading to the name and the name itself constitute a unique identifier.

Now, if you choose to migrate to just one domain from this sort of structure, it will cause you problems. All names, users, and groups will migrate to one, flat space on the NT server that may cause an administrative nightmare. However, you can migrate your various NetWare 4.x containers to multiple domains in NT and solve the problem completely.

Using multiple domains produces the same multilayering effect as organizing your network with containers. Not only can you create separate administrative entities, these entities can be isolated or linked to other entities for the purpose of sharing resources and centralized administration. For information about multiple domains, see Chapter 15, "Managing Multiple Domains." For information about migrating from NetWare 4.x to multiple domains, see Chapter 10, "Using the Migration Tool with NetWare."

Administration

I'm concerned about learning a whole new operating system. Is there any way I can jump in and learn more quickly?

Yes, you can give the Administrative Wizards a try. A Wizard is Microsoft's guide-me process that offers step-by-step instructions to completing tasks. Open the Administrative Wizards by choosing Start, **P**rograms, Administrative Tools, Administrative Wizards. The Getting Started with Windows NT Server dialog box appears. You can choose from the following Wizards:

Add User Accounts
Group Management
Managing File and Folder Access

Add Printer
Add/Remove Programs
Install New Modem
Network Client Administrator
License Compliance

Read each Wizard dialog box and follow the instructions as they are presented to you.

How can I govern the use of resources, such as share directories and files?

The Server Manager enables you to view the shared resources for any computer connected to the server. You also can create new shares and stop sharing resources for any computer you're managing. See Chapter 14, "Advanced Network Management," for more information.

Can I disconnect users from the server remotely?

Yes, from the Server Manager, you can select any computer connected to the server and disconnect that computer. You also can disconnect users from any shared resources they're using. Additionally, you can send a message to the users so they can save their work and close out files before you disconnect them. See Chapter 14 for more information.

Client Software

What do I do about my DOS and Windows 3.1 clients when I migrate servers?

You can upgrade your workstations, of course, and use a Windows NT Workstation or Windows 95 client; or you can attach a DOS and Windows 3.1 workstation to the network and access resources, with the right client. NT Server includes a Network Client Administrator tool that enables you to create the DOS client on a set of installation disks or on an installation startup disk. After you install the DOS client, you can connect the workstation to the NT server. Instructions for creating the client software and for connecting to the server are in Chapter 12, "Client Considerations."

Where do I get a client for Windows 95 machines? Windows NT Workstation machines?

Windows 95 comes with a Microsoft Networks service that enables you to attach to the NT server. You can configure the network components—protocol, client service, and adapters—in the Network dialog box in Windows 95. See Chapter 12 for more information.

Windows NT Workstation doesn't need a client, but you will need to install the adapter and protocol to enable access to the NT server and network. See Chapter 12.

What do I do about my Macintosh clients?

NT includes Services for Macintosh that enables the clients to attach to the network and access files, printers, and other resources. Chapter 13, "Tying Up Loose Ends," covers this subject briefly.

Domains

What is a domain and do I have to use it on my system?

A domain can be a department, one floor of an office building, or even an entire building. A domain is an administrative unit with centralized user account information stored on a primary domain controller that authenticates users. You do not have to organize your network into domains, but it is more beneficial to you and your clients if you do.

Your choice other than using domains is to set up a workgroup, similar to the peer-to-peer Windows for Workgroups setting. In a workgroup, you could of course use servers and clients; however, if your network grows larger than 5 to 10 users, administration could be a nightmare. Additionally, workgroup security is based per computer; each workstation maintains its own set of user accounts.

Administration of a domain makes access to resources more efficient, improves security, enables remote administration, and generally, is more convenient for both clients and administrators. See Chapter 2, "Concepts Comparison," for more information about domains. See Chapter 6, "Preparing for the Migration," for more information about multiple domains.

How do I set up the domain? What if my corporation already has domains and I want to join them with my network?

NT supports various domain types, from simple to complex. You may want to set up one domain for your entire office, keeping administration to a minimum while benefiting from the security and resource-sharing features. You can also set up and/or access multiple domains, preserving security while enlarging the number of resources available to your clients. For information about domain models, see Chapter 6.

How do I manage multiple domains on my network?

NT supplies administration tools for supervising and administering domains. You can set up trust relationships for security purposes; to schedule events, administer services; and so on. See Chapter 15, "Managing Multiple Domains," for more information.

Do members of a domain have to be in the same physical area? Can they be in separate buildings or on separate segments of the network?

Members of a domain do not necessarily have to be in the same office, building, city, or even the same country. A domain is simply a way of organizing groups of clients and servers; you can arrange the users and groups in your domain to the way most convenient and efficient for your work. See Chapter 15 for more information about domains.

Files and File Systems

Do I have to use NT's file system?

No, you do not have to use the NTFS (New Technology File System) on the server. NT also enables you to use the FAT (File Allocation Table) file system. But one advantage of using the NTFS system is the security features it affords you. Additionally, using NTFS, you can better control access to directories, files, and other network resources. NTFS also exploits Windows NT's fault-tolerance features, performs well with very large disk volumes, provides data-logging capabilities, supports long file names as well as DOS 8.3 file names, and provides for file compression. See Chapter 2 or more information about the file systems.

What if some of my client computers are MS-DOS-based using the FAT file system and the NT Server uses the NTFS file system? What kinds of problems will NT's long file names cause the DOS computers?

None whatsoever. When using the NTFS file system, NT does support long file names (up to 256 characters including spaces); in addition, NT creates a DOS-compatible file name to maintain DOS adaptability. Using an algorithm, NT truncates the long file name to fit the eight-character DOS standard, often using a tilde (~) in the name. NT truncates not only file names but directory names as well.

Can I compress files in NT?

Yes, if you're using the NTFS file system on the volume on which you want to compress files. You can use the Explorer to compress files: right-click any directory or file and choose Properties to compress or uncompress. Additionally, remember these guidelines about compression:

- If you compress a directory, all new files created in the directory are automatically compressed.
- When you copy or move a compressed file, it retains its compression state even if you move it to an uncompressed directory.
- Subdirectories within a compressed directory retain their compression unless you specify to uncompress them.

Gateway Services

Why would I want to use a Gateway Service?

You might try the Gateways service for several reasons. Perhaps you're considering a migration to NT but you're not really sure yet. The Gateway gives you a chance to work on the NT server and explore the possibilities before making a decision. For more reasons to use a Gateway Service, see Chapter 8.

Can I use the Gateway Service for NetWare instead of migrating so that I can integrate my NetWare and NT networks?

Yes. The Gateway Service for NetWare provides a bridge between the networks, enabling the NT clients to access NetWare resources without installing the NetWare client software to the workstations. However, using the Gateway Service does tend to slow client access to NetWare resources. For more information, see Chapter 8, "Considerations for Using a Gateway Service."

Do I need to install the Gateway Service before migrating?

Yes. You must install the Gateway Service before NT enables the Migration Tool. Installing the Gateway Service provides NT with a bridge for communication between the two servers and the NWLink transport protocol, also needed for migration. For information about installing and configuring the Gateway Service for NetWare, see Chapter 9, "Using the Gateway Service for NetWare."

If I connect a Gateway between NetWare and NT, can my NT clients print to NetWare printers?

Yes, you can install the printer drivers for the NetWare printers to the NT server, thus making it available to your NT clients. For more information, see Chapter 8.

If I install and use the Gateway Service for NetWare, can I use my NetWare utilities from NT?

Yes, you can use some of the NetWare utilities from within NT; additionally, you can use some NetAware utilities. For more information, see Chapter 8.

Hardware

Do I need a special UPS for the server or will the one I've used with the NetWare server work?

Check with Microsoft's Hardware Compatibility List (HCL) to see if your UPS is listed; make sure to confirm that the serial cable is also compatible. If they are, then you should have no problems. You configure UPS options—including the serial port, the warning signal for a low battery, whether to signal during a power failure, timing for warning messages, and so on—in the Control Panel. For more information, see Chapter 13, "Tying Up Loose Ends."

I use a SCSI adapter. How can I configure it for NT?

NT supports many SCSI devices; check the Hardware Compatibility List to make sure yours is supported. Then, see Chapter 13 for information about viewing SCSI adapters and installing drivers.

How can I use my tape drive with NT to perform backups?

NT supports many tape drives (consult the HCL) and you can configure your tape device in a special utility in NT's Control Panel. Additionally, you can use NT's Backup program to back up an entire drive, a volume, a directory, or just selected files to a tape. See Chapter 13 for more information.

Login Scripts

What about login scripts? Can I transfer my NetWare scripts to NT?

NT doesn't support NetWare's login scripts, and therefore they do not transfer during the migration. NT reduces the need for login scripts by maintaining a list of permanent network connections (as viewed and accessed in the My Computer Window and Explorer) and automatically reinstating them at login.

Additionally, you can set a home directory, map drives, and have NT perform other tasks automatically on login using other tools included with NT Server. You can also create login scripts to run in NT, if you want; and you can use User Profiles to perform many of the services a login script performs. For more information, see Chapter 3, "Working with Users and Groups," and Chapter 13, "Tying Up Loose Ends." For information about user profiles, see Chapter 14, "Advanced Network Management."

Migrating from NetWare to NT

Which files, directories, and/or users migrate?

You choose the files and directories you want to migrate from NetWare to NT. You also select the users and groups to transfer during the migration. See Chapter 10, "Using the Migration Tool with NetWare," for information.

Do Directory Services migrate?

Not directly. You can migrate users and groups within containers but not the containers themselves; you can migrate files and directories. However, if your network depends on a multilayered directory services implementation, you'll want to fully understand how NT performs the same functions before determining whether migration to NT is right for you.

Can I migrate more than one NetWare server at a time?

Yes. When you use the NT Migration Tool, you can choose to migrate one server or multiple servers. See Chapter 10 for information.

When I click the Migrate button, is that it? Can I go back?

First of all, click the Trial Migration button first. The trial migration performs a mock migration and records all activity to logs you can view. In these logs, all transfers are recorded—both successful moves and errors—so you can study them and correct any possible problems you run across. For more information, see Chapter 10, and Chapter 11, "Running a Migration."

Next, if you choose to migrate, you're not losing any data on the NetWare server, you're simply transferring the data to the NT server. You can always go back to NetWare if you change your mind. For more information, see Chapter 13, "Tying Up Loose Ends."

I'm running NetWare 4.1. How much difference is there in migrating from this version than from version 3.1x?

The main difference is in the directory services. You must use bindery emulation in NetWare 4.x servers before you can migrate to Windows NT Server. See Chapter 10 for more information.

Networking

I'm used to using Windows for Workgroups in a workgroup system. How will it work in a domain?

A workgroup situation is less secure and more difficult to centrally manage than a domain setting; workgroups emphasize sharing rather than security. Although you could continue to use workgroups, I suggest you set up a single domain instead. You can integrate the Windows for Workgroups client easily into the NT domain, sharing files, directories, and printers supplied by the server. Additionally, you can limit the client's access to any resources on the server and network by assigning rights and permissions.

How do I add adapters and protocols to the Windows NT Server computer?

You add and configure adapters, protocols, services, bindings, and the computer's identification in the Network dialog box, accessed by choosing Start, Settings, Control Panel. Double-click the Network icon to open the dialog box. For more information, see Appendix A.

Will my NetWare troubleshooting experience help me troubleshoot NT?

That will be difficult, since the two systems are so different; however, if you're at all familiar with previous versions of Windows, you already have a head start in understanding some of how Windows works. Additionally, NT supplies an effective on-line help system (Start, Help), and in that Help, you can often find a troubleshooting section for networking, communications, and other problems you may run across. Finally, many common problems and solutions with NT networking, installation, printing, and so on are listed in Appendix D, "Common Problems and Solutions."

How do I connect to the Internet?

NT Server and NT Workstation software supplies an Internet access application—the Internet Explorer—you can use with your Internet Service Provider to access the Internet. You can also configure an NT Server to act as a DNS, WINS, or other Internet server. Appendix E, "TCP/IP Issues," covers the protocol and utilities briefly; but I suggest you buy a book dedicated to using Windows NT Server with the Internet to thoroughly familiarize yourself with these topics. Stephen A. Thomas' book, *Building Your Intranet with Windows NT* published by John Wiley & Sons, is a great source book for information about using TCP/IP with your network, setting up a name server, using electronic mail, creating a web site, and more.

Printing

Can I set up a dedicated print server?

In NT, you can create a dedicated print server by assigning a member server (a computer running NT Server software but not set up to authenticate users) as a print server. You can set up various configurations of print devices and printers, create printing schedules, manage print queues, and so on. You also can, if your network is small, use a member server as a print server and a file server; or you can use one computer, running the NT Server software as the primary domain controller that authenticates users, the file server, and the print server. For more information, see Chapter 5, "Managing Print Services."

Will I need an additional NT Server license to set up a dedicated print server?

Yes. Any time you install Windows NT Server 4.0 to a computer, you must purchase an additional license for that computer.

Is there one central location in which I set up and manage all of my printers?

You can install all of the printers on the network to one server—the primary domain controller if your network is small or a member server if you want one machine to act as a dedicated file and/or print server. You also can install printers to different servers on the network, and manage them remotely from one central location.

You could, possibly, use a computer running NT Workstation as a print server; however, NT Workstation software limits the number of connections to 10, but if you have a small network, this will work fine.

How does NT deal with the various fonts my client computers use?

NT has an extensive font management system that enables you to use TrueType fonts, printer fonts, bitmapped fonts, and so on. The TrueType fonts are probably the best bet for your clients to use because of their construction; TrueType fonts print exactly the way they look on the screen, no matter which printer you use. For more information about font management, see Chapter 5.

Can I use a computer running NT Workstation as a print server?

You can if you have no more than 10 connections, no Services for Macintosh, or Gateway Services for NetWare attached to the workstation. Unless your network is very small, 10 workstations or less, then you would be better off to use a computer running NT Server software as a print server. For more information, see Chapter 5.

Does NT use spooling as a method of processing documents to be printed?

Yes, in NT the print spooler is a collection of DLLs (Dynamic Link Library) that receive, schedule, and distribute documents to the printer. NT does write the contents of the document to a file on disk and holds it until it can be printed.

Protocols

What protocols can I use with NT Server?

You can use any of several protocols on your NT network, depending on your clients, on gateways you might use, and on additional connections such as the Internet. NT supplies NetBEUI/NetBIOS, an IPX/SPX-compatible protocol, and TCP/IP for connections to many networks. For more information about protocols, see Chapter 2; Chapter 9, "Using the Gateway Service for NetWare"; Appendix A, "Installing Windows NT Server and Configuring the Network," and Appendix E, "TCP/IP Issues."

The Registry

What is the Registry and what can I do with it?

The Registry is a database that maintains configuration information. When you configure any system settings in NT—in the Control Panel, User Manager for Domains, Network dialog box, for example—those changes are recorded in the Registry. The Registry takes place of the INI files used in previous versions of Windows.

You use the REGEDT32.EXE, or Registry Editor, to modify the Registry; but be aware that the Registry Editor is potentially the most dangerous tool you can use in NT. Making changes to the Registry, even the most minor ones, can render your system unstable and even useless. Be very careful when editing the Registry; I suggest you research the tool and the database and become very familiar with its contents before editing or modifying the file.

Editing the Registry is beyond the scope of this book; for information about the Registry, as well as about NT architecture, Remote Access Service, and a host of other networking issues, refer to John Ruley's book *Networking Windows NT 4.0: Workstation and Server, Third Edition*, published by John Wiley & Sons, Inc.

Replication

Is replication the same thing in NT as it is in NetWare?

No. In NetWare 4.x, you replicate a partition, container, and objects to a local server to make logins and authentication easier on another server. In NT, you replicate directories, files, and login scripts as a backup, to keep shared resources current, or to relieve bottlenecks on a server. You can use replication to maintain identical directory trees on multiple servers, to balance the work load, for example. You can replicate directories and files between two domains or within the same computer. For more information, see Chapter 14.

Security

What happens to NetWare rights assigned to users and file attributes when I migrate to NT?

NT also uses rights and attributes (permissions in NT) to restrict users and limit file and directory access. During migration, many rights and attributes are transferred; however some are not. For a complete list of how the Migration Tool handles NetWare rights and attributes, see Chapter 7, "Planning the Migration." For information about NT's user rights and file and directory permissions, see Chapter 4, "Managing Security Policies."

In NT, what's the difference between rights and permissions?

Rights in NT are similar to rights in NetWare. Rights are assigned to users and groups, and control access to the network and its resources. NT's permissions are similar to NetWare's attributes. Permissions are assigned to files, directories, and printers, and limit use of that resource. See Chapter 4 for more information.

Which of my NetWare rights and attributes will transfer during the migration?

Many individual user rights and administrative account rights transfer to NT from NetWare during the migration, and several file and directory attributes move to NT as permissions. For a complete list of NetWare rights and attributes that transfer during the migration, see Chapter 7, "Planning the Migration."

Server

What happens to my NetWare server after I migrate?

The NetWare server remains intact after a migration. You can continue to use the machine by changing its data and/or operating system. If you want to keep the NetWare server and just change data, you can keep it attached to the NT network using the Gateway Service; see Chapters 8 and 9. For more information about using the NetWare server after a migration, see Chapter 13.

Can I migrate containers and their contents from my NetWare 4.1 server?

Yes. You'll have to set the bindery context for each container you want to migrate, but you'll have no problem migrating users and groups from individual containers. You will, however, want to consider checking for duplicate user and group names in multiple containers and changing any you find before you migrate. For information about setting the bindery context, see Chapter 8.

Do I have to use NT's peer-to-peer capabilities? Can't I just set up a client/server system as I do in NetWare?

You can use a computer running NT Server as a dedicated server, and you probably should, if you have many users on the network, if the computer serves as both a file and print server, if you're using Remote Access Services, and so on.

You'll want one computer running NT Server to use as the primary domain server, or the computer that authenticates the users who log on to the network. On this computer, you can manage users and groups, audit security and system activities and events, and otherwise mange the network. You may also want to use this computer as a print server. This computer should be a dedicated server, although you can use it for word processing, e-mail, and other light work-related activities.

As an alternative to using the primary domain controller as a print server, you may want to add another computer that runs the NT Server operating system. This second computer, which does not authenticate users, is called a member server; for a full definition, see the question, "What is a member server," later in this section. Use this computer as a file server, print server, workstation, or all three. For more information about domain servers and member servers, see Chapters 2 and 3. For more information about print servers, see Chapter 5.

If I use the computer running NT Server as a workstation, what kind of security is available?

When you start the NT server, you must log on to the system. Only members of the Administrators group have the rights and abilities to manage the server and the system. When you're finished with the server, you can log off of it; thus in effect, you're locking the server until you or another member of the Administrators group logs back on to the server. For more information about the Administrators and Users groups, see Chapter 4.

If I have all of my users and groups defined on one server for authentication, is there a backup feature in case something happens to the server?

Yes. The first server you install to your network is called a primary domain controller (PDC); this computer contains all user and group accounts and authenticates users when they log on to the network. By rights, you could also use this same server as a print and file server without installing other servers to the domain.

For safety and security purposes, however, you'll most likely want to install a second server to the domain. This second server should be designated as a backup domain controller. NT automatically replicates and updates user and group accounts from the primary domain controller to the backup domain controller. If something should happen to your primary domain controller, you can promote the backup domain controller to the primary status; users continue with their work, none the wiser. You can also use this computer as a file and print server. For more information, see Chapters 2 and 6 and Appendix A.

Do I have to have more than one server in an NT network?

You do not necessarily need more than one server in your NT network; but, depending on the number of users, printers, and other resources, you may want more than one server. The first server (a computer running the NT Server 4.0 software), the one server you must have, as just noted in the previous question, is the primary domain controller, which contains all user and group information and therefore authenticates anyone who logs on to the network. You can also use the PDC as a file and print server, if your network is small and network traffic is at a minimum. There is one PDC per domain.

You can install additional servers—backup domain controllers or member servers—to the network, but you do not have to do so.

What are the requirements for a computer that will run NT Server software?

Basically, the hardware requirements for Windows NT Server are:

- 32-bit x86-based microprocessor or Intel Pentium
- VGA or higher resolution
- 123M minimum free disk space
- 3.5-inch floppy disk drive plus a CD-ROM drive
- 16M RAM recommended
- Mouse or other pointing device recommended
- One or more network adapter cards

Appendix A covers this list in more detail.

If I want, can I add users and groups from a computer other than the NT server?

NT enables you to administer certain tasks from a computer running NT Workstation software or a computer running Windows 95. Using the Network Client Administrator, you can load the necessary files to run the User Manager for Domains, the Event Viewer, and other server tools to an NT Workstation or Windows 95 machine and then administer the network from that workstation. A computer running NT Workstation enables you to install and use more server tools than does a computer running Windows 95. For more information, see Chapter 12.

Can I use a computer running Windows NT Workstation 4.0 as a server on my network?

No. NT Workstation software doesn't contain the necessary tools for administrating a network, such as User Manager for Domains, Network Client Administrator, Server Manager, and so on. Further, a computer running NT Workstation can have only a maximum of 10 connections at any time.

Can I use a computer running Windows NT Workstation 4.0 as a dedicated print server?

Yes, if your network is small and you will have no more than 10 connections to the computer at any one time. The NT Workstation software has the same tools for adding a printer and managing a print queue as NT Server software. See Chapter 5 for more information.

What is a member server?

A member server is a computer running NT Server 4.0 software but not configured as a domain controller; you configure the domain controller when you install the software (see Appendix A). A member server can be used to run applications dedicated to specific tasks, such as a database; or use a member server as a file or print server.

Member servers support up to 256 simultaneous remote connections, have advanced fault tolerance, and enable Macintosh access to Windows NT Server File and Print services.

Users and Groups

Will my NetWare 3.12 groups, such as User Account Managers and Printer Server Operators, transfer during the migration?

Some groups will transfer with similar rights to NT group accounts that are equivalent, but other groups will not. For example, NT has an equivalent to the Print Server Operators group in NetWare and so all users in that group and all rights for that group transfer to NT. On the other hand, NT doesn't have an equivalent for the Print Queue Operator group, so it doesn't transfer that. instead, you can create a Print Queue Operator group in NT and assign the rights and the users you want to place in that group. For more information about groups, users, and rights that transfer during migration, see Chapter 7.

Can I choose the users I want to migrate or must I migrate everyone on the NetWare server?

You can select only the users, groups, and/or files you want to migrate. You also can select to transfer only files or only users and groups, then choose within those parameters the files, users, and/or groups to transfer. For more information, see Chapter 10, "Using the Migration Tool with NetWare."

Can I set a work environment for the users and make it compulsory that they use that environment?

Yes, you can create a work environment—including desktop and application settings, home directories, mouse, display, keyboard, and other settings—as a mandatory user profile. For more information, see Chapter 14, "Advanced Network Management."

Utilities and Applications

Does NT have a utility similar to the File Manager in Windows 3.1?

Yes, the NT Explorer is very similar to the File Manager of previous Windows' versions. Use the NT Explorer to create directories, move and copy files and directories, view file and directory details, share files and directories, open files, map drives, and more. For information about the NT Explorer, see Chapter 4.

Which applications does NT support?

Windows NT supports most Windows 95, Windows 3.x, MS-DOS, and 16-bit character-based OS/2 applications. If an application isn't designed for NT or Windows 95, it may need an updated device driver to communicate with the system; you can generally contact the manufacturer of the application to obtain an updated driver designed to run with Windows NT.

You'll definitely need a device driver specifically designed for NT for most fax, scanner, and terminal emulation cards. You may also need the updated driver for disk maintenance applications and for applications that rely on their own graphic device drivers.

What about running DOS programs in NT?

As with Windows 95, you may find some problems when running DOS applications, especially accounting software or industry-specific applications, in a DOS window with NT; however, you can easily store the data files and program files on the server for DOS and Windows 3.x clients to access.

Workstations

What type of clients can I use with NT Server?

Windows NT Server supports MS-DOS, Microsoft Windows (including Windows NT Workstation 3.51 and 4.0, Windows 95, and Windows for Workgroups 3.11), OS/2, Macintosh, and UNIX. Additionally, NT Server includes a Network Client Administrator utility that enables you to create network installation startup disks for many operating systems and clients, as well as a remoteboot feature that starts MS-DOS and Windows workstations over the network. For more information, see Chapter 2.

What's the difference between NT Workstation 4.0 and NT Server 4.0?

Both NT Workstation and Server are NT operating systems. Although they share a common interface, accessories, programs, utilities, and so on, the major difference between the two is in the administrative tools included with NT Server. NT Server enables the administrator of the network to manage users and groups across the domain (and across multiple domains), to manage security for the entire network, enable print services to clients, measure performance, and monitor activities and errors and other administrative duties. Any security, auditing, and other such features available on NT Workstation apply only to that computer, whereas the features on NT Server apply to the entire network, domain, and multiple domains.

Do I need NT Workstation?

You do not need to run NT Workstation on the client computers when running NT Server on the server machine. You can also use Windows 95 clients, Windows for Workgroups, and so on. You might want to use NT Workstation for its security features, file sharing security, and file access auditing; however, the problem with this operating system is that most clients on your network will probably not be powerful enough or have enough memory to run the software. If you have to upgrade all of your clients, NT Workstation may not be practical.

If you choose to use NT Workstation software, you'll need at least 12M RAM, a 486 or Pentium processor, VGA or higher display, 120M free disk space, 3.5-inch floppy disk drive, mouse, and network adapter card. Naturally, you'll need to purchase the Windows NT Workstation software for the client.

How does a Windows 95 client work with an NT Server network?

Windows 95 and Windows NT 4.0 have similar interfaces and procedures for setting up a network. You can use either the NetBEUI/NetBIOS protocol or TCP/IP. Administering Windows 95 clients is easy; when you designate shared resources, Windows 95 clients can easily attach to the network and access files, directories, and printers. Most NT security features apply to Windows 95 clients as well. For more information about NT Server and clients, see Chapter 8, and Chapter 12, "Client Considerations."

What are the hardware requirements for Windows NT Workstation 4.0 software? Can I install that software to my present client computers or will I have to upgrade?

You'll most likely need to upgrade your client computers to use Windows NT Workstation 4.0 or Windows 95 as client software. For NT Workstation 4.0 or Windows 95, you'll need a 32-bit 486- or Pentium-based microprocessor, VGA or higher-resolution monitor, about 120M free disk space, 16M RAM (recommended), mouse, and network card. Chapter 12 discusses client considerations.

What about using workgroups on my network as opposed to using a domain?

Workgroups and domains exist separately on a Microsoft NT network. A workgroup is a group of computers in which each computer controls its own user and group account information and doesn't share that information with other computers in the group. In a domain, the domain controller (server) controls this information and does share it with other members of the domain, both server and client.

If you're using workgroups instead of a domain, you're using a peer-to-peer network in which the administrator gives up all control to the individual workstations. If you use a workgroup in addition to a domain, the workgroup computers can share each other's resources.

If security is important on your network, you're better off to use a domain instead of workgroups; that way, you have the control over all clients and resources.

Chapter 2, "Concepts Comparison," gives you an overview of Windows NT Server 4.0 plus a comparison of NetWare and NT terminology.

2 Concepts Comparison

As a network administrator, you're familiar with the terminology and concepts you need to manage your NetWare network, and you may be apprehensive about changing operating systems and your network software. You'll be happy to know that many of the Windows NT and NetWare concepts are similar and only the name of the terms have changed.

This chapter defines many concepts and terms for Windows NT by comparing them to NetWare terms you're used to seeing and using. Additionally, translations of NT terminology to NetWare are sprinkled throughout this book. In this chapter, you'll learn about the following:

- Basic Operating System Information
- NT Overview
- Directory Services
- User and Group Accounts
- Security Issues
- Printing Issues

Basic Operating System Information

For your information, the following is a brief synopsis of the two versions of NetWare and of NT, presenting basic information about the operating systems for comparison. Since you're already familiar with NetWare, NT Server is described in greater detail in the next section, throughout this chapter, and throughout the book.

NetWare 3.1x is a 32-bit operating system that runs on 80386 processors and later. Version 3.1x is suitable for large, multisegment networks. Also, version 3.1x can access up to 4GB of RAM and up to 32TB of storage. Disk mirroring, disk duplexing, and UPS monitoring (Uninterrupted Power Source) are all available with this network software.

NetWare 4.x adds to the 3.1x advantages, support for optical disks, CD-ROMs, data compression, and improved login security mechanisms. In addition, version 4.x replaces the bindery of previous versions with NDS (NetWare Directory Services) . Version 4.x is suitable for larger, multisegment internetworks, and it includes a set of user and administrator utilities that feature a graphical user interface.

Novell has also added features to ensure the integrity of data on the network to version 4.x, including protecting data against surface defects that develop on the disk and storing redundant copies of system data, such as file indices, file allocation tables, disk duplexing, disk mirroring, and RAID (Redundant Array of Inexpensive Disks) techniques.

Windows NT Server is a 32-bit, multitasking operating system. NT requires 16MB RAM and an 80486/25 processor or higher, and supports computers with up to four microprocessors. NT is also is suitable for larger, multisegment internetworks. For a complete list of hardware and memory requirements, see Appendix A, "Installing Windows NT Server and Configuring the Network."

TIP: Windows NT can also run on an RISC-based (Reduced Instruction Set Computing) microprocessor such as the MIPS (Million of Instructions Per Second)1 R4x00, Digital Alpha AXP, or a powerPC.

NT contains a graphical user interface and can run Windows and DOS applications, as well as OS/2 16-bit character-based applications. Of course, it also can run 32-bit apps designed specifically for NT 4.0 and Windows 95. C2 is the NT security level, which requires an individual level of login by password, with an audit mechanism (also found in NetWare). In addition to the NTFS (New Technology File System), NT also supports FAT (File Allocation Table) and HPFS (High Performance File System) file systems, as well as multiprocessing and peer-to-peer networking. NT Server provides centralized network management and security functions, disk mirroring, disk duplexing, RAID, and UPS monitoring.

NT Overview

Windows NT Server has changed from previous PC-based server products in architecture, functions, and features. Support for multiple processors, multitasking,

Concepts Comparison

event logging, and more make NT more suitable for today's computers and for the future.

> **Note:** Microsoft features two NT operating systems: NT Server and NT Workstation. Although both software packages look and act similarly, NT Server offers utilities and tools for working on a network, controlling network and server access, sharing resources, managing users, and so on. NT Workstation is client software, similar to Windows 95 or Windows for Workgroups. In this book, NT refers to NT Server and the NT network, unless specifically written as NT Workstation.

NT's architecture isn't based on any processor; it is not specifically designed to implement on an x86 chip. Independent of any processor's architecture, NT Server can be easily installed to a RISC or a PC. When the network needs a bigger server, therefore, the administrator can purchase a simple, fast, streamlined machine that has been designed to act as a LAN (Local Area Network) server to provide service to hundreds of users.

In addition to providing support for faster processors, NT's design sustains up to four processors. Whether you're using one processor or more, NT also provides for true multitasking, meaning one machine can run several different programs at once. Not only is NT's multitasking preemptive and priority-driven, it also supports multithreaded programs, which means faster screen redraw and more efficient use of your programs. This applies to both NT Server and NT Workstation.

> **Note:** NT includes a specially-written Hardware Abstraction Layer (HAL) included in the software that enables NT Server to support up to 16 processors. The HAL is a small piece of the NT code that is machine-specific and controls the part of the operating system that implements NT on a new processor type.

NT Server also offers many advantages to the enterprise networks using many servers and workstations (see Figure 2.1). Following are just a few of those advantages:

- Remote access service offers support for call-in connections to the network (Windows NT Workstation, Windows for Workgroups 3.11, and Windows 95 include the client software for remote access service).
- Event logging and auditing keep track of who logs on to the network and which resources they use; in addition to security issues, you can view an applications log and a problems log to review any errors or other questions about the network.

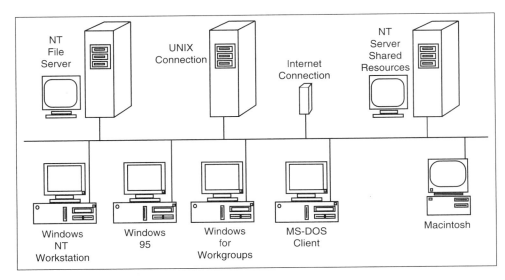

Figure 2.1 NT Server can manage various clients and multiple servers.

- You can assign security rights on a number of workstations and on multiple servers, all the way down to the file and user level in NT.
- NetWare and Macintosh connectivity means the NT Server network can communicate and share resources with other networks within an enterprise system.

Network Components

The basic theories of administering a network with Windows NT Server and NetWare software are similar, although the terms and procedures are different. This section lists some of the common NetWare concepts and translates them to NT, adding any details that differ between the two systems. Appendix B, "NetWare to NT Server Terms," presents NetWare terms translated into their NT counterparts, and Appendix C, "Glossary," defines much of the terminology you'll see in this chapter and throughout the book.

Directory Services

Basic to the operation of a network server is the ability to track user accounts in a secure database. Each account includes information about the user: the user's name, password, and any group memberships, for example. Additionally, this database contains information about servers and network configuration.

Concepts Comparison **25**

In NetWare version 3.1x, that database is called a bindery. In NetWare 4.x, NetWare Directory Services (NDS) replaces the bindery of previous versions, although version 4.x includes a bindery emulation feature that provides backward-compatibility with other versions that use the bindery. Both types of NetWare databases maintain information on and provide access to every resource on the network: users, groups, printers, volumes, and servers. The NDS also manages all network resources as objects, independent of their actual physical location.

In Windows NT, the same type of database system is used to track and maintain user accounts, and is called a *directory database*. *Directory services* are operating system services that facilitate the use of the database. The directory database stores all security and user account information for a domain. NT stores the directory database on one server and replicates copies of the database to backup servers on a regular basis.

TIP: You may see the term Security Accounts Manager database (SAM) referred to in some Microsoft documents; this is another name for the directory database.

Domains

NT uses a domain structure to organize users in the database; a domain can describe one computer, a whole department, or a complete site. Additionally, the group of servers and computers that belong to a domain share common security policies, so that when a user logs on to a domain, he or she has access to each computer and server in the domain. Figure 2.2 illustrates a simple domain structure on an NT network, which may or may not include all of the machines shown in the figure.

The advantages of the domain structure include the following:

- A user can connect to many servers and resources with a single network logon.
- Users can access multiple network domains with one password and user name.
- Users must remember only one password to access available resources.
- Users, groups, and resources can be viewed from any workstation on the network for easier management of the network.
- The network and resources are easier to view and recognize when the entire network is grouped into domains.
- Administrators manage only one account for each user, for one or several servers, and for one or several domains, thus saving time and energy.

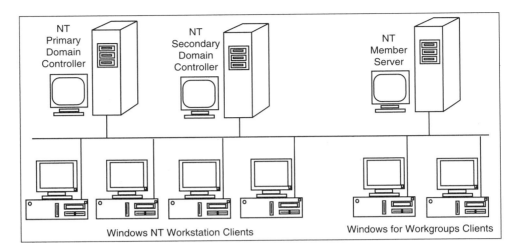

Figure 2.2 A simple domain structure can include one or multiple servers.

Domain Controllers

NT designates domain controllers as gatekeepers of all the shared items in the domain. The domain controller simply keeps the database of security information and uses that information to validate requests for network resources from workstations.

A domain's master security database (which approves or rejects requests for resources on the network) is located on the *primary domain controller* (PDC). Any and all changes made to user accounts for the domain are made to the PDC. There is only one PDC per domain.

However, the responsibility of maintaining the directory database can be shared among multiple NT servers, also called *backup domain controllers* (BDC). The backup domain controller contains a copy of the database and periodically and automatically updates it with the PDC. Multiple BDCs can exist within a domain. If something should happen to the PDC, the BDC can be reassigned as a PDC and work continues on the network as if nothing has happened.

The first NT Server you install in a domain should be designated as the primary domain controller; the second should be a backup domain controller. See Appendix A, "Installing Windows NT Server and Configuring the Network."

Note: In addition to domain controllers, you may have other computers on your system that run the Windows NT Server software. These computers, called member servers because they do not contain the database of users, can be used as workstations, file servers, print servers, and so on.

> ### Trust Relationships
>
> If your organization and network are small, you'll probably use only one domain for storing accounts and resources; but if you have multiple domains, you'll need to understand *trust relationships*. A trust relationship is a link that combines two domains into one administrative unit that authorizes access to the resources on both domains.
>
> NT's Directory Services provides two types of trust relationships: one-way and two-way. The one-way trust relationship represents one domain that trusts another to use its resources. The first domain enables users on the trusted domain to access its resources, but its users are not trusted to use the second domain's resources. The two-way trust relationship enables users in either domain to access resources in the trusted domains. Naturally, using the resources in any domain is subject to permissions and rights. For more information about trusting domains, see Chapter 15, "Managing Multiple Domains."

File System

NetWare uses the FAT (File Allocation Table), an index table that points to the disk areas where a file is located. NetWare accesses the FAT from the DET (Directory Entry Table). The DET is a table that contains basic information about files, directories, directory trustees, and other entities on the volume.

The New Technology File System (NTFS) supports up to 256 characters for file names, a wide range of permissions for sharing files, a transaction log that allows NT to complete any incomplete file-related tasks before continuing if the operating system is interrupted (comparable to NetWare's TTS (Transaction Tracking System), and supports FAT and HPFS (High Performance File System used for OS/2 systems) file systems as well.

TIP: NetWare's server utility, Add Name Space, creates space for long, non-DOS (8 characters plus 3-character extension) file names for UNIX and/or Macintosh clients; however, NT automatically supplies the long file-name capability. NT can also truncate long file names for use with DOS and other systems. See Chapter 4, "Managing Security Policies," for more information.

You can install NT to a FAT or NTFS machine; the benefit of using the NTFS file system, however, is in security issues. You cannot apply NT's file and directory permissions to a FAT file system. For more information about directory and file permissions, see Chapter 4, "Managing Security Policies."

Workstations

Both NetWare and NT support various types of workstations so you'll have little if any worries about migrating your users quickly and easily.

NetWare lets you use DOS, Microsoft Windows (including Windows NT Workstation and Server, Windows 95, and Windows for Workgroups), OS/2, Macintosh, and UNIX operating systems as clients for the network; however utilities for administering the network are available only for DOS, Windows, and OS/2 workstations.

Windows NT Server supports DOS, Microsoft Windows (including Windows NT Workstation, Windows 95, and Windows for Workgroups), OS/2, and Macintosh clients, as well. NT also provides protocols and utilities that enable you to share data and communicate with UNIX machines and the Internet.

Additionally, NT Server includes a Network Client Administrator utility that lets you to create network installation startup disks for many operating systems and clients, including NT Server versions 3.51 and 4.0, NT Workstation versions 3.51 and 4.0, Windows 95, Windows for Workgroups version 3.11, and MS-DOS. See Chapter 6, "Preparing for the Migration," for more information about preparing the clients and users of the network; see Chapter 13, "Tying Up Loose Ends," for information about installing client software.

NT Server also provides a remoteboot feature that starts MS-DOS and Windows workstations, with or without a hard disk, over the network from software installed to the server. The workstations need only an adapter card with a Remote Initial Program Load ROM chip to retrieve startup and configuration software from the server. Remoteboot offers the network administrator more control over applications and resources, as well as a reduced cost to networking.

Protocols

NetWare's primary protocol is IPX/SPX (Internet Packet Exchange/Sequenced Packet Exchange), although you can also load TCP/IP (Transmission Control Protocol/Internet Protocol). Workstations must also use the IPX/SPX protocol to communicate with the NetWare server.

NT, on the other hand, can use a variety of protocols to communicate with workstations and other systems. You can also install and use more than one protocol at a time to your NT workstation so the client can communicate with a variety of systems across the network.

NT's default protocol is NetBEUI (NetBIOS Extended User Interface). NetBIOS (Network Basic Input/Output System) provides an Application Program Interface (API) with a consistent set of commands for requesting lower-level network services to transmit information from node to node, thus separating applications from the underlying network operating system. NetBEUI is a refined NetBIOS that communicates with the network interface card via the NDIS (Network Driver Interface Specification). NDIS is an interface between the network card driver and a protocol stack. NDIS provides protocol multiplexing so that multiple protocol stacks can be used at the same time with the same computer.

NT can use TCP/IP to communicate with Windows NT Servers and Workstation, other Microsoft networking systems, and even non-Microsoft systems such as UNIX systems and the Internet. Although TCP/IP has long been the standard for internetworking, it is quickly becoming a favorite for local area networking as well because most modern operating systems offer TCP/IP support. In addition, TCP/IP is widely accepted protocol for connecting dissimilar systems, and provides the foundation needed to connect and use Internet services. For more information about TCP/IP, see Appendix E.

NT's NWLink IPX/SPX Compatible Protocol conforms to the Novell IPX Router specification so that workstations on the NT network can access a NetWare 3.1x or 4.x server that is also on the network. You can use NT's IPX/SPX in addition to other protocols so a workstation can connect to different types of networks, such as NetWare and Microsoft, at the same time.

NWLink supports the sockets application program interface (API). Because some NetWare-based application servers using NLMs (NetWare Loadable Modules) use sockets to communicate with clients, NWLink makes the NT client act like a NetWare-based client. You'll use the NWLink protocol when installing the Gateway Service for NetWare and for the migration to NT; for information about installing NWLink and using the Gateway Service, see Chapter 8, "Considerations for Using a Gateway Service," and Chapter 9, "Using the Gateway Service for NetWare."

Security Issues

One of the most important functions of a network is to provide security for files, folders, resources, and users. Windows NT not only offers reliable security for your network, but makes network security easy to administer. Most security features in NT work most efficiently with the NTFS file system; if you use the FAT system, you'll be greatly limited in the NT security innovations you can access.

Note: NetWare terminology uses the word directory but Windows NT names the same thing a folder; both refer to the hierarchical file system for organizing and group files and subdirectories, or subfolders.

Users

Just as with NetWare, NT assigns an account to each user. An account is used for administrative, security, and communication purposes, as well as for use of online services. A user account identifies a subscriber by name, password, server or domain, and information about the groups to which the user belongs. The account policy is a set of rules that defines whether a new user is permitted to access a system and its resources; in NT, the account policy also defines the way passwords are used in a domain or on an individual computer.

In NT Server, you use the User Manager for Domains to manage accounts on the local domain and to any other domain or server to which you have access. Figure 2.3 shows the User Manager for Domains window, which lists users and groups. For more information about using the User Manager for Domains, see Chapter 3, "Working with Users and Groups."

NT supplies two built-in user accounts: Administrator and Guest; and a third account—IUSER or Internet User—is added if your server is set up for Internet

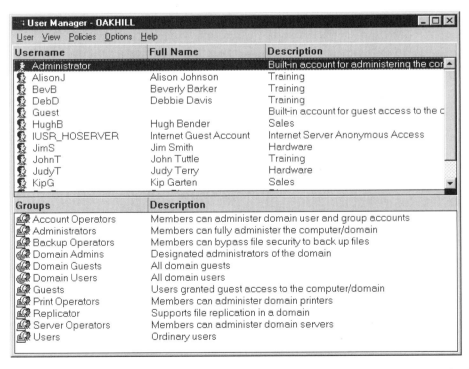

Figure 2.3 *User Manager for Domains enables you to add, delete, and manage individual users and groups on the domain.*

Concepts Comparison **31**

access. The built-in Administrator account has rights to create and manage users. Similarly in NetWare, the ADMIN is a NetWare 4.x and the Supervisor is a 3.1x user object created during installation that has the right to create and manage other objects. The Guest account in NT is a built-in user that can log on to a workstation or member server, but that is all; you can assign additional rights to the Guest user, if you want.

Groups

To make administering rights easier and quicker, you usually assign rights to groups and then assign each user to a group, although you can assign rights to individuals. Unlike NetWare, NT supplies built-in groups, each with rights assigned; however, you can edit the assigned rights to any built-in group. Or you can create and remove your own groups in NT.

Note: NetWare 3.1x does supply the Everyone group, which has no assigned rights initially; NetWare 4.x does not supply built-in groups.

Rights, in both NetWare and NT, are privileges granted to a user or group of users by the network administrator that determine the operations users can perform on the system. In NetWare 3.1x, rights include read, write, erase, create, modify, access control, and file scan. In NetWare 4.x, rights are grouped as directory, file, object, and property.

In NT, rights include access to a workstation; the capability to back up and restore files and directories, change the system time, load and unload device drivers, and manage auditing and security logs; and to shut down the system. In addition, NT offers some advanced user rights, including adding workstations to the domain, debugging programs, creating shared objects, as well as others dealing with the operating system.

Permissions

Another security feature of a network is the protection of files and directories, or folders. In NetWare, you assign attributes to control access to and properties of files and directories within a file system. File attributes used in NetWare include Archive, Read, Write, Create, Execute, and Shareable; file and directory attributes include: Delete inhibit, Hidden, Purge, Rename inhibit, and System.

NT uses similar attributes for file and folder protection, but calls these attributes permissions. They include: No Access, List, Read, Add, Add & Read, Change,

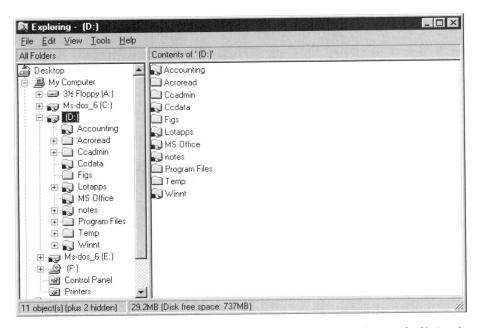

Figure 2.4 The NT Explorer enables you to assign permissions for specific files and folders, as well as perform other file management tasks.

and Full Control. In addition, you can set the following special directory and/or file access for any group: Read, Write, Execute, Delete, Change Permissions, and Take Ownership. NT permissions are set in the Windows NT Explorer (see Figure 2.4). For more information, see Chapter 4, "Managing Security Policies."

Note: The Windows NT Explorer lists all files and folders on the local drive, the network, floppies, CDs, and other peripherals. You can copy, delete, move, rename, and otherwise manipulate files and folders; you can also create and remove folders, open files, share files, and map drives from the Explorer. The Explorer is the NT 4.0 version of the Windows File Manager in previous versions of Windows.

Accessing the Network

Similarities and differences exist between NetWare and NT networks as far as accessing the server and other workstations on the network. One major difference between the two networks is that you cannot use the NetWare 3.1x or 4.x server as a workstation; to access a NetWare server, you must log on from a workstation that's attached to the network. NT, on the other hand, enables you to access the server from same computer or from a workstation attached to the network.

Naturally, using NT Server as a workstation may slow the system, but it can be done. Actually, most NT Server member servers are used as workstations in addition to being used as file or print servers. If you have one server (which is the primary domain controller) that you use as a file and print server as well as for logging on users, I suggest you use that as a dedicated server. However, if you use a primary domain controller for user authentication only, and use several member servers as file and print servers, all can easily be used as workstations as well. Assess your system to see what works for your network.

Other similarities between the two networks include logging on to the network, logging off the network, and attaching to a different server to make its resources available to you. In NetWare 3.x, you use the workstation utility ATTACH to attach to servers other than the current server; in NetWare 4.x, you use the LOGIN utility instead. In NT, you use the Attach As command in the Network Neighborhood. The procedures are similar and the results are the same for these basic tasks. For other tasks, the procedures are vastly different.

Note: When logging on to the network with NT Server or Workstation, you enter your user name, password, and domain. As administrator, you can log on to the network from any workstation or server. You can also log off of the network so your security rights are not compromised.

Viewing and Accessing Network Resources

One very significant difference between NetWare and NT networks is in viewing and accessing network resources. You'll certainly want to know which directories, or folders, on the server and other workstations are available to users. NetWare makes it somewhat difficult, compared to NT, to view and use the network resources.

You can use a variety of NetWare utilities to view the network and access directories. For example, from DOS you can use the NetWare version 3.1x utility SESSION to view a directory (no files) and to map directories. In NetWare 4.x, you use the NETUSER utility to accomplish the same thing.

You can use the NetWare shell (NETX), a program loaded into each workstation's memory, to allow the workstation to access the network in NetWare 3.1x. The shell captures the workstation's network requests and forwards them to a Net-

Ware server. The term shell is not used in NetWare 4.x; instead, the NetWare DOS Requester, or VLM (Virtual Loadable Module), replaces NetWare shell on a DOS client.

NetWare User Tools for Windows 3.1 is a NetWare 4.x utility that allows users to perform a variety of network tasks: access network resources, map drives, manage printing, and send messages. This utility loads only when you load VLMs; therefore it's not available with NetWare 3.1x unless you have loaded the DOS requester on workstations attached to 3.12. VLMs are shipped with version 3.12.

Note: In NetWare, SYS:PUBLIC is a public directory created during installation that allows general access to the network and contains utilities and programs for network users. Public files located in SYS:PUBLIC directory can be accessed by all NetWare users. There are no folders created by NT specifically for sharing files and utilities; however, you can create folders on the server and choose to share them. Additionally, if you migrate to NT, the PUBLIC directory and its contents will migrate as well.

Now consider the Windows NT Network Neighborhood. With the Network Neighborhood, users on the server, or on a Windows NT or Windows 95 workstation, can view and access the entire network as long as they have access rights and permissions (see Chapter 4 for more information). Figure 2.5 shows the Network Neighborhood from an NT Workstation. In the Network Neighborhood window, you see the Entire Network icon, the Director's computer, and the server: HOSERVER.

In the Network Neighborhood, you can access the server and network to which you're attached, multiple servers and workstations, and multiple networks. For example, if a workstation belongs to both a NetWare and a Microsoft network, the user can switch back and forth between the networks and the servers from the Network Neighborhood by double-clicking the Entire Network icon. You can also access folders and files on a server or other workstation by double-clicking the icon representing the computer, as long as you have rights and permissions; you can even open files to view and edit from the Network Neighborhood.

Note: Although NT Workstation and NT Server have a similar interface and offer similar procedures to performing network and other tasks, the difference between the two operating systems is that NT Server supplies the utilities and tools needed to administer the network, domains, users, and so on.

Concepts Comparison

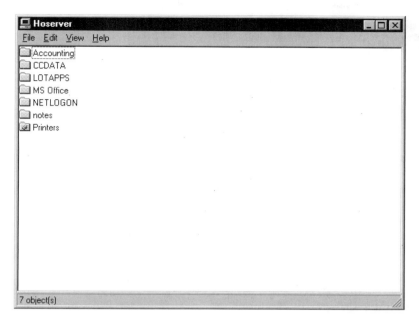

Figure 2.5 *The Hoserver window displays available folders and printers on the NT Server.*

You can also perform the following tasks in the Network Neighborhood, as long as you have rights and permissions:

- Copy, delete, and move files and folders.
- List details about files.
- Launch applications.
- Search for specific files, folders, and even text.
- Create new folders.
- Access printers an other resources.
- Map network drives.

Mapping Drives

Mapping drives is a very important part of using a NetWare network.. The process is as follows. MAP is a NetWare 4 utility that lets users create, view, or change network drive mappings, or assign a drive letter to represent a complete directory path statement. NetWare provides local drive mapping (local hard and floppy disks), network drive mapping (volumes and directories on the network),

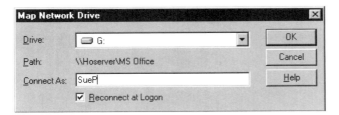

Figure 2.6 NT *provides a dialog box in which you can quickly and easily map drives and resources.*

network search drive mapping (to directories containing DOS files or apps), and directory map objects (which map drives to directories containing frequently used files, like apps).

NT enables you to perform drive mapping as well, in the Network Neighborhood. To assign a drive letter to a shared network resource in Windows NT, you open the Map Network Drive dialog box (see Figure 2.6) and choose the drive letter from the **D**rive drop-down list box. Next you enter the **P**ath to the directory on the server or workstation; and, optionally, enter the user name you want to connect as in the **C**onnect As text box. You can even choose to reconnect at logon, if you want.

Another, perhaps easier method, is to first access the workstation or server; and then open the folders you need to get to the directory you want to map. You select the directory and choose **F**ile, **M**ap Network Drive to automatically enter the path in the Map Network Drive dialog box. All that's left to do is choose a drive letter to represent the path.

After you map drives in NT, those drives then appear in the My Computer window and the Windows NT Explorer for quick access. Figure 2.7 shows mapped drives as they appear in My Computer window. From this window, you can open and view the mapped drives and access any resources for which you have permissions and rights.

Printing Issues

Both NetWare and NT enable a variety of printing services, and use similar methods for accomplishing the specific printing tasks, whether you're dealing with print servers or print queues. In both NetWare and NT, for example, you can set up a computer as a print server to manage and control the printing traffic on the network. In NetWare, you can run the PSERVER.NLM to add a print server to a file server. Additionally, you can use any low-end computer as a dedicated print server for NetWare networks using the PSERVER.EXE.

Concepts Comparison **37**

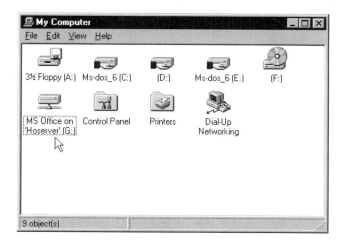

Figure 2.7 *Map drives and choose to reconnect at logon so the resources are always available to you.*

In Windows NT, you also can set up a print server on a file or database server. Naturally, file operations have first priority over printing services. The only requirement for a file and print server is 16MB RAM for a server controlling a small number of print devices; more devices and/or larger documents, naturally, will require more memory. Disk space for a print server is minimal. You could, of course, assign a dedicated print server in NT; but that is only recommended if there are many heavily used printers on the network or if there is a security concern with the file and print server.

Note: NT enables you to assign more than one printer to a print device so that you can use a printer in different ways, such as stagger printing times, create different priority levels, and so on; NetWare only enables priority levels.

You can use printers attached to workstations running Windows NT and other Microsoft operating systems and to NetWare printers. In addition, NT enables printing to a network-attached TCP/IP print device and to devices physically attached to most UNIX computers, to provide flexibility in your printing setup. You can even provide print services to a Macintosh client connected to an NT server. You can also perform these services with either version of NetWare; however, it is not normally done because of the degree of difficulty.

The print queue, a holding area in which documents wait to be printed, works in a similar manner in both types of networks. The print queue in NetWare is created through NETADMIN (DOS utility for version 4.x), NWADMIN (Windows utility for version 4.x) or PCONSOLE (version 3.1x and 4.x). A corresponding directory is created for each print queue; in 3.1x, the print queue directory is placed in the SYS:SYSTEM directory of the current server. In 4.x, the print queue directory is placed in QUEUES directory on the specified volume by default. NT stores all print queues in a Printers folder, from which you manage document printing and network printers.

Just as in NetWare, NT supplies the features and commands you need to control a print queue, some relating to the printer and others to the documents. The print queue in NT looks and behaves similarly to the one in previous versions of Windows. You can, for example, control a printer by viewing a list of documents waiting to be printed, pause and resume printing, and purge all documents waiting for a printer. You can further control each document in the queue by pausing and resuming printing, restarting the printing of a document from the beginning, deleting a document, and editing document priority and other settings.

Whereas NetWare administrators can create Print Queue Operators to manage print queues, an administrator or anyone with Full Control access in NT can manage a print server from any Windows NT client on the network, controlling such elements as printer properties and creating new printers.

Finally, any network users can check on the status of a remote printer and manage any documents of their own in the print queue, although they cannot manage others' documents unless they have the rights to do so. For more information about printing services, see Chapter 5, "Managing Print Services."

PART II

Understanding NT Networks

3 Working with Users and Groups

Windows NT Server includes administrative tools that enable you to create, edit, and manage users and groups on the network. Just as in NetWare, NT users are those allowed to access the network; NT groups are sets of users that have the same level of security. Further, a user account in NT is a security mechanism used to control access to the network; it defines the user's name, password information, and information about any group to which the user belongs.

You create and manage users and groups with the NT User Manager for Domains tool, much like the SYSCON tool in NetWare 3.1x or NETADMIN or NWADMIN for Windows in NetWare 4.x.

This chapter shows you how to do the following in NT Server:

- Edit users.
- Create users.
- Manage user accounts.
- Configure the user's environment.
- Manage existing groups.
- Create and edit groups.

User Manager for Domains

In NT, the User Manager for Domains is the administrative tool for managing user accounts, groups, and security policies in domains. The network administrator controls all rights and permissions for user and group accounts to the resources on the domain. See Chapter 4, "Managing Security Policies," for information about user rights and object permissions.

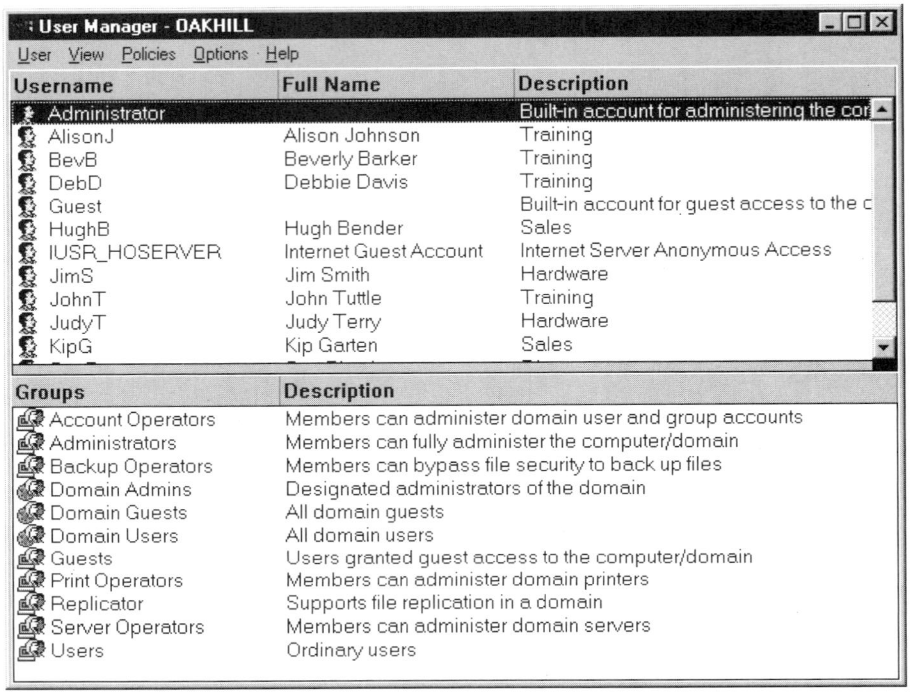

Figure 3.1 View, edit, create, and otherwise manage users and groups in the User Manager for Domains.

The User Manager for Domains is only available on a computer running NT Server and configured as a primary domain controller or a backup domain controller. On member servers and computers running the NT Workstation software, the utility is the User Manager, which only enables you to control access to the computer on which you are working.

To open the User Manager for Domains, choose the Start button on the Taskbar, and select **P**rograms, Administrative Tools, and User Manager for Domains. Figure 3.1 shows the User Manager for Domains on an NT Server, primary domain controller. Listed in the upper pane of the window are the individual users of the network; listed in the lower pane are groups.

Note: NetWare provides two predefined users in NetWare 3.1x (Supervisor and Guest) and one predefined user in 4.x (Admin). Similarly, NT provides the Administrator user with assigned rights for administering the network and a Guest user; the IUSR (Internet User) is added if you have Internet service on the NT

Working with Users and Groups

Server. NetWare 3.1x provides the Everyone group, but 4.x provides no predefined groups by default. NT, on the other hand, provides eight groups, each with predefined rights. You can edit the rights of any user and/or group in NT.

Domain Information

In NT, a domain is a logical group of network servers and workstations that share common security and user account information. A domain can exist within one office or in several cities or countries. It may have one server or several, a few workstations or as many as 26,000, and as many as 250 groups. The number of accounts can be as high as 5,000, depending on the power of the computer.

Most organizations need only a single domain. Administration and user management is easy within a single domain because one administrator can manage all network servers. You might, however, want to split your system into domains for organization purposes; doing so enables you to assign various administrators the task of managing their own departments. For more information about multiple domains, see Chapter 15, "Managing Multiple Domains."

The possible computer members of a domain include primary and backup domain controllers, member servers, and workstations. A domain controller is a computer running Windows NT Server that shares one directory database and manages all aspects of user-domain interactions. (Chapter 2 contains details about domain controllers.) A member server is a computer running Windows NT Server software but has not been designated as a domain controller. Member servers don't have a copy of the directory database and cannot authenticate accounts; they usually serve as file, database, and/or print servers, and can double as a workstation. Finally, any clients attached to the network are workstations, which may or may not share their resources with others on the domain.

Note: A workgroup, as opposed to a domain, is a group of computers that share directories and other resources over the network but do not share a common directory database; therefore, members of a workgroup cannot share resources with computers in a domain, only with members of their workgroup. For the most part, you'll want to assign your workstations to a domain instead of a workgroup.

The User Manager on a server running Windows NT Server looks similar to the User Manager in any client computer running Windows NT Workstation. The difference between the two tools is in the operating system running the computer. The User Manager on the server, called the User Manager for Domains, lets you manage user and group accounts on the local domain and on any domain to which you have access. The User Manager on a client or workstation enables you to manage only users and groups that access the workstation.

TIP: You can run User Manager for Domains on a computer running Windows NT Workstation, if you've installed it using the Network Client Administrator so that the server can be managed remotely from a workstation, similar to NetWare's RCONSOLE. For more information, see Chapter 13, "Tying Up Loose Ends."

If your server is a member of more than one domain, notice that the domain name precedes the user name to indicate where the user's account was created; for example HughB from the Product domain might appear as PRODUCT\HughB.

Editing Users

When you migrate from NetWare to NT, all user accounts will transfer to NT; nevertheless, you'll probably want to modify some accounts, or at least check them to make sure rights and restrictions transferred the way you wanted them to. You can edit any user account in the User Manager by first double-clicking the user's name, which opens the User Properties dialog box, as shown in Figure 3.2.

TIP: Chapter 7, "Planning the Migration," compares a list of NetWare user rights to NT user rights, and lists comparisons of administrative accounts and file and directory attributes.

TIP: To edit several users at one time and apply the same properties—such as password restrictions—select the first user and hold the Ctrl key as you select each subsequent user. Then choose **U**ser, **P**roperties. All of the user names appear in the User Properties dialog box, and all modifications apply to those names listed. Table 3.1 describes each of the options in the User Properties dialog box.

Working with Users and Groups

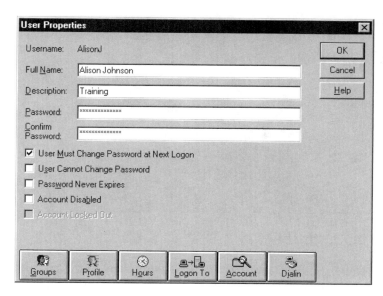

Figure 3.2 *In this dialog box, you edit user properties, such as password, group membership, and profile issues.*

Table 3.1 User Properties

OPTION	DESCRIPTION
Username	The user name used for logon purposes.
Full Name	Enter or edit the user's name as you want it to appear in the User Manager and on the user account; only the user name is needed for logon to the network
Description	Optionally, enter or edit the user's description.
Password	Enter the password the user must type to log on to the network; enter the password again in the Confirm Password text box to verify.
Password Options	From the check boxes, choose any or all restrictions for the user's password: User Must Change Password at Next Logon, User Cannot Change Password, and/or Password Never Expires.
Account Disabled	Select this option to prevent the user from accessing the network temporarily; the account remains in the database but cannot be used until you enable it again.
Account Locked Out	This option is grayed unless the account becomes locked out automatically; lockout occurs when a user fails to enter the appropriate password three times in a row.

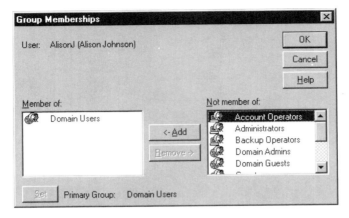

Figure 3.3 Add or remove groups you want the user to belong to.

To continue configuring a user, you can choose any of the buttons at the bottom of the User Properties dialog box: **G**roups, **P**rofile, **H**ours, **L**ogon To, **A**ccount, or **Di**alin, as described in the following sections.

TIP: To change a user name in the User Manager, select the user and then choose **U**ser, **R**ename.

Groups

The Groups button leads to the Groups Memberships dialog box (see Figure 3.3) which enables you to select the groups to which the user will be a member. If the user was a member of a group on the NetWare network, that group will be created on the NT Server during the migration and will appear in the Group Memberships dialog box.

By default, every user is a member of the Domain Users group, as shown in the **M**ember of list box. To add a group to the user's account, select the group in the **N**ot Member of list and choose the **A**dd button. To remove a group from the user's group memberships, select the group in the **M**ember list and select the **R**emove button. When you're done, choose OK to close the dialog box and return to the User Manager for Domains. For a list of built-in groups and their assigned rights, see the section "Managing Groups," later in this chapter.

At the bottom of the dialog box is the **S**et button. Use Set only when the user is running the Macintosh client or POSIX applications. Set changes the primary group to which the user is a member.

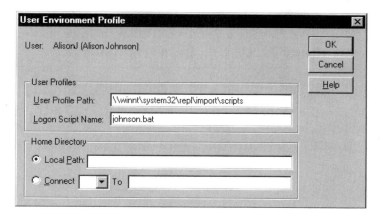

Figure 3.4 Specify a home directory, path to a logon script, or enter a path to customize the user's environment.

Profile

Computers running Windows NT Server and Windows NT Workstation have user profiles that automatically create and maintain a user's desktop settings: screen colors, desktop items and settings, mouse settings, window size and position, and network and printer connections. No matter which workstation the user logs on to, the user's personal settings follow. The user profile is created when the user logs on to the workstation the first time. User profiles provide the user with a consistent working environment, even if the workstation is used by several people.

Note: User profiles only apply to computers running Windows NT Server and Workstation; computers running MS-DOS, UNIX, or OS/2 are not affected. You can apply user profiles to computers running Windows 95, if you enable them. On the Windows 95 computer, open the Passwords icon in the Control Panel and choose to enable user profiles.

The User Environment Profile dialog box appears when you click the **P**rofile button in the User Properties dialog box, as shown in Figure 3.4. The User Profiles area of the dialog box designates the user's desktop environment information. Optionally, enter a path to the folder that contains the information in the **U**ser Profile Path text box in the following format: \\director\profiles\bessieb.

Note: The desktop environment includes screen colors, network connections, and other settings that the user has control over. You can, alternatively, designate a mandatory user profile. To do so, open the Control Panel, click on the System icon and choose the User Profiles tab. Copy the predefined user profile to the path location and then rename the NTUser.dat file to NTUser.man.

The **L**ogon Script Name contains the path and name of the script file. You can use a BAT, CMD, or EXE file. Save the script file to the \\WINNT\SYSTEM32\REPL\IMPORT\SCRIPTS directory and enter this as the path in the User Environment Profile dialog box.

Logon Scripts

Just as with NetWare, the logon script assigned to a user's account runs each time that user logs on to the network. You can assign a logon script to one user or to multiple user accounts by assigning the script to a group.

To create a logon script, use a text editor; then assign the script to users in the User Manager. Following are some special parameters you can use when creating logon scripts for multiple users:

%HOMEDRIVE%	Defines the user's local workstation drive letter that is connected to the user's home directory.
%HOMEPATH%	Represents the full path of the user's home directory.
%OS%	Represents the operating system of the user's workstation.
%PROCESSOR_ARCHITECTURE%	Defines the processor type of the user's workstation.
%PROCESSOR_LEVEL%	Defines the processor level of the user's workstation.
%USERDOMAIN%	Represents the domain containing the user's account.
%USERNAME%	Represents the user name.

The logon script is downloaded from the domain controller server that authenticates the user's logon request. If you have multiple domain controllers in the domain, you should copy all logon scripts for user accounts to every primary and backup domain controller, because any controller could authenticate the user's logon request.

TIP: Clients running the MS Network Client for MS-DOS, Workgroups for Windows, Windows NT 3.1, or LAN Manager 3.x must use the BAT file extension for logon script files.

In the Home Directory, choose either the Local **P**ath (local computer) or the **C**onnect To (network) text box to enter the path to the user's home directory. In NT as in NetWare, the home directory is the user's own private space on the server. Conversely, In NT, the home directory is used as a default directory for the Save As and Open dialog boxes of applications, for the command prompt, and so on. If you choose to place the home directory on the network and the directory does not already exist, User Manager for Domains creates it for you. If you do not assign a home directory, the default on the user's local drive is used: \USERS\DEFAULT.

CAUTION: As in NetWare, if the home directory already exists when you assign it to a user, you must grant the user permission to his or her home directory before he or she can access it. In NT, you grant object permissions from the NT Explorer. For more information, see "Granting Permissions," in Chapter 4.

TIP: If you're configuring multiple users, you can substitute %USERNAME% for the last item in the home directory path. NT will substitute the username of the user account for you. If you're using the FAT file system, however, you cannot user %USERNAME% because of the 8.3 limitation.

Hours

NT enables users to log on 24 hours a day, every day, by default; however, you can limit the logon hours in the User Properties dialog box by choosing the **H**ours button. As you can see in Figure 3.5, the Logon Hours dialog box contains a one-week calendar with logon hours in one-hour increments. One box represents one hour in the calendar. The first box, for example, represents 12:00 A.M. to 12:59 A.M.; the last box represents 11:00 P.M. to 11:59 P.M.

Filled boxes indicate the hours a user can connect to a domain server; empty boxes indicate hours of no access. If a user exceeds the set logon hours, NT Server responds either by disconnecting the user or by denying the user new connections. You set the response you want in the Account Policy dialog box (see Chapter 4 for more information).

50 Chapter 3

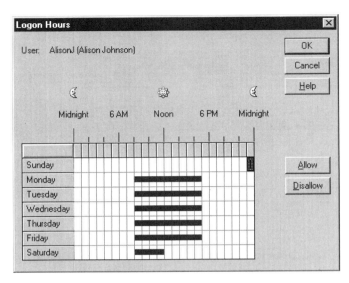

Figure 3.5 *Set the logon hours to your business and your preferences in the Logon Hours dialog box.*

You set the hours in the calendar first by dragging the mouse across a time block to select it and then choosing the **A**llow or **D**isallow button.

Logon To

You use the **L**ogon To button to specify which of the workstations on the network the user may access. Depending on the services set up in your network, different options may appear in the dialog box. Figure 3.6 shows the most common options on a server set up for domains in an NT network.

The default option, User May Log On To **A**ll Workstations, can be changed to User May Log On To **T**hese Workstations, and then only certain computers can be named for access. If your network has additional services, such as one or more NetWare workstations, options to limit access to those services are included in the dialog box.

Account

NT also lets you determine such account information as an account expiration date and account type. Figure 3.7 shows the Account Information dialog box, opened from the User Profiles dialog box by choosing the **A**ccount button.

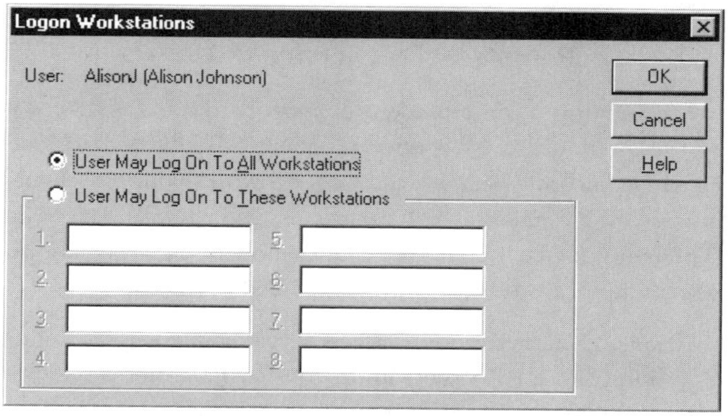

Working with Users and Groups

Figure 3.6 *Here you choose which workstations a user has access to.*

The default option in the Account Expires area is **N**ever, but you can change the data by choosing the **E**nd of option and adding the month, date, and year for the account to expire. When an account expires, the account is disabled (not deleted); the user, therefore, cannot log on again unless you enable the account.

In the Type of Account area, you can choose to make the account either global or local. Global is the default setting and is the account for the normal user in his or her home domain. You might choose the local account type for a user from a domain that is not trusted, thus limiting access to your domain.

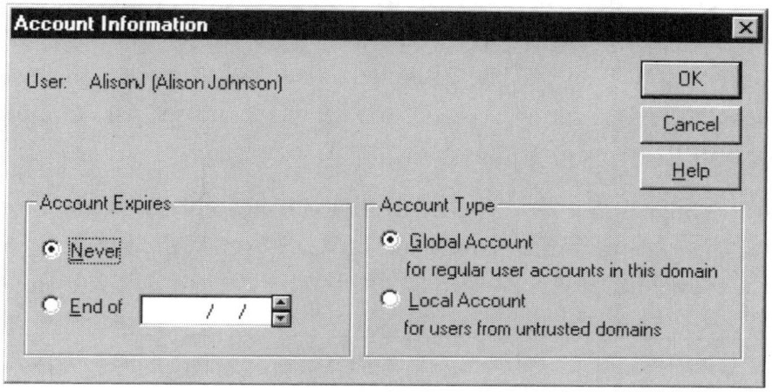

Figure 3.7 *Set an expiration date and the type of account for a user in the Account Information dialog box.*

> ### Remote Access Service (RAS)
>
> Users who work away from the office can connect to the NT network and its resources using the Remote Access Service supplied by NT. RAS includes file and print services, messaging, and database access. RAS works with any client computer running Windows NT, Windows for Workgroups, MS-DOS, LAN Manager, or a PPP client. The user must have a 9600 or higher modem, X.25, or ISDN card. Additionally, the remote access software must be installed to the client.
>
> You will also need a dedicated remote access server for best results and improved performance. You install the RAS program to control the remote access server; your server will need a multiport adapter or modems and analog telephone lines or other WAN connections. If you're planning to provide access to the network, the server will also need a separate network adapter card installed and connected.
>
> NT Server's RAS feature permits up to 256 clients to dial in to the network. You can further configure RAS to provide access to all network resources, or you can limit access to the RAS server only.
>
> In addition to the LAN protocols—TCP/IP, IPX, and NetBEUI—NT supports remote access protocols, including PPP (Point-to-Point Protocol), SLIP (Serial Line Internet Protocol), and Microsoft RAS Protocol. The LAN protocols are used to integrate the RAS clients with the rest of the network; remote access protocols control the transmission of data over a WAN (wide area network). NT automatically picks up any LAN protocols installed to the network when you install the remote access service.
>
> RAS also enables NT to provide services to the Internet. You could, therefore, configure an NT Server computer as an Internet Service Provider and offer dialup Internet connections to a PPP client. The PPP client must use TCP/IP, IPX, or NetBEUI to access the RAS server; the NT RAS software needs no special configuration for non-Microsoft PPP clients.
>
> Installing and configuring a remote access service is beyond the scope of this book; however, you can get more information about RAS from Windows NT Server documentation and on-line help.

Dialin

Remote Access Service (RAS) is a service provided by NT that enables remote and mobile users to connect to the network over a modem, ISDN, or X.25. All

Working with Users and Groups **53**

services provided by the RAS are usually the same as services available to a LAN-connected user.

The **Di**alin button leads to the Dialin Information dialog box. Use this dialog box to set permission for remote users to connect to the network through dialup networking. You can also set call back options in this dialog box.

Adding and Deleting Users

You can add as many users as necessary in the User Manager, and for each user you add, you can set properties as previously described in the section "Editing Users." You can add one user at a time or add multiple users. You can always delete a user, too, when you no longer want that person on the domain.

> **Note:** When you add a user on the NT Server domain controller, you're adding the user to the domain; on the other hand, if you add a user from a member server or a workstation, you're adding that user only to the individual computer.

Adding Users

Try to be consistent when adding usernames because NT presents the list of user accounts sorted by usernames. Using a standard for naming users means you can more easily find the one you want in the list.

To add a new user in the User Manager, choose **U**ser, New **U**ser. The New User dialog box appears, looking exactly like the User Properties dialog box (refer to Figure 3.2). To add more than one user, enter the information for the first user and then choose the Add button; the text boxes clear, ready for the next user.

As in NetWare, the user name must be unique. The password is also case-sensitive. The user name can be as long as 20 characters and can contain any uppercase or lowercase characters except the following:

" \ / [ ] ; : = + , * ? < >

> **Note:** Similar to NetWare, user and group accounts in NT include a unique number assigned as a security identifier (SID) for internal processes in NT. If you delete an account and then create another account with the same name, the new account will have a new SID and therefore will not have the same rights as the original account.

Adding Multiple Users

If you have a lot of users to add, NT Server Directory Services provides a method by which you can copy an existing account and then just change the user name, full name, password, and whatever else needs to be changed.

To copy a user account, select the user in the User Manager and choose **U**ser, **C**opy. The Copy of dialog box appears (looking exactly like the User Properties dialog box). All properties are set like the original user; all you have to do is fill in the names and password.

You can also create a template that contains all of the information you want a group of users accounts to contain and copy that template when creating your users. For security purposes, disable the template account in the User Properties dialog box when you're not using it so no one can log on with that account. Copied accounts are enabled by default.

Deleting Users

To delete any user, select that user in the User Manager pane and press the Delete key. A confirmation dialog box appears; choose OK to delete the user. Select several users for deletion by holding the Ctrl key as you click on each username.

Managing Groups

Groups are collections of users with certain rights. Unlike NetWare, NT supplies eight built-in groups with rights already assigned to make administration of users easier. Instead of assigning individual rights to each user, you assign a user to a group with the rights you want that user to have.

You can edit and modify the rights to any built-in group to customize them for your users and network. Additionally, you can add groups to your network and set the rights you want from scratch. This section covers a description of NT's built-in groups, editing group properties, adding groups, and deleting groups. For information about assigning rights and permissions, see Chapter 4, "Managing Security Policies."

Note: Permissions in NT are similar to attributes in NetWare. You assign permissions to files and folders and these permissions control various users' access.

Groups Description

NT Server supplies eight built-in local groups and three built-in global groups to which you can assign users for quick rights management and control. In addition to specific rights, each group may or may not be granted certain abilities to perform tasks on the server and/or network. Rights include such actions as accessing the server or network, shutting down the system, backing up files and folders, changing the system time, and loading device drivers. Abilities include such tasks as adding a workstation to the domain, creating and managing user accounts and groups, assigning user rights, locking the server, formatting the server's hard disk, and so on.

Note: NT supplies nearly the same set of built-in groups for both NT Server and NT Workstation (Server Operators are not available on NT Workstation), but the rights and abilities are not always the same for both operating systems. In this book, we're discussing only NT Server groups.

Local Groups

Following is a brief description of each group in NT Server; for more information about group rights and permissions, see Chapter 4. For information about how NetWare groups translate to NT groups during a migration, see Chapter 7, "Planning the Migration."

The Administrators group grants full control access of the network to its members, and is the only group that does, by default. Administrators can access workstations, files, and folders; manage and control users and groups; choose which resources to share, such as printers, CD-ROM drives, and so on; and more. The Administrator has all rights and abilities on the NT Server and Workstation.

The Server Operator group grants its members the rights and abilities needed to administer the primary and backup domain controllers: logging on locally to the server, shutting down the system, backing up and restoring files, locking and unlocking the server, sharing resources, and so on.

Members of the Account Operators group can manage and create accounts for users and groups using the User Manager for Domains. Additionally, an Account Operator can log on locally to the server and shut down the system. An Account Operator cannot, however, modify the Administrators, Servers, Account Operators, Print Operators, or Backup Operators local groups or any local groups that are members of these local groups

Print Operators can also log on to the server and shut down the system, but they can only create, edit, delete, and manage printer shares.

Backup Operators are granted the control necessary over the server to perform backup and restores. In addition to accessing the server from the network, the Backup Operators can shut down the system, back up files and folders, and restore files and folders. No abilities are granted the Backup Operator.

> ### Local and Global Groups
>
> Microsoft supplies two types of groups, local and global, for use with security and organization. Local groups are collections of users that are available to receive permissions and rights in a single domain, or locally. You can put users and global groups into a local group; however, you cannot put one local group into another. Global groups are those that can contain only users, and these users can only be from the domain in which the global group was created. In a single-domain NT Server network, global groups are basically irrelevant; however, if you plan to join a multiple-domain network, you'll need to understand local and global groups. With a global group, you can combine user accounts on multiple domains and workstations.
>
> Remember the following points in relation to local and global groups:
>
> - You must use the local group if your members need rights and permissions in one domain only.
> - You must use a local group if you want a group that can contain other groups as well as users.
> - You must use a local group if your group is to contain users from multiple domains. Since a local group can only be used in the domain in which it is created, you must manually create the local group in every domain.
> - You must use a global group if you want to combine users of one domain into a single unit for use in other domains.
> - You must use a global group if you want the user of an NT Workstation to grant permissions to any groups.
>
> A member of a built-in local group has the rights to perform various tasks on the domain controllers, member server, and/or workstation in the domain. By default, every new domain user is a member of the Domain Users global group and, therefore, a member of the Users built-in local group.

The Replicator group does not have actual users as members; instead, an account is used to log on to the Replicator services of the primary domain controller and the backup domain controllers of the domain.

Users group members have no rights nor abilities on the server, unless you assign them. Finally, Guests have no rights nor abilities on the server.

NT also includes the following special groups you may see in a list, but you cannot modify the members of these groups: Everyone (anyone using the computer), Interactive (anyone using the computer locally), Network (all users connected over the network), System (the operating system), and Creator Owner (for permissions sake, the creator of a file or directory).

Note: NT Workstation and member servers also include the Power Users group, whose members have rights to the local computer and shut down rights, as well as the ability to use the User Manager for the specific computer and create groups, users, and shares.

Global Groups

In addition to the previously described groups, there are three global groups built in to a domain's primary and backup domain controllers: Domain Admins, Domain Users, and Domain Guests. Domain Admins is a member of the Administrators local group; the built-in Administrator user account is a member of the Domain Admins global group. An Administrator can administer the domain, the primary and backup domain controllers, and all other computers running both NT Server and Workstation in the domain.

Domain Users is a member of the Users local group for the domain and of the Users local group for every NT Workstation and member server on the network. Domain Users have normal user access.

The Domain Guests group contains the domain's built-in Guest user account, to which rights are limited. You could move any Domain Users to the Domain Guests group to limit their rights and permissions.

Managing Groups

You can change the description of any group at any time. You also can add and remove members from the group, whether the group is built in or you create the group yourself. See the following section, "Adding Groups," for more information.

To manage a group, follow these steps:

1. In the User Manager for Domains, double-click on the group you want to edit; alternatively, select the group, and then choose **U**ser, **P**roperties. The Local Group or Global Group Properties dialog box appears (see Figure 3.8).

2. To edit the description, select the text in the **D**escription text box and enter new text.

3. To remove a member, select the member and choose the **R**emove button; NT removes the user without warning or confirmation.

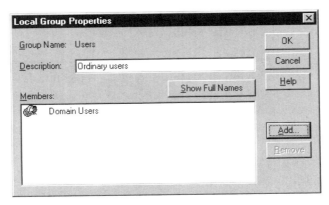

Figure 3.8 View a list of members to a group, add new members, or edit the description of the group in the Local Group Properties dialog box.

4. To add a member, choose the **A**dd button; the Add Users and Groups dialog box appears, as shown in Figure 3.9.
5. In the **L**ist Names From drop-down list box, choose the server containing the names of the users and/or groups you want to add.

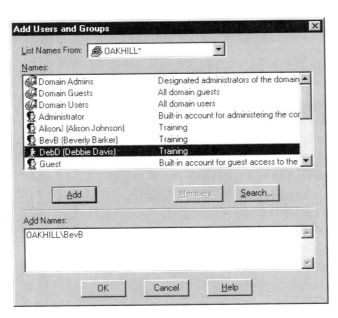

Figure 3.9 Add users and groups from the domain to the local group in the Add Users and Groups dialog box.

Working with Users and Groups 59

6. In the list of **N**ames, select the name you want to add and then choose the **A**dd button. The name appears in the **Ad**d Names list at the bottom of the dialog box; add all of the names you want to the list box.

Note: You can search for any member or group name by choosing the **S**earch button. The Find Account dialog box appears. Enter the user or group name for which you're searching and choose the **S**earch button.

---

7. To view the members of any group, select the group name in the Add Users and Groups dialog box and then select the **M**embers button. A list of that group's members displays at the end of the users list of **N**ames.
8. When you're done, choose OK to close the dialog box and return to the Local Group Properties dialog box. Choose OK to close the box and return to the User Manager.

Adding Groups

You might want to add new groups to your system for organizational and management purposes; for example, add a group for users who belong to a specific department or office, or for users who require only certain resources. When you add a group, you can assign users and rights to the group, edit the group, and otherwise manage the new group.

TIP: The same naming rules apply to groups as apply to naming users.

You might also add a new local group so you can grant permissions to files, directories, and other resources to the group and its members. Or add a global group to organize users based on the type of work they do. Suppose you have a printer you want to limit access to:

1. First create a local group that has permission to use the printer.
2. Next create a global group containing users who are allowed to use the printer.
3. Add the global group to the local group and then control access to the printer by adding or removing members to the global group.

Note: You cannot rename a group after you create it.

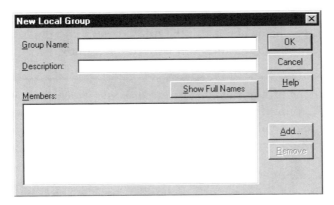

Figure 3.10 Add users and groups from the domain to the local group.

Local Groups

You can create a new local group and add its members from scratch; or you can copy any existing group and its members as a foundation for the new group. When you copy a new group, the permissions and rights of the original group are not copied to the new group, only the members are the same. To add a group, follow these steps:

1. In the User Manager for Domains, choose one of the following:

   Select the group you want to copy in the User Manager for Domains Group list; or
   Choose the **U**ser menu, New **L**ocal Group command.

   The New Local Group dialog box appears, as shown in Figure 3.10.

2. Enter the new group's name in the **G**roup Name text box; this name must be unique and can contain up to 256 characters, *excluding* the backslash character.

3. In the **D**escription text box, optionally enter a description of the group.

4. In the **M**embers list box, you can add more members to the group by choosing the **A**dd button. The Add Users and Groups dialog box appears (see Figure 3.11).

   TIP: To display the full names in the **M**embers list box, choose the **S**how Full Names button.

5. In the **L**ist Names From drop-down list box, choose the server or domain from which you want to choose groups and users.

Working with Users and Groups

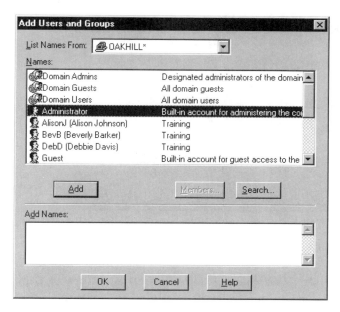

Figure 3.11 Choose users and/or other groups to add to the new local group.

6. Select the users and/or groups from the **N**ames list to add to the new group. You can add one name at a time or several. To add names in the list that are adjacent to each other, hold the Shift key as you click on the first and last names you want to add; all names in between are also selected. To add names that are not adjacent to each other in the list, hold the Ctrl key as you click on each name.

7. Choose the **A**dd button. You can change servers and/or domains and add more names, if you want. If you cannot locate the users or groups you want to add, choose the Search button to display the Find Account dialog box; enter the name of the user or group, and choose the **S**earch button. When NT locates the user or group, choose the **A**dd button to attach that name to the list.

8. When you're done, choose OK in the Add Users and Groups dialog box to return to the New Local Group dialog box. Choose OK to close the dialog box and return to the User Manager. The new group is listed in the Manager.

Global Groups

Creating a global group is similar to creating a local group; you can either copy an existing group or start a new one. In the User Manager for Domains, choose **U**ser,

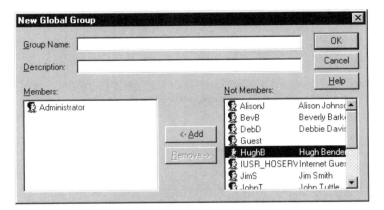

Figure 3.12 In the New Global Group dialog box, choose users and/or other groups to add to the new global group.

New **G**lobal Group to start a new group; choose **U**ser, **C**opy to copy an existing group. The New Global Group dialog box appears, as shown in Figure 3.12.

Enter the **G**roup Name and, optionally, a **D**escription. In the **N**ot Members of list, choose the users to add and then select the **A**dd button. Unfortunately, you can add only one user at a time instead of selecting multiple users in this dialog box. When you're done, choose OK to close the dialog box.

You can assign rights to the new group, as you would with an existing group. For more information, see Chapter 4, "Managing Security Policies."

Deleting and Editing Groups

You can delete and edit groups you create, just as you can delete and edit built-in groups. To delete a group, select the group in the User Manager for Domains Group list and choose **U**ser, **D**elete. NT warns you with a message dialog box that once you delete a group, you cannot restore access to resources without completely re-creating the group and reassigning rights. Choose OK and confirm the deletion in another dialog box to erase the group from the list.

To edit a group's properties, select the group name and choose **U**ser, **P**roperties. The Local Group Properties dialog box appears, in which you can edit the description of the group and add and remove members.

4 Managing Security Policies

In Chapter 3, "Working with Users and Groups," you learned about various built-in groups supplied by Windows NT Server. Each group has specific rights and abilities assigned to it, enabling the members of that group access to the network and its resources. As administrator of the network, you can modify the rights and abilities to any group, assign rights to new groups, and designate which groups your users belong to.

In addition to user and group rights, you can set specific permissions for directories, files, and other resources, such as printers. Similar to NetWare's attributes, permissions designate access to the specific resource; for example, you might set a read-only permission to a file, a read and write permission to a directory (folder), or full control to a printer on the network.

TIP: In this chapter, I generally use the words directory and subdirectory instead of folder and subfolder; however, the terms are interchangeable and mean: a convenient way of organizing and grouping files and other directories in a hierarchical file system.

In this chapter, you learn to:

- Understand the difference between rights, abilities, and permissions.
- Manage the user rights policy.
- Understand sharing resources.
- Sharing and stop sharing.
- Grant permissions for files, directories, and other resources.

Using Rights, Abilities, and Permissions

Rights and abilities authorize users and groups to perform certain tasks, such as logging on to the server, managing security logs, adding users to the domain, and so on. NT's built-in system of security grants these rights and abilities to predetermined groups of users. The Administrators group, for instance, has full control over the network; a member of the Administrators group has all rights and abilities so he or she can perform all of the tasks necessary to administer the network. A member of the Print Operators group, on the other hand, has only the rights necessary for performing his or her job: logging on to the server, shutting down the system (file server), and sharing and stopping the sharing of printers.

NT segments rights among the different groups to divide the workload. The Administrator could perform all of the tasks, as necessary; however, it's easier and more efficient to assign specific users to perform such tasks as managing printers, user accounts, and backup operations. It is up to you to assign the users of your network to the specific groups that match the rights and permissions you want them to have.

Client/Server vs. Peer-to-Peer

Some NetWare administrators may be concerned about the work involved with running an NT Server network; administration may seem more like a peer-to-peer network using NT groups, rights, and permissions, than like a true client/server network. With NetWare, users cannot access another workstation and its resources; all resources made available to a user must be placed on the server. The NetWare client/server setup makes administering the network easier than a peer-to-peer because you don't have to be concerned about who has permission to use that file, or whether that printer is shared or not, and so on.

By default, in NT, members of the Administrators group have full control over the network, and members of the Users group have no rights or controls, whatsoever. As administrator of the network, you choose which users to assign to which groups. If you want, you can assign all users to the Users group and leave the Users group as is, with no special rights granted to its members. You also can set up permissions from the server so that everyone has rights only to those files, programs, and other resources you specify. You can set up a dedicated print server to take care of the printing needs of all users. NT offers flexibility and control. You make the decisions; you set up the network in the way that makes it comfortable to work with.

NT Server Rights and Abilities

Rights and abilities apply to tasks the user can perform on the network. There are regular rights you can assign as well as advanced rights. For the most part, you'll work with the regular rights, since advanced rights deal with programmers writing applications running on NT. Some advanced rights are create a pagefile, debug programs, increase quotas for objects, log on as a batch job, and so on. For more information about advanced rights, see Windows NT Server help.

Abilities are built-in devices or rights that enable users to perform tasks. For example, all users have the ability to create and manage their local group; that is, the group of users who access their own machines. Following is an explanation of the abilities and the groups to which they're assigned.

Note: The ability to create and manage local groups applies only to workstations running Windows NT Workstation software (versions 3.5, 3.51, and 4.0); workstations running MS-DOS, Windows for Workgroups 3.11, and so on, do not have the software abilities to create and manage a local group even though they have the network's permission to do so.

Rights are granted and restricted on the domain level. Rights apply to group members on all primary and backup domain controllers in the domain. However, rights assigned on Windows NT Workstation computers or NT Server member computers apply only to that single computer.

You use the User Manager for Domains on a primary or backup domain controller to assign rights for the domain; you use User Manager on a member server or NT Workstation computer to assign rights to local groups and users. For more information about the User Manager for Domains, see Chapter 3.

Describing Rights and Abilities

You can assign rights to a user or to a group. You'll save time and effort by assigning rights to groups, however, and then place the users in those groups. See Chapter 3, "Working with Users and Groups," for more information. Abilities are built in. You cannot assign abilities as you would rights; however, you can assign users to the groups with built-in abilities.

Rights

Following is a description of the regular rights assigned from the file server, User Manager for Domains:

Log on locally. Enables a user to log on locally to the server computer. Groups granted this right by default include the Administrators, Server Operators, Account Operators, Print Operators, and Backup Operators groups.

Access this computer from the network. Enables the user to connect and use the server's resources over the network. Groups granted this right by default include the Administrators and Everyone groups.

Take ownership of files. Allows the user to take ownership of files and objects owned by other users; when a user has ownership of a file, he or she can read and edit the file, move the file, even delete the file from the drive. Groups granted this right by default include the Administrators group.

Manage auditing and security log. NT includes the Event Viewer program that can be set to monitor events such as unsuccessful logons and other breaches to security. The events that are monitored are recorded in a security log. This right enables the user to specify the type of events that are monitored, as well as the type of resource events that will be audited. Additionally, the user can view and/or clear the security log in the Event Viewer if granted this right. Groups granted this right by default include the Administrators group.

Change the system time. Allows the user to set the time for the internal clock in the server computer. Groups granted this right by default include the Administrators and Server Operators groups.

Shut down the system. Enables the user to shut down the entire NT network from the server. Groups granted this right by default include the Administrators, Server Operators, Account Operators, Print Operators, and Backup Operators groups.

Force shutdown from a remote system. Allows the user to shut down the network from any workstation or remote access system. Groups granted this right by default include the Administrators group and Server Operators group.

Back up files and directories. Allows the user to create backups of the files and directories (folders) on the network. This right overrides any file and directory permissions set on individual computers or the server. Groups granted this right by default include the Administrators, Server Operators, and Backup Operators groups.

Restore files and directories. Enables the user to restore backed up files and directories. This right overrides any file and directory permissions, as well. Groups granted this right by default include the Administrators, Server Operators, and Backup Operators groups.

Load and unload device drivers. Users can load and unload device drivers to the server for operation of hardware. Groups granted this right by default include the Administrators group.

Managing Security Policies **67**

Add workstations to the domain. In addition to being a built-in ability for the Administrators and Account Operators groups, this is also a right that enables the user to add workstations to the domain. This right is granted to no one group in particular; however, members of the Administrators or Account Operators groups can assign this right to others.

Built-in Abilities

Abilities are built in, by default, so you cannot assign or change them. Abilities simply apply to certain groups. Following are descriptions of the abilities and the groups granted them:

Add workstation to domain. Users can add a workstation to the home domain, for instance, when a new workstation is added to the network. Groups granted this ability by default include the Administrators and Account Operators groups.

Create and manage user accounts. Users can open the User Manager for Domains and create, delete, edit, and otherwise control user accounts for the domain. Groups granted this ability by default include the Administrators and Account Operators groups; however, members of the Account Operators group cannot modify the accounts of the Administrators, Domain Admins global group, or the Administrators, Servers, Account Operators, Print Operators, or Backup Operators local groups (or any global groups that are members of these local groups), but they can modify all other accounts.

Create and manage global groups. Users can create and manage global groups in the User Manager for Domains. Again, the Administrators and Account Operators groups are granted this ability by default, and the Account Operators group is limited in which groups it can manage (see previous paragraph).

Create and manage local groups. Users can create, edit, and manage local groups. The abilities are granted to the Administrators and Account Operators groups, by default, and the same limitations apply to the Account Operators groups as outlined in the previous paragraph. In addition, users have this ability, but they cannot create local groups on the server if they do not have the ability to log on to the server or access to the User Manager for Domains tools.

Assign user rights. Users can assign user rights to any member of the domain. Groups granted this ability by default include the Administrators group.

Lock the server. Users can lock the server so no changes to configuration can be made. Groups granted this ability by default include the Administrators, Server Operators, and Everyone groups; although the Everyone group has the ability to lock the server, only those who can log on to the server can actually lock it.

Override the lock of the server. Users can unlock the server if it has been locked. Groups granted this ability by default include the Administrators and Server Operators groups.

Format server's hard disk. Users can format the server's hard disk, thus erasing all data from that disk. By default only the Administrators group is granted this ability.

Create common groups. Users can create groups. Groups granted this ability by default include the Administrators and Server Operators groups.

Share and stop sharing directories. The ability to share and stop sharing directories means to designate any directory on the server as one that can be accessed by others on the network. Groups granted this ability by default include the Administrators and Server Operators groups. See the section "Sharing Resources" later in this chapter for more information.

Share and stop sharing printers. Sharing a printer designates that resource as one others on the network can access and use. Groups granted this ability by default include the Administrators, Server Operators, and Print Operators groups. See the section, "Sharing Resources" later in this chapter for more information.

Assigning Rights to Users and Groups

To assign or revoke rights, you use the User Manager for Domains on the primary domain controller. Following are the steps used to assign and revoke rights. For more information about users and groups, see Chapter 3.

Note: Use the User Manager on any computer running NT Workstation or on a member server running NT Server software to control the rights for that particular computer. You can create and edit users and groups, assign rights and permissions, and otherwise manage the resources to that computer.

---

1 Open the User Manager for Domains by selecting the Start button, **P**rograms, Administrative Tools, and User Manager for Domains. Figure 4.1 shows the User Manager for Domains tool.

2. Choose **P**olicies, **U**ser Rights. The User Rights Policy dialog box appears (see Figure 4.2).

3. In the Right drop-down list, choose the right you want to assign (refer to the list of rights and descriptions in the previous section).

4. To add users or groups to the **G**rant To list, select the **A**dd button. The Add Users and Groups dialog box appears, as shown in Figure 4.3.

Managing Security Policies **69**

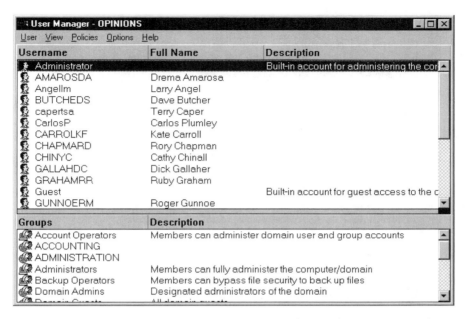

Figure 4.1 *Use this tool to control users and groups for the entire domain in the User Manager for Domains.*

5. In the **L**ist Names From drop-down list box, select the domain or computer you want to work with.
6. Select a group from the **N**ames list and choose the **A**dd button. The domain name and group name appear in the **Ad**d Names list at the bottom of the dialog box. You can continue to add users and groups to the list without closing the dialog box in between.

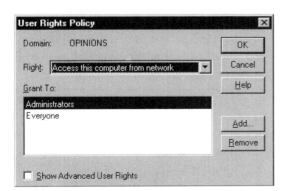

Figure 4.2 *Grant rights to groups in the User Rights Policy dialog box.*

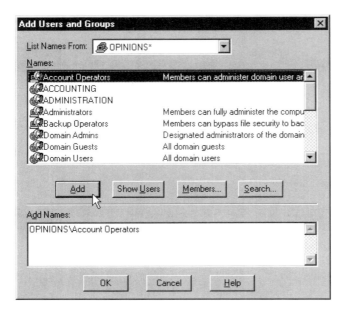

Figure 4.3 *In the Add Users and Groups dialog box, choose the names to add to the list for granting rights.*

7. You can also choose from the following:

    To display the users in the domain, choose the Show **U**sers button.

    To display the members of any group, choose the **M**embers button.

    To search for a group or member not listed, choose the **S**earch button and enter the name in the Find **U**ser or Group text box and choose the **S**earch button.

Note: If you accidentally add a user or group and you want to remove it, you can either cancel the dialog box and start again or you can choose OK and remove the one name from the User Rights Policy dialog box by selecting the name and choosing the Remove button.

---

8. Choose OK to close the Add Users or Groups dialog box. The names appear in the **G**rant To list in the User Rights Policy dialog box. To remove any name in the dialog box, select the name and choose the **R**emove button.

9. You can choose OK to close the User Rights Policy dialog box and save the changes, or you can choose another right from the drop-down Righ**ts** list and add or remove users and/or groups to that list.

Managing Security Policies 71

Setting Account Policies

Similar to NetWare, NT provides account policies that govern password restrictions. In NetWare, you set default password policies and then create your users so that they all begin with those restrictions. In NT, the process is nearly the same. You set a general password and lockout policy in the Account Policy dialog box and then, if necessary, set user-specific policies in the User Properties dialog box as explained in Chapter 3. The account policy in NT governs password restrictions, length, and uniqueness, and account lockout for all users on the domain. You set the account policies for all users in the User Manager for Domains.

To open the Account Policy dialog box, in the User Manager for Domains, choose the **P**olicies menu, **A**ccount command. Figure 4.4 shows the Account Policy dialog box; Table 4.1 describes the options in the dialog box.

TIP: For information about how the Migration Tool transfers user rights from NetWare to NT, see Chapter 7, "Planning the Migration."

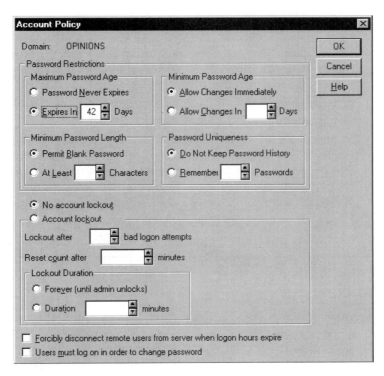

Figure 4.4 Manage passwords and account lockouts in the Account Policy dialog box.

Table 4.1 Account Policy Options

PASSWORD RESTRICTIONS AREA	
Maximum Password Age	Choose either Password **N**ever Expires or **E**xpires In *x* Days and fill in the number of days in the text box to limit the time users can use their password; the number ranges from 1 to 999.
Minimum Password Age	Choose either **A**llow Changes Immediately or Allow **C**hanges In *x* Days to govern when the users can change their own passwords; the number ranges from 1 to 999.
Minimum Password Length	Choose either Permit **B**lank Password or At **L**east *x* Characters to govern whether the user can press Enter instead of using a password and the minimum length of the password; the number ranges from 1 to 14.
Password Uniqueness	Choose either **D**o Not Keep Password History or **R**emember *x* Passwords to control the users' implementation of the same password over and over again; you can choose from 1 to 24 passwords if you select the **R**emember option.
Account Lockout	Choose either No Account Lockou**t** or Account Loc**k**out.
ACCOUNT LOCKOUT AREA	
Lockout after *x* bad logon attempts	If you choose the Account Loc**k**out option, enter the number of failed logon attempts NT should accept before locking the account out; number ranges from 1 to 999.
Reset count after *x* minutes	Enter the number of minutes you want NT to wait before another logon attempt; the number ranges between 1 and 99999.
Lockout Duration	Choose either Fore**v**er, or Dura**t**ion *x* minutes to indicate that the lockout lasts until the administrator unlocks it in the user's User Properties dialog box or the length you want the lockout to remain in place; the number ranges from 1 to 99999.
Users must log on in order to change password	Select to require a user to log on before the password can be changed (if this box is not checked, the users can change their expired passwords without notifying the administrator).

Setting Audit Policies

One final security policy you can set in the User Manager for Domains is the audit policies. Audit policies determine the tracking of certain user activities and the recording of those activities in a security log. You can then view the security log in a Windows NT Server utility called the Event Viewer (see "Viewing a Security Log in the Event Viewer").

Managing Security Policies

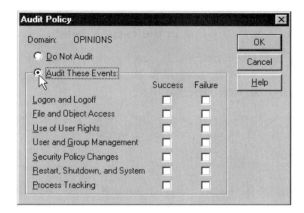

Figure 4.5 Activate tracking of certain events for security purposes in the Audit Policy dialog box.

To set auditing policies, choose **P**olicies, Au**d**it in the User Manager for Domains. The Audit Policy dialog box appears with the default option, **D**o Not Audit, selected. To activate the auditing of certain events, choose the **A**udit These Events option and then select the events you want to audit. When selecting each event, you can choose to log successful occurrences of the event and/or failed occurrences of the event. Figure 4.5 shows the Audit Policy dialog box and Table 4.2 describes the types of events.

Table 4.2 Audit Policy Event Types

Logon and Logoff	Applies to a user logging on or off the server or making a network connection.
File and Object Access Management	Records when a user accesses a directory, file, or printer that is set for auditing.
Use of User Rights	Records any exercised user right other than logging on or off the network.
User and **G**roup Management	Reports a user account that has been created, edited, deleted, renamed, disabled, or enabled or when a password has been set or changed.
Security Policy Changes	Documents any change to the User Rights or Audit policies.
Restart, Shutdown, and System	Records when a user shut down or restarted the server or some other event that affects the entire system.
Process Tracking	Provides tracking of events such as program activation, indirect access of an object, process exit, and so on.

> **Viewing a Security Log in the Event Viewer**
>
> The security log records events that change the security system of the network and identifies any possible breaches to security. Only members of the Administrators group can view the security logs in the Event Viewer.
>
> View the security log in the Event Viewer by choosing Start, **P**rograms, Administrative Tools, and the Event Viewer. In the Event Viewer window, select the **L**og menu, Se**c**urity command to display the security log. Events are listed by date and time, with the source of the event, category, event name, user, and computer listed as well.
>
> To view details about any one event, double-click that event. The Event Detail dialog box displays a description of the event for more information that's displayed in the log window. You can sort, or filter, events so that you view the events from a specific time period or type of event; choose **V**iew, Fi**l**ter Events and fill in the appropriate time and dates.
>
> Finally, you can choose **L**og, **S**elect Computer to display the computers on the network in the Select Computer dialog box. Select the computer whose events you want to view and choose OK. The security log for that computer appears in the Event Viewer. When you're finished viewing events, choose **L**og, E**x**it to close the Event Viewer.

Sharing Resources

As with NetWare, NT Server enables you to designate resources you want to share across the network, including files, directories, and printers; and NT lets you restrict the use of resources to certain users and groups. NetWare uses attributes to limit access to files and directories; NT calls the same limits "permissions."

Before you set the permissions on a file or directory, you must designate the directory as a shared directory. Users cannot access any file or directory on the server or other network computer unless it is shared. When you share a directory, all subdirectories and files in that directory are also shared. Then you set permissions to control access to the shared resources.

You designate shares with the NT Explorer, which looks and acts similarly to the File Manager in previous version of Windows. Open the NT Explorer by choosing Start, **P**rograms, and Windows NT Explorer. Figure 4.6 shows the Explorer; the left window pane displays the hard drive plus folders on that drive, floppy drives, tape and/or CD drives, the Network Neighborhood, and other items on the Desktop. The right pane displays the folders and files of any element selected in the left pane.

Managing Security Policies

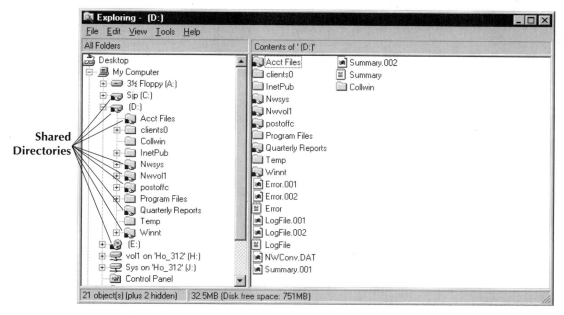

Figure 4.6 The NT Explorer lets you manage the files and directories on the server and on other computers attached to the network.

Sharing Resources Guidelines

When you share a directory on an NTFS volume, all files and directories within that directory become available to the network users. You can, however, place restrictions on any file or subdirectory to limit access with permissions (see the following section, "Granting Permissions").

Users can view shared drives from their Network Neighborhood (Windows NT Workstation, Windows NT Server, and Windows 95) in the Connect Network Drive dialog box (Windows for Workgroups) or from the command prompt (DOS workstations).

When sharing a directory, you choose a share name that represents it to the users; normally, it's easier to use the directory's given name as a share name. Since Windows NT enables the use of long file names, you can use up to 80 characters (including spaces) if your clients use only Windows NT and/or Windows 95 operating systems. If you do have DOS users (including workstations using Windows for Workgroups) on the network, follow the 8.3 DOS file-naming convention for share names you assign to directories; DOS users will not be able to access shares that don't follow this convention.

You can still use the long file names for files and directories, even if you do have DOS clients on the network. NT provides name mapping that assigns a file or

> ### Using the NT Explorer
>
> You can use the Explorer to create and delete folders and subfolders (subdirectories), copy and move files and folders, rename files and folders, map network drives, view details about files, open applications and network drives, and more. Following are just a few instructions on the use of the Explorer; invoke Explorer Help to find out more. Notice that the Explorer uses the term "folder" in place of "directory," and displays folder icons to represent the organization of the drives.
>
> To view the contents of any drive, folder, or other element in the left pane of the Explorer window, click the element one time; its contents appear in the right pane. In the right pane, double-click on a folder to open it; double-clicking on a file will open it, as well.
>
> Following are other tasks you can perform in the Explorer:
>
> - Choose **V**iew, **D**etails to view file size, creation or modification date, and attributes.
> - Choose **T**ools, **F**ind, **F**iles or Folders or **C**omputer to search for an item you cannot locate.
> - Choose **T**ools, **M**ap Network Drive to map drives on the network.
> - Select a file or folder and choose **E**dit, **C**opy or Cut; then select the folder or drive in which you want to place the file or folder; choose **E**dit, **P**aste to insert the file or folder to its new location.
> - Choose **F**ile, Ne**w**, **F**older to create a new folder on the selected drive or folder.

directory a second name, in addition to the long file name, that follows the 8.3 convention. NT converts long file names using the following these guidelines:

- Removes all spaces.
- Changes characters not allowed in DOS names to an underscore (_).
- Truncates the name to its first six characters, adds a tilde (~) and a digit (1, 2, and so on).
- If the name has a period in it, NT uses the first three characters after the period as the extension in the DOS name.

Note: You can still use applications that do not support long filenames in NT, but if the application opens a file with a long file name, the long name is lost and only the short name remains.

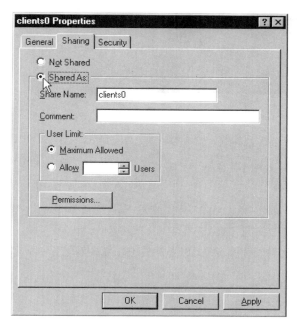

Figure 4.7 *Choose to share a directory and then set the options for the share.*

Sharing NT Server Resources

To share the resources on the server, you use the NT Explorer to designate those shares. You must be logged on to the domain controller as a member of the Administrators or Server Operators group or have the right to create permanent shared objects to designate shared directories on the domain. The Explorer represents shared directories and files with an outstretched hand icon (refer to Figure 4.6).

To share a directory, follow these steps:

1. In the Explorer, select the directory you want to share.
2. Choose **F**ile, **P**roperties; the directory's Properties dialog box appears.
3. Choose the Sharing tab. To activate sharing, select the **Sh**ared As option and the sharing area becomes available (see Figure 4.7).
4. If you want to change the share name, enter a new name in the **S**hare Name text box; users will identify the resource by its share name.
5. Optionally, enter text in the **C**omment text box; this text will be displayed for users to see.
6. You can set a limit to how many users can access the directory at one time. In the User Limit area, choose one of the following options:

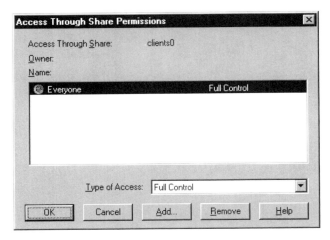

Figure 4.8 By default, Everyone has permission to access the directory.

Maximum Allowed enables the highest possible number of users to access the directory at one time.

Allo**w** *x* Users enables you to set a limit as to how many users can access the directory at one time.

7. Click the **P**ermissions button to view the list of users and groups that can access the directory. The Access Through Share Permissions dialog box appears (see Figure 4.8).

8. You can decide who has access to the directory:

    To add users and/or groups, choose the **A**dd button. The Add Users and Groups dialog box appears (refer to Figure 4.3). Add users and/or groups and then choose OK to close the dialog box.

    To remove Everyone, or any other group or user, select the name in the **N**ame list and choose the **R**emove button.

9. To set the access level for anyone on the list, select the name and choose the **T**ype of Access drop-down box; you can select Full Control, No Access, Read, or Change.

10. Choose OK to close the dialog box and choose OK again to close the Properties dialog box.

Stopping Sharing

You can stop sharing a directory at any time from the NT Explorer. Select the directory and choose **F**ile, **P**roperties; alternatively, you can right-click a directory

Managing Security Policies **79**

Designating Shares with the Server Manager

NT Server also supplies a Server Manager that you can use to designate and view shared drives. The Server Manager enables you to manage directory replication, control services, send messages to connected users, and more. For more information about the Server Manager, see Chapter 15, "Managing Multiple Domains."

You must be logged on as a member of the domain Administrators local group to designate shared directories using the Server Manager. Any member of the Administrators or Server Operators group can also use the Server Manager to designate shared resources.

To open the Server Manager, choose Start, **P**rogram, Administrative Tools, and Server Manager. To set shares, select the server or other computer and choose **C**omputer, Shared **D**irectory. The Shared Directory dialog box displays only shared directories.

You can add a share by choosing the **N**ew Share button. In the New Shared dialog box, enter a share name, the path to the directory, any comment you want to add, and choose the User Limit (the same as you would in the Sharing tab of the Properties dialog box for any directory). Choose OK to close the dialog box or choose the Pe**r**missions button to set access permissions.

To stop sharing a directory, in the Shared Directory dialog box, select the directory and choose the **S**top Sharing button. To close the dialog box, choose the Close (X) button. Click the Close button (X) in the title bar of the Server Manager to close the utility.

---

and choose S**h**aring from the shortcut menu. Choose the Sharing tab of the Properties dialog box and select the N**o**t Shared option. Choose OK to close the dialog box.

Printer Sharing and Permissions

Users logged on to a domain controller as a member of the Administrators, Domain Admin, Server Operators, or Print Operators can choose to share or stop sharing printers. A shared printer can be used by anyone on the network, unless specific permissions are applied. After you share a printer, you can set access permissions that govern the printer.

TIP: You also can share CD-ROM drives, floppy drives, tape backups, and other resources using similar steps as for sharing directories; just locate the item in the Explorer and designate it as shared.

Figure 4.9 *All network printers appear in the Printers dialog box.*

For more information about installing a printer to the network, print queues, and other printing issues, see Chapter 5, "Managing Print Services."

Sharing a Printer

To share a printer, you use the Printers folder instead of the NT Explorer. Follow these steps:

1. Choose Start, **S**ettings, **P**rinters. The Printers folder window appears (see Figure 4.9).
2. Select the printer you want to share and choose **F**ile, S**h**aring. The printer's Properties dialog box appears, as shown in Figure 4.10.
3. In the Sharing tab, choose the **S**hared option.
4. In the Share Name text box, accept the default name or enter a name for users to see when they access the printer.
5. If necessary, choose additional drivers to install for users to access from the network; you must have your NT Server CD to install new drivers.
6. Choose OK to close the dialog box.

Setting Printer Permissions

You can also set permissions on printers. Since printer permissions are similar to directory access permissions, I'll discuss those in this section rather than in the next. To set permissions for a printer, follow these steps:

1. Open the printer's Properties dialog box by choosing Start, **S**ettings, and **P**rinters.

Managing Security Policies

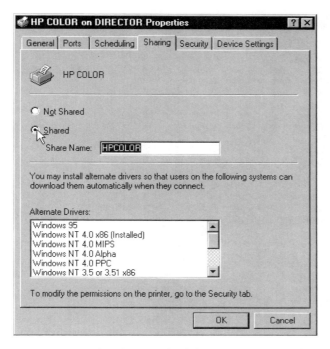

Figure 4.10 The Sharing tab of the Properties dialog box appears, ready for you to modify.

2. Choose **F**ile, **Sh**aring.
3. Choose the Security tab in the printer's Properties dialog box, as shown in Figure 4.11.
4. Choose the **P**ermissions button to display the Printer Permissions dialog box (see Figure 4.12).
5. To add groups and/or users, choose the **A**dd button to display the Add Users and Groups dialog box. Select the names you want to add and then choose OK to close the dialog box. To remove any names from the list in the Printer Permissions dialog box, select the name and choose the **R**emove button.
6. Select the name in the list and then choose the access you want to apply from the **T**ype of Access drop-down list. You can choose from the following permissions:

    No Access. User or group does not have permission to print or otherwise use the printer.

    Print. Grants permission to print to the printer.

Chapter 4

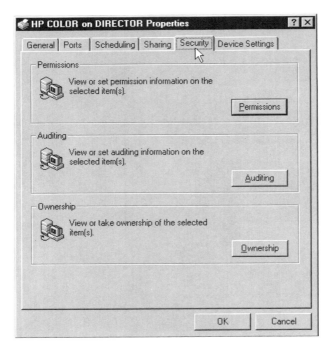

Figure 4.11 Set printer permissions in the Security tab of the Properties dialog box.

Figure 4.12 Set access permissions for users and/or groups in this dialog box.

Managing Security Policies **83**

> **Manage Documents.** Grants permission to open the print queue and rearrange printing order, delete or pause printing, and otherwise manage the printing of the documents in the queue.
>
> **Full Control.** Grants permission to print, manage print jobs in the queue, and manage the printer.

7. Choose OK to close the Printer Permissions dialog box, and choose OK again to close the printer's Properties dialog box.

Granting Permissions

When you designate a shared directory, all files and subdirectories it contains are also shared. You can limit access to the shared directory by setting access permissions, as described in the last section. Additionally, you can set file and directory permissions for each file or subdirectory you share. You set file and directory permissions in the NT Explorer. Some limits apply, depending on whether you use the NTFS or FAT file system.

Directory permissions can be granted to local groups, global groups, and individual users in the server's domain; global groups and individual users from trusted domains; and special groups: Everyone, System, Interactive, and Creator/Owner. Permissions apply to both users working on the local computer and users accessing the computer's resources over the network. The following guidelines and rules apply to permissions:

- Permissions are cumulative. If a user is a member of several groups, each group's permissions apply.
- The No Access permission overrides all other permissions.
- Newly created subdirectories and files inherit permissions from the directory.
- The owner (or creator) of a file or directory controls access to that file or directory.
- Members of the Administrators group can take ownership of files and/or directories.

TIP: User rights take precedence over object permissions; for example, the Backup Operator has rights to get to your files, even no access files.

File Systems and Sharing

NT's permissions are more effective when used on an NTFS (New Technology File System) than when used with the FAT (File Allocation Table) file system.

When using NTFS volumes, you can set not only directory permissions but also file permissions. NTFS permissions apply to users and groups, both locally and over the network.

Volumes that use the FAT file system are somewhat limited as far as permissions are concerned. You can protect files but only at the directory level, and only over the network. You first choose to share the directory, then you can protect it by specifying permissions that apply only to a directory. File-level permissions aren't available on FAT volumes; only directory-level permissions are valid.

Directory and File Permissions Described

Directories inherit their permissions from their parent directories, and files inherit their permissions from the directory in which they reside. The standard permissions that you can apply to a file or directory are described in Table 4.3.

Directory and file permissions consist of combinations of the standard permissions listed in Table 4.3. Table 4.4 describes the directory permissions. The standard permissions in the first set of parentheses refer to permissions for the directory itself, and in the second set of parentheses, the individual permissions that apply for new files subsequently created in the directory.

TIP: For information about how the Migration Tool transfers NetWare file and directory rights to NT during a migration, see Chapter 7.

Table 4.3 Standard Permissions

Permission	Description
Read (R)	Allows display of a directory or file's contents, attributes, owner, and so on.
Write (W)	Permits creation of subdirectories and files, changes to file's data and attributes, display of permissions and owner.
Execute (X)	Allows display of attributes, permissions, and owner, changing to subdirectories, and running program files.
Delete	Enables deletion of a directory or file.
Change Permissions (P)	Permits changes to the file's or directory's permissions.
Take Ownership (O)	Allows changes to directory's or file's ownership.

Table 4.4 Directory and File Permissions

Permission	Description
Directory Permissions	
No Access (none) (none)	Cannot access the directory in any way, not even to view directory, subdirectory, or file contents.
List (RX) (not specified)	List subdirectories and files in the directory and change to a subdirectory; cannot access new files created in the directory.
Read (RX) (RX)	Read file contents and run applications in the directory.
Add (WX) (not specified)	Add files to the directory; cannot read or change the contents of current files.
Add and Read (RWX) (RX)	Add files to directory and read current files; cannot change files.
Change (RWXD) (RWXD)	Read and add files, change contents of current files.
Full Control (all) (all)	Read and change files, add files, change permissions for the directory and its contents, and take ownership of the directory and its files.
File Permissions	
No Access	Cannot access the file in any way.
Read (RX)	Read file contents and run application files.
Change (RWXD)	Read, change, and delete the file.
Full Control (all)	Read, change, delete, set permissions for, and take ownership of the file.

Setting Permissions

You set directory and file permissions in the NT Explorer. The procedures for setting permissions for files and directories are the same; only the permissions you choose change. To set directory and/or file permissions, follow these steps:

1. In the Explorer, select the directory or file.
2. Choose **F**ile, **P**roperties; alternatively, right-click the file or directory and choose **P**roperties from the shortcut menu. The folder's Properties dialog box appears.

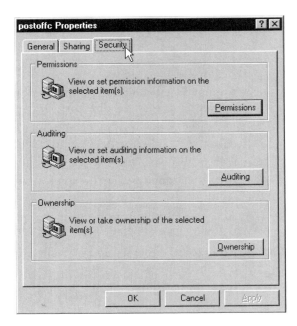

Figure 4.13 Set permissions in the Properties dialog box.

3. Choose the Security tab (see Figure 4.13).
4. Choose the **P**ermissions button; the Directory or File Permissions dialog box appears (see Figure 4.14).
5. By default, directory permissions apply only to the directory and its files. You can, however, choose one of the following options in the Directory Permissions dialog box:

    Replac**e** Permissions on Subdirectories. A check in the box applies the permissions to all subdirectories.

    Replace Permissions on Existing **F**iles. Clear the check box to apply permissions to the directory only.

6. In the **N**ame list box, a list of the groups and users who have permission to use the file or directory appears. Select a group or user and choose the permission you want to set from the **T**ype of Access drop-down box.
7. You also can add or remove groups and users:

    To add users or groups, choose the **A**dd button to display the Add Users and Groups dialog box.

    To remove names, select the name and choose the **R**emove button.

Managing Security Policies

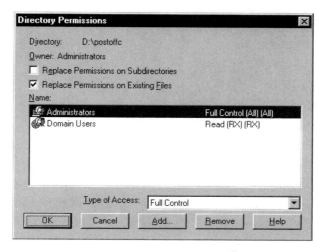

Figure 4.14 The Directory Permissions dialog box provides two Replace options that the File Permissions directory dialog box does not.

8. Choose OK when you're done to close the dialog box; choose OK again to close the Properties dialog box.

Note: NT provides special directory access and file access permissions you can set to customize permissions. In the Directory or File Permissions dialog box, select the user or group for which you want to customize permissions and then choose the **T**ype of Access drop-down list and from it select either Special Directory Access or Special File Access. In the Special Access dialog box, choose the permissions you want to apply and choose OK.

Taking Ownership

Members of the Administrators group control permissions set on files and directories; however, the user who created the files and/or directories is also the owner and can control permissions. This way, users can keep their files on the server private.

TIP: The Creator/Owner, a specialized group introduced in Chapter 3, applies to the creator of a file or directory.

Figure 4.15 View or take ownership of a file or directory.

Members of the Administrators group generally create and own most files on the server because it is the administrator who installs applications and creates directories. Individual users often create only data files to store on the server, and those are usually stored in the users' home directories.

Note: When you migrate files and directories from NetWare to NT, the NT Administrator becomes the owner of all files and directories.

The administrator can take ownership of a file or directory at any time by following these steps:

1. Open the directory's or file's Properties dialog box and choose the Security tab.
2. Choose the **O**wnership button. The Owner dialog box appears (see Figure 4.15).
3. Choose the **T**ake Ownership button and then close the dialog box.

Auditing Security Events

You can use the Directory and File Auditing feature to audit the use of a file or directory by users and groups. You view the results of the auditing in the Event Viewer. See Chapter 3 for information about viewing and auditing events.

Note: Before you can audit security events, you must activate the security log in the User Manager for Domains. Open the User Manager for Domains and choose **P**olicies, Au**d**it. In the Audit Policy dialog box, choose to **A**udit These Events and choose **S**ecurity Policy Changes. Choose OK to close the dialog box. For more information about the User Manager for Domains, see Chapter 3.

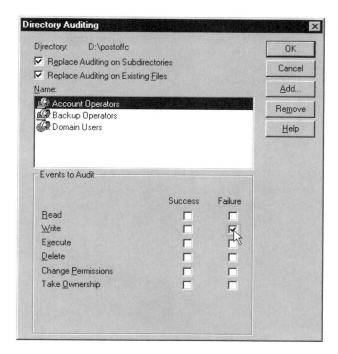

Figure 4.16 *Audit the use of directories and files.*

By default, auditing changes on a directory apply only to the directory and its files. The Directory Auditing dialog box offers two options not found in the Files Auditing dialog box. A check mark in the Replace auditing on Subdirectories check box applies auditing to all subdirectories; clearing the check box in front of Replace Auditing on Existing Files applies the auditing to the directory only. To audit events, follow these steps:

1. Open the directory's or file's Properties dialog box and choose the Security tab.
2. Choose the Auditing button to display the File or Directory Auditing dialog box (see Figure 4.16).
3. The currently audited groups and users appear in the Name list. You can add or remove groups and users to the list by doing the following:

    Add names by choosing the Add button and selecting users and groups from the Add Users and Groups dialog box.

    Remove names by selecting the user or group in the Name list and clicking the Remove button.

4. Select a group or user in the **N**ame list and then choose the event you want to audit by selecting the appropriate check box for auditing Success or Failure of the event.

5. Choose OK to close the dialog box. Choose OK to close the Properties dialog box.

5   *Managing Print Services*

Printing is one of the most important tasks on a network; if the users cannot print, the network is worthless. Users must be able to use network printers easily and efficiently, and it's the administrator's job to make sure they can.

Many familiar NetWare terms are also used with NT. A *print server* is the computer to which the printer is connected and on which the printer drivers are stored. The *print device* is the actual printer; whereas the *printer* is the interface between the operating system and the print device. Finally, the *queue* in NT is a list of documents waiting to be printed, whereas in NetWare, it's a directory to which print jobs are spooled until the printer is ready for them. Generally, the queue holds the jobs waiting to be printed.

In this chapter, you learn how to do the following:

- Plan and set up a print server.
- Configure a printer.
- Connect to a shared printer.
- Control printing through a print queue.

Advantages of the NT Print Server

With NT, you can use one computer as a print server whether that computer is the domain controller, a member server, or a computer running NT Workstation. That same computer can serve as a file server as well, depending on the number of clients and the traffic on your network.

If your network is small—10 clients or fewer—you can use a computer running NT Workstation as a print server. NT Workstation is, however, limited to only 10 connections; therefore, a larger network will need to use a computer running NT Server instead. Further, NT Workstation does not support Macintosh services or Gateway services for NetWare, thus it is impractical if your network administers to those clients.

NT Server software, on the other hand, is perfectly suited to use as a print server. Consider the following features NT offers:

- Using various methods—Network Neighborhood, Add Printer Wizard, Print Setup dialog box of Windows NT and Windows 95 clients—clients can browse the network for available printers.
- Clients can use network printers supplied by other operating systems, such as LAN Manager 2.x.
- An administrator can remotely administer the NT print server, printers, documents, and printer drivers.

As in NetWare, NT also supports the use of network-interface printers; that is, printers containing built-in network cards and connected to the network by cable rather than requiring a parallel or serial connection. Although you can use the network-interface printer directly, it's better to connect through a print server because there is no print queue associated with a network-interface printer.

Note: Windows NT and Windows 95 clients can install and update printer drivers using drivers loaded to the NT print server. MS-DOS and Windows for Workgroups clients can also access Windows NT printers; however, they must redirect the output ports to the appropriate *\\server\sharename*. Finally, non-Windows NT clients must install the printer driver manually and then connect to the server.

Planning Your Printing

You probably already have print devices you've used with your NetWare network, as well as a computer you want to use as a print server. Following are just a few guidelines for choosing the equipment you need to work with NT. More important, however, you'll want to think about how to set up your NT printers for the most efficient use of your print devices. This section offers some options for setting up print servers.

Print Devices

NT supports most print devices: dot-matrix, inkjet, and laser printers, as well as network-interface print devices and network-aware print devices connected to the network using AppleTalk or TCP/IP protocols. For an updated version of the Windows NT Hardware Compatibility List (HCL), see the Microsoft World Wide Web site at http://www.microsoft.com.

Note: When installing a network-interface print device, you install the DLC (data link control) protocol, AppleTalk protocol, or the Microsoft TCP/IP Printing service from the Network icon in the Control Panel folder. See "Using NT's TCP/IP Printing Service" for more information.

When choosing the print devices to use with NT, or any network, consider the following: printer speed, graphics support, quality, and durability. Consider, too, which of the add-on features you'll need, such as double-sided printing, dual paper bins, and so on.

Print Servers

A computer that serves as a print server on NT can also be used as a file or database server or as a dedicated print server (unlike in NetWare). You can choose to use the computer running NT Server software any way you like. Unless you have truly heavy traffic to the printer, you'll probably want to use the server as a file and print server rather than a dedicated print server. Either way, the computer onto which you load the NT Server operating system must have a license to run the software.

The computer should have at least 16MB RAM for a small number of print devices; more memory will be needed to manage a larger number of print devices or many large documents. Disk space is minimal. Remember, if you have more than 10 users attached to the network, you'll want to use NT Server software on the print server.

If you choose to use one server as both a file and print server, there are a few guidelines to be aware of. File operations always take first priority over printing transactions, although the impact printing has on file access and vice versa is insignificant. You will want to use a dedicated print server only if you'll have heavy traffic to multiple printers. The only other consideration with using one computer as a file and print server is security. A print server needs to be available to all users; but you might want to physically isolate a file server for security's sake.

Access to Printers

You can set up the users' access to printers in various ways with NT. You can set up a single printer to a single print device, multiple printers to a single print device, or a single printer to multiple identical print devices. This final option provides the most flexibility.

Using multiple printers leading to one print device, you can schedule printing times for specific print devices; for example, postpone the printing of less important documents until nonwork hours. You also can set different priority levels to control printer access, by assigning different groups to each printer and rights to the groups so that you prioritize documents by user instead of the actual document sent to the printer.

Another option to manage users access to the print devices is a printing pool. A pool consists of multiple, identical print devices associated with one printer. The idle print device, then, receives the next document to be printed. When the document is printed, NT's Messenger Service (if active) notifies the client and identifies the printer port to which the document was printed.

All of the print devices in a printing pool are the same hardware model, and they act as a single unit; therefore, all print settings apply to the entire pool. Ports, however, can be the same type or mixed: parallel, serial, and/or network. If one print device in the pool stops working for some reason—paper jam, runs out of paper, and so on—it holds the last document sent to it until someone fixes the problem; other documents sent to the pool continue to print from other devices.

Note: NT supports an unlimited number of serial and parallel ports; however, finding an available IRQ level may be difficult. The standard devices are assigned to IRQs as follows: LPT1 = IRQ7, LPT2 = IRQ5, COM1 = IRQ4, and COM2 = IRQ3. To see the current IRQ settings on your computer, run the Microsoft Diagnostics program by choosing Start, **P**rograms, Administrative Tools, Windows NT Diagnostics. NT analyzes your hardware and displays the results on the various tabs in the Diagnostics window.

Creating Printers

After you attach the print devices, you must create a printer on the print server by choosing a port, printer manufacturer, model, and otherwise defining the printer. To create a printer on the domain controller, you must be a member of the Administrators, Server Operators, or Print Operators group. To create a printer on a member server or NT Workstation, you must be a member of the Administrators or Power Users group; the Power Users group has rights and abilities on the NT Workstation or member server that are similar to a Server Operator's rights on the NT Server.

To create a printer, follow these steps:

Managing Print Services

Using NT's TCP/IP Printing Service

Clients on your network can output to most print devices attached to UNIX computers if you install the TCP/IP protocol and the Microsoft TCP/IP Printing service to the print server on the network.

Open the Control Panel and double-click the Network icon. Choose the Protocols tab and then select the **A**dd button. From the list of protocols, choose the TCP/IP protocol and choose OK. Configure the protocol by selecting TCP/IP in the Protocols tab of the Network dialog box and then choosing the **P**roperties button. Set the IP address, DNS, routing, and other options in the Microsoft TCP/IP Properties dialog box.

To install the Microsoft TCP/IP Printing service, open the Network icon from the Control Panel and choose the Services tab. Choose the **A**dd button and select the service from the list. Choose OK to close the dialog box and OK again. You'll have to reboot the computer to complete the service and protocol additions.

When you install the Microsoft TCP/IP Printing service, you also install the LPD (line printer daemon) service, which enables the print server to receive documents from line printer remote (LPR) utilities running on client systems, much like that on a UNIX system. The LPD services must be set to run automatically; in the Control Panel, choose the Services icon and change the startup options for the TCP/IP Print Server service.

---

1. Choose Start, **S**ettings, **P**rinters. The Printers window opens (see Figure 5.1).
2. Double-click the Add Printers icon. The first Printer wizard appears. Choose the N**e**twork printer server option (see Figure 5.2).

Figure 5.1 *Installed printers and the Add Printer icon appear in the Printers folder window.*

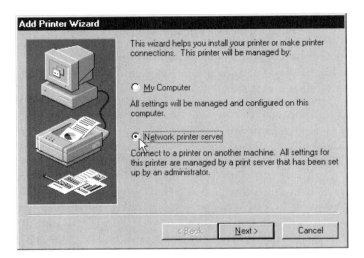

Figure 5.2 The Printer wizard leads you step by step to installing a printer in NT.

3. Choose the **N**ext button. The Connect to Printer dialog box appears.
4. Select the print device; if you do not see the print device, double-click the network, server, or computer attached to the print device to display the printer, as shown in Figure 5.3.

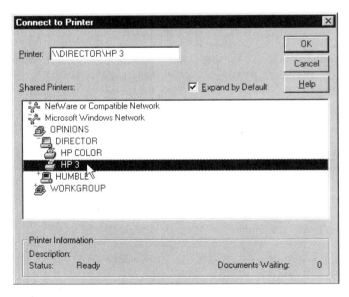

Figure 5.3 Select the print device in the Connect to Printer dialog box.

Managing Print Services **97**

Figure 5.4 *You'll need to install the driver to the server.*

5. Choose OK; a message may appear stating the server doesn't have an installed printer driver and asking if you want to install the driver, as shown in Figure 5.4. Choose OK.
6. In the next printer wizard dialog box that appears, choose the manufacturer of the printer from the **M**anufacturer's list and then choose the model in the **P**rinters list (see Figure 5.5).
7. Choose OK and insert the NT Server CD if prompted. NT copies the necessary printer drivers and then displays the specific printer's Properties dialog box. Figure 5.6 shows an HP LaserJet properties dialog box; naturally, the options in the dialog box change depending on the selected printer.
8. Choose the settings such as paper tray, font cartridges, paper size, and so on. When you select a setting in the upper window of the dialog box, the options in the lower portion of the dialog box change to related options.

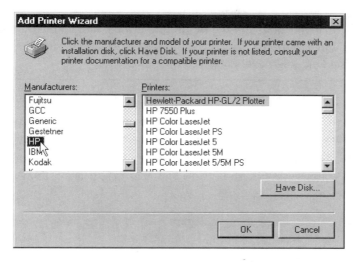

Figure 5.5 *Select the manufacturer of the printer to display available drivers for specific models via the Add Printer Wizard.*

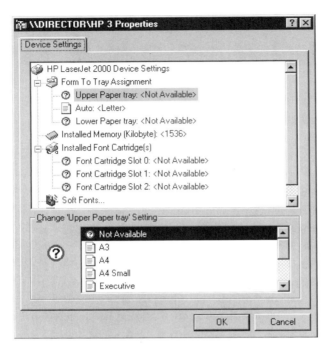

Figure 5.6 Settings are specific to the selected printer.

> **TIP:** You can change the settings for the printer at any time by opening the Printer window, right-clicking the printer to display the shortcut menu, and selecting Document Defaults from the menu.

9. Choose OK to close the Settings dialog box. The next Wizard dialog box asks if you want to use the printer as a default printer for the programs on the server (see Figure 5.7). Choose **Y**es or **N**o and then select **N**ext.
10. The final wizard box appears stating that the printer installation was successful. Choose the Finish button. The printer appears in the Printers window, as shown in Figure 5.8.

> **TIP:** You can set up additional printers for the same print device by using the same steps for creating a printer.

Managing Print Services

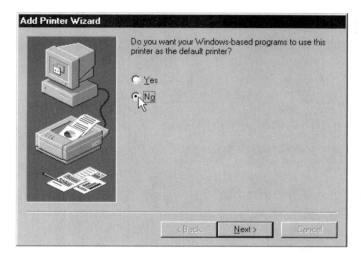

Figure 5.7 The default answer is not to use the printer as a default printer.

Configuring a Printer

When you configure the printer, you set up ports, separator pages, scheduling and priorities, spooling options, and so on. You can modify a printer's properties at any time by opening the Printers folder window and right-clicking the printer. From the shortcut menu, choose the **P**roperties command; the printer's Properties dialog box appears. Various tabs within the dialog box control the settings and configuration, as described in the following sections; depending on the type of print device you've installed, some of the options described here may or may not be available.

Figure 5.8 It is from the Printers window that you can set printer properties and control the print queue.

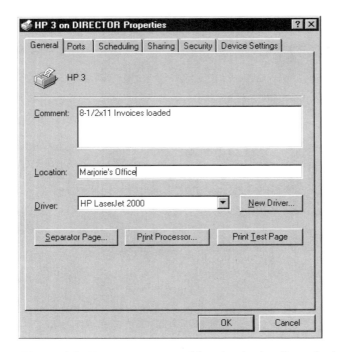

Figure 5.9 Enter comments and location in the General tab.

General Tab

The General tab of the Properties dialog box covers such information as the printer driver, separator page, print processor and so on. Figure 5.9 shows the General tab, and Table 5.1 describes the options in the dialog box.

Table 5.1 General Tab Options

OPTIONS	DESCRIPTION
Comments	Enter any remarks you want the users to see when browsing the network printers.
Location	Enter the physical location of the print device.
Driver	Set or change the print device type (for example, from an HP LaserJet 4MP to an HP LaserJet 5P).
New Driver	Select this button to choose a new driver.
Separator Page	Print one or more separator pages at the beginning of each document.
Print Processor	Install or select a print processor.
Print Test Page	Click this button to print a test page to the printer.

Managing Print Services **101**

Note: NT enables you to use any of its three built-in separator pages, or you can create your own custom pages. You must enter the file name of the separator page in the General tab of the printer's Properties sheet to use it. SYSPRINT.SEP prints a page before each document, and is compatible with PostScript; PCL.SEP switches the printer to PCL printing and prints a page before each document; and PSCRIPT.SEP switches the printer to PostScript printing without printing a separator page. To set up a custom separator page, rename and modify one of the supplied files.

Ports Tab

The Ports tab of the printer's Properties dialog box enables you to set a port, add or delete a port, and configure ports. Figure 5.10 shows the Ports tab. In the list of Ports, select a check box to select or deselect that port; a check mark in the check box means the port is selected.

Add a port by choosing the Add Po**r**t button. You can choose from such ports as digital network port, local port, and so on. To delete a port, select it in the list and choose the **D**elete Port button. The **C**onfigure Port option enables you to

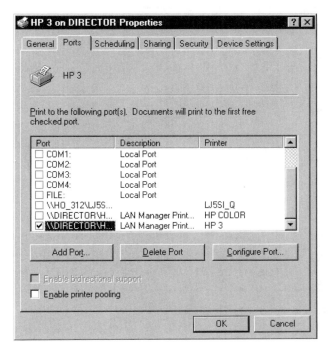

Figure 5.10 Configure the printer ports via the Ports tab.

modify settings for serial or parallel ports. Settings include baud rate, data bits, parity, stop bits, flow control, and so on. Be careful when you adjust settings for a serial or parallel port, because you affect not only the printer but the entire system.

Scheduling Tab

Figure 5.11 shows the Scheduling tab of the printer's Properties dialog box. You can choose when the printer will be available: Available Al**w**ays or **F**rom and set certain times. Use the spinner arrows or enter the time in the text box; make sure to add A.M. or P.M. to the time. You can also choose the document priority by moving the **P**riority slide bar from low to high, ranging from 1 (lowest) to 99 (highest). These scheduling options enable you to ease traffic to the print devices. You can also choose spooling options in the Scheduling tab, as described in Table 5.2.

TIP: Use the Print spooled documents first and Start printing immediately options together for more efficient printing.

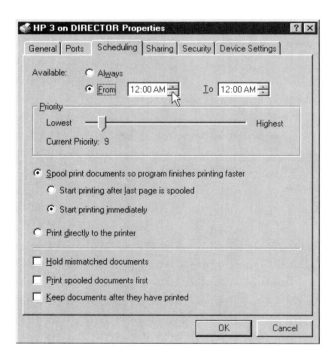

Figure 5.11 Set scheduling and spooling options for the printer using the Scheduling tab in the Properties window.

Managing Print Services

Table 5.2 Spooling Options

Option	Description
Start printing after last page is spooled	Select this option to prevent delays caused by a fast print server.
Start printing immediately	Select to print pages as quickly as possible.
Print directly to the printer	Use this option to send documents directly to the printer instead of first writing them to the server's hard disk.
Hold mismatched documents	Select to have spooler hold documents that do not match the available form.
Print spooled documents first	Use to have the spooler print the documents in the order in which they finish spooling instead of the order in which they start spooling.
Keep documents after they have printed	Select this option to keep documents in the print queue so users can resubmit a document for printing without going back to the original application.

Sharing Tab

You use the Sharing tab to designate printers as shared and to designate drivers for the clients to use. Choose **S**hared to share the printer and then enter a shared name (see Figure 5.12). For more information about sharing printers, see Chapter 4, "Managing Security Policies."

Note: Remember, when creating a share name for a printer, don't use long names containing spaces or special characters if your network has some clients who will not recognize those names, such as MS-DOS-based clients

Because different hardware platforms and operating systems require different printer drivers, you can designate drivers in the Sharing tab that clients can download when they connect to the print server. Select each version/hardware platform you want to add from the dialog box and follow any directions that may be displayed.

Security Tab

Use the Security tab to assign permissions to users and groups who will use the printer, and to set auditing policies and ownership of the resource; by default, all

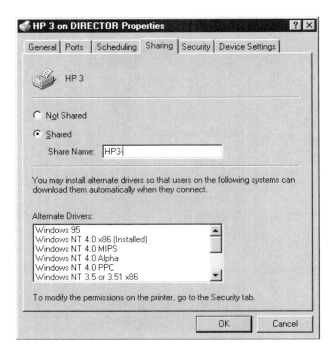

Figure 5.12 *You must designate a printer as shared before clients can see it on the network.*

shared printers are available to all network users. You must be the owner of the printer or have Full Control permission to change permissions on the printer.

The four types of permissions you can set to a network printer are: No Access, Print, Manager Documents, and Full Control. Permissions and the Security tab are covered completely in Chapter 4, if you need more information. Figure 5.13 shows the Security tab of the printer's Properties dialog box. You also can set auditing and ownership information in the Security tab, as explained in Chapter 4.

Device Settings

Device settings govern the physical configuration of the print device, including memory, paper trays, and so on. This is the same dialog box you see when you create a printer (see Figure 5.14).

Set printer memory, print forms (discussed in the next section), and font types in the Device Settings tab of the printer's Properties dialog box. Depending on your printer, your options may differ from those shown in the figure. After you create and share a printer, the printer appears in the network printer browse list for clients to view and use.

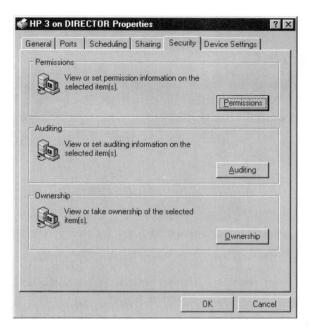

Figure 5.13 *By accessing the Security tab, you can assign permissions to those users and groups using the printer.*

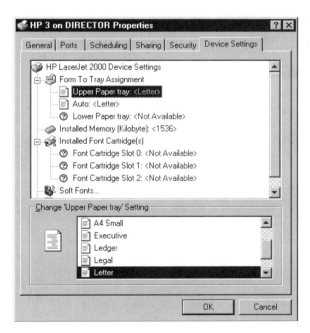

Figure 5.14 *Default settings work for most printers; however, you can change the print device's configuration if you need to.*

Configuring Server Properties

Server properties govern port settings for all ports on the server, the creation of custom forms made available to all printers on the server, and spooling logging and notification. To open the Server Properties dialog box, select the printer in the Printers folder window and then choose **F**ile, S**e**rver Properties.

Forms Tab

A form defines the paper size and margin size of the paper that can be printed to the printer. You must have Full Control access to create forms. Figure 5.15 shows the Forms tab from which you can define a new form for the printer to use.

In the list of paper and envelope sizes, select a form to use as a base. Choose **C**reate New Form and enter a new name in the **F**orm Description for text box. Enter the paper size and printer area margins in the appropriate text boxes and then choose **S**ave Form. New forms are added to the print server's database and can then be accessed by the clients. After you create a from, specify its use with a specific print device in the printer's Properties Settings dialog box.

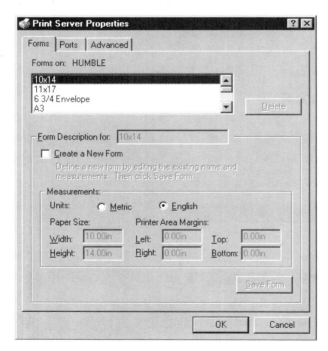

Figure 5.15 Create and save new forms to use with the printer.

Managing Print Services

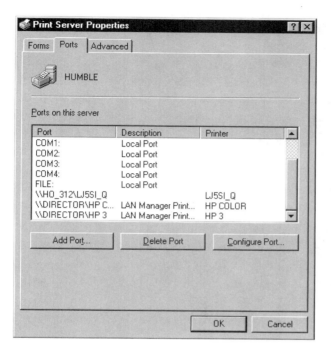

Figure 5.16 Add or delete ports; configure serial or parallel ports.

Ports Tab

Settings similar to those in the Server Properties Ports tab appear in the Port tab of the printer's Properties dialog box (see Figure 5.16). You can use the Ports tab of the Server Properties dialog box to add, delete, and configure ports as discussed previously. The only difference between the two Ports tabs is that you must use the printer's Properties Ports tab to increase or decrease the number of printers in a print pool and to change the port to which a printer is connected.

Advanced Tab

The Advanced tab of the Servers Properties dialog box enables you to set the spool folder location, enable spooler event logging and to set notification options for printing. Figure 5.17 shows the Advanced folder.

IMPORTANT: If the spool folder is located on an NTFS drive, users must have the Change permission to print; see Chapter 4 for more information about granting users and groups permissions.

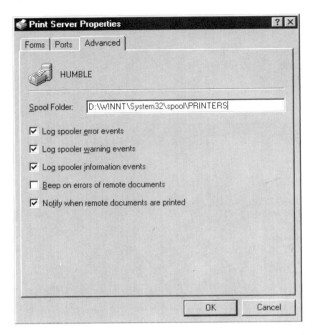

Figure 5.17 Set spooling and notification options in the Advanced tab.

To log spooling events in the system log, choose any or all three of the logging options for spooling; you can log error events, warning events, and/or information events. To view the events, open the Event Viewer (Start, **P**rograms, Administrative Tools, Event Viewer). Additionally, you can choose to have the print server beep when there is an error in remote printing. Finally, choose to notify the client when the document has finished printing.

Using the Print Queue

Members of the Administrators, Print Operators, and Server Operators groups (and anyone else who has Full Control access) can manage documents in the printer server's print queue by changing the printing order, pausing printing, purging the printer, and so on. The print queue for any printer enables you to control both the printer and the documents in the queue.

To open the print queue for any printer, open the Printers folder window and double-click the printer you want to view. The print queue opens, displaying all of the print jobs in the queue and their status (see Figure 5.18). Also displayed for each document are the following: document name, owner, pages, size, port, and the person or machine that submitted the document.

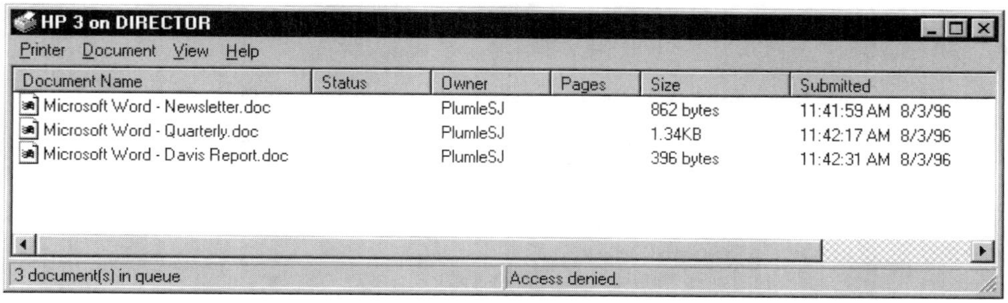

Figure 5.18 You can control the printing of documents in the print queue.

To control the printer, use the **P**rinter menu. You can choose the **Pa**use Printing command to suspend all printing; select the command again to resume printing. Choose the **Pu**rge Print Documents command from the **P**rinter menu to delete all jobs in the print queue.

To set up document defaults for a printer—including page size, paper source, copies, and so on—open the print queue and choose **P**rinter, Document Defau**l**ts. The printer's Default Document Properties dialog box appears, as shown in Figure 5.19.

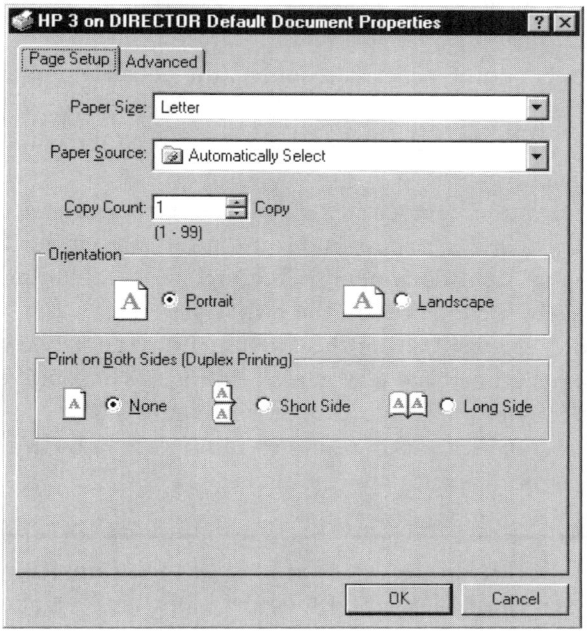

Figure 5.19 Set defaults for all documents sent to this printer.

Figure 5.20 View the settings for default documents for this specific printer.

In the Page Setup tab, choose paper size, source, the default number of copies, page orientation, and whether or not to print both sides of the page (dependent on your printer). Use the Advanced tab (see Figure 5.20) to view a summary of printer settings or to change paper size.

Control individual or multiple documents by first selecting the documents and then choosing any of the following commands on the **D**ocument menu: **Pa**use to suspend printing of the selected document(s); **Re**sume to continue printing; and **C**ancel to delete a selected document from the print queue.

You also can choose **Pr**operties from the **D**ocument menu to view a selected document's properties, including page size, pages printing, owner, and to set priority and scheduling restrictions for that document (see Figure 5.21).

Finally, choose **V**iew, Re**f**resh at any time to display any jobs that have been sent to the printer since you opened the print queue.

Note: If you have Full Control access, you can manage the print server from any NT workstation or server on the network. Open the Network Neighborhood and select the printer. Change its properties or even create new printers. You can also

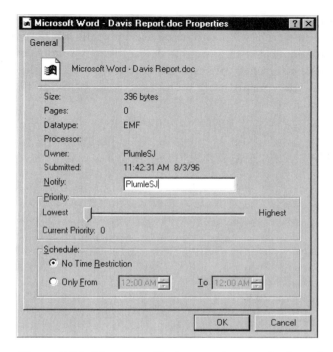

Figure 5.21 View a specific document's properties from the print queue.

manage document printing by rearranging the order of documents in the queue, deleting documents to be printed, and so on.

Clients can view printers and the progress of their documents at any time; however, clients cannot manage any documents other than their own unless they have Full Control or Manage Documents permission.

Font Management

Printing to any print device can be troublesome when it comes to fonts, especially when you're using different client operating systems. As you know, a print device can use any of three types of fonts: device fonts, screen fonts, and downloadable soft fonts. Any device fonts that reside in the print device or a font cartridge can be used with NT and NT clients. NT can also use screen fonts; you can install screen fonts using the Control Panel, Fonts option on the print server. Downloadable soft fonts, on the other hand, should be installed locally to the client computers; clients can then print to the NT print server.

NT software supplies TrueType fonts (the same font type as with previous versions of Windows). Since TrueType fonts are device-independent, the font you see on the screen can be duplicated in any print device. TrueType fonts are versatile, high-quality, and easy to use; if you can use TrueType fonts all the time, you should if only because documents using them are compatible with any print device, application, or system.

NT also supports raster, or bitmapped, fonts. Raster fonts are device-dependent; if a print device doesn't support them, they don't print. Vector fonts, such as those used as pen plotters, are also supported by NT.

PART III

Planning and Preparing for Migration

6 *Preparing for the Migration*

Before you begin a migration, you will need to make some preparations. The actual migration takes very little time, but the groundwork you lay in advance can save you and your users time, energy, and headaches. You'll need to prepare your system—both servers and clients—as well as your users for the changes about to take place. This chapter covers some important system guidelines and some considerations you'll want to review before migrating from NetWare to NT Server. This chapter covers the following:

- Requirements for the server
- Workstation preparations
- Peripherals
- Application considerations

Server Considerations

Before you can migrate to NT, you must have a computer with NT Server 4.0 software installed. But before you install the NT Server operating system, consider your options, such as hardware, file system, protocols, and so on. This section covers some choices you'll make about your network.

NT Server Hardware Requirements

The NT server, like most any server you use in your network, must be a fairly powerful computer. This book addresses only the x86- and Pentium-based computers; RISC-based microprocessors—such as MIPS R4x00, Digital Alpha AxP, or

PowerPC—are not covered here. Hardware requirements for an NT server include the following:

- 32-bit x86-based microprocessor or Intel Pentium
- VGA or higher resolution
- 123M minimum free disk space
- 3.5-inch floppy disk drive plus a CD-ROM drive
- 16M RAM minimum recommended (more always welcomed)
- Mouse or other pointing device (recommended)
- One or more network adapter cards

Note: Before running the installation for NT Server software, check all hardware—sound card, CD-ROM, video card, and so on—with the Hardware Compatibility list included with the software's documentation. If any piece of hardware is not on the compatibility list, your installation may fail. (See Appendix A, "Installing Windows NT Server and Configuring the Network," for instructions on formatting a drive to NTFS, making a server a primary or backup domain controller, and installing the NT Server 4.0 operating system to the server.)

If you prefer your server's drive to contain volumes, you can format the NT drive and partition it during installation of the Windows NT Server software. Then, when you migrate, you can migrate a volume from the NetWare server to a volume on the NT server.

IMPORTANT: For your NetWare trustee rights to transfer to NT directories and files, you must install the NT Server software on an NTFS drive. You cannot assign NT permissions to files on a FAT file system

Protocols and Gateway Service for NetWare

Regardless of the protocol type you will use between the NT server and the workstations on the network, you must install the NetWare Link IPX/SPX Compatible Transport (NWLink) and the NWLink NetBIOS to each NT server you'll be migrating, so it can communicate with the NetWare server. The NWLink protocol ships with NT and is compatible with NetWare's IPX/SPX stack. NWLink supports the sockets application program interface (API). NWLink NetBIOS also ships with NT and is a Microsoft-enhanced implementation of Novell's NetBIOS.

NWLink NetBIOS enables the transmission of packets between the NetWare server and the NT server. Microsoft's version of the IPX/SPX compatible protocol and NWLink NetBIOS can successfully coexist with other protocols on the same adapter card.

You install NWLink protocol and NWLink NetBIOS from the Network dialog box (Control Panel, Network option), Protocol tab, when you install the Gateway Service for NetWare. The Gateway Service creates a bridge through which the NT server can access the NetWare resources, including files, printers, directories, and so on. You cannot start the Migration Tool if the Gateway Service isn't installed and working. For information about installing NWLink and the Gateway Service for NetWare, see Chapter 9, "Using the Gateway Service for NetWare."

Choosing One or Multiple Domains

If your network is a small one—one or two servers, for example—you can easily set up one NT domain for your entire system. You can use member servers to perform as file and print servers and install one primary domain controller (PDC) and one backup domain controller (BDC). You can, depending on the size of the network, use just one NT server as a primary domain controller, file server, and print server, although it is always a good idea to have a backup domain controller as well.

If, on the other hand, you have several NetWare servers and you want to migrate to several NT servers divided into different departments, you'll want to use multiple domains on your NT network. For more information about domains and domain controllers, see Chapter 2, "Concepts Comparison."

Domain Controllers

In NT, the domain controller is a computer running NT Server software and containing the database for authentication of users who access the server and the network's resources, and tracks changes made to user accounts. The primary domain controller is the first server on the domain, the server that authenticates the users as they log on. You may or may not have a backup domain controller, which maintains a copy of the user database and serves as a replacement in case something should happen to the primary domain controller; but it's a very good idea. There is only one primary domain controller per domain but multiple backup domain controllers can exist within a domain.

If you're migrating one NetWare server to one NT server, your NT server must be configured as a primary domain controller. If you're migrating multiple servers, you can use both NT primary domain controller and backup domain controllers.

Single Domain Model

In a domain, users can reach all domain resources with one user name and password. Account administration is handled on the primary domain controller, and changes made to the PDC affect all servers in the domain. When you migrate user and group accounts from the NetWare server to the NT server, the accounts are automatically created on the PDC of the domain. At the end of the process, accounts are automatically replicated on the backup domain controller in the domain. In most cases, you'll want to use the single domain model (see Figure 6.1).

A single domain model enables you to centralize the management of your user accounts, thus making administration of the network easier. You can administer all network servers and domain accounts on the PDC. Generally, if you have enough servers capable of handling the network resources, up to 26,000 users and groups can be successfully managed in a single domain. This book assumes you'll be migrating to a single domain model; however, you can apply the instructions to multiple domains, as well.

Multiple Domain Models

If you are migrating several NetWare servers to NT servers in different departments, you may want to organize your network into multiple domains. Using

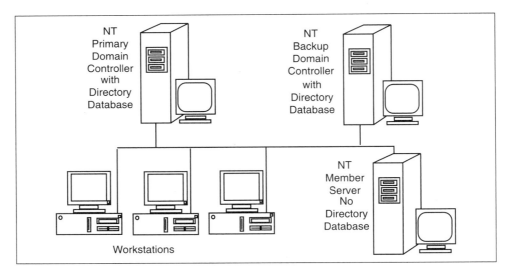

Figure 6.1 A single domain model includes only one PDC, but may consist of a BDC, a member server, and multiple workstations.

multiple domains normally means you'll need multiple administrators, one for each domain, because of work load. Before deciding, consider all of your network resources, servers, and workstations. Perhaps create a chart on how the current resources are used and how you plan to use them.

There are two methods of organizing multiple domains: the single master domain model and the multiple master domain model. The easiest method of organizing multiple domains in NT is to use a single master domain model. You can split the network into domains for organizational purposes using this model and you'll still have centralized administration. The multiple master domain model is more difficult to administer and to guarantee security on because of the two-way trust relationships between domains. For more information about trust relationships, see Chapter 2, "Concepts Comparison," and Chapter 15, "Managing Multiple Domains."

Single Master Domain Model

The single master domain model consists of a master domain and one or more resource domains. The master domain contains all user and group accounts, and the resource domains share their resources—such as printers and file servers—with the users and groups in the master domain. All users log on to the master domain. All resources are located in other domains. The resource domains establish a one-way trust with the master domain, which enables the users access to the resources.

One administrator can easily manage this one master domain as well as the resource domains. Alternatively, administration of each resource domain can be assigned to different administrators. Using the single master domain model, users need only log on to the domain once but can still use all resources on the network. Figure 6.2 illustrates a single master domain model.

TIP: If your company has an IS (Information System) department that integrates data from all the departments, you should place the master domain administration in that department.

In summary, use the single master domain model when you need centralized account management (decentralized resource management is acceptable and perhaps even preferred), and when resources can be grouped logically to correspond with local domains. The single master domain model can handle as many as 25,000 to 40,000 users and groups divided into as many resource domains as necessary and as permitted by your system resources.

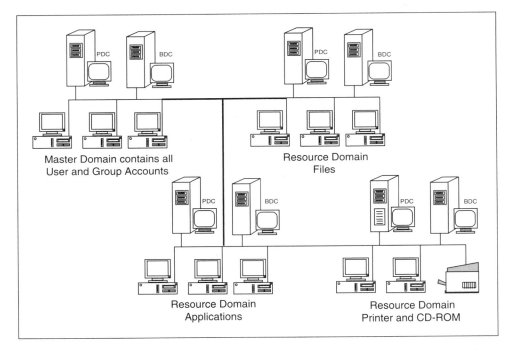

Figure 6.2 A master domain contains all domain accounts, and the resources are stored within other domains on the network.

Multiple Master Domain Model

You could also use the multiple master domain model, in which you use two or more single master domains to serve as user and group account domains. Other domains on the network are resource domains, as in the single master domain model.

The trust relationships in a multiple master domain model differ from the single master domain model in that every master domain is connected to every other master domain in a two-way trust relationship. All resource domains have a one-way trust with each master domain, as well. With this model, every user account can use any master domain and any resource domain.

Generally, the multiple master domain model is used in organizations with 40,000 users or more, but it can be adapted to networks with any number of users. You may also want to use this model if you have many mobile users, if centralization of administration doesn't matter, or if you want to share resources over a WAN.

> **NetWare Features You'll Wish You Had in NT**
>
> Windows NT Server is a great operating system. It supplies some fantastic features for administering a network. Unfortunately, there are some NetWare features you won't find in NT; but, you may be able to find workarounds for some of them; if you do, let me know.
>
> - First, NT does not have an equivalent to the File Scan right and so all users can see the contents of a directory if they have permissions to that directory.
> - Second, NetWare lets you limit the amount of volume space a user can use for creating and saving files. NT doesn't have an equivalent restriction for those users who want to back up their hard drive to their home directory, unfortunately.
> - Third, NetWare limits the stations from which a user can log in. For example, if the user normally logs in to a workstation that is diskless for the purpose of securing data, he or she cannot log in to another computer to copy that data. Again, NT has no comparable restriction.

Other Elements

It is important to check your NetWare volumes, and change or remove any duplicate names for users, groups, directories, and files. Additionally, check for duplicates on the NT server, and change the names that you can change. You'll be able to choose options for dealing with duplicate names during the migration and you can try different methods during a trial migration to see which works best for your transfer.

You'll also want to plan the order of the server migration, if you have more than one server to move. The easiest way to choose is to migrate the NetWare server with the greatest number of user and group accounts first. Then, as you migrate additional servers, you have more control on how to handle any duplicate user and group accounts that slipped by.

Workstation Issues

You'll want to consider the client software on your workstations before completing a migration; you can install the client software after the migration. Workstations running NetWare client software should be upgraded to provide connectivity to the Windows NT Server. If you upgrade the workstations to Microsoft client software, you'll be able to take advantage of some or all of the services and features provided by NT Server. Microsoft client software includes MS-DOS, Windows for Workgroups 3.11, Windows 95, Windows NT 3.51 or 4.0 Server, and Windows NT 3.51 or 4.0 Workstation. NT even provides server services for Macintosh computers.

Note: Microsoft provides a separate product—File and Print Services for NetWare—that enables an NT Server computer to provide file and print services directly to NetWare client computers; using FPNW, you can also migrate login scripts. Although login scripts do not migrate from NetWare, you can create NT logon scripts (see Chapters 2 and 14) or you can create user profiles that provide many of the same features a NetWare login script does (see Chapter 14).

If the client computers you use implement an operating system other than Windows NT Server or NT Workstation, they can most likely interact within the NT Server domain; however, they may not have the same logon security to protect their own resources from others on the network.

Computers running either NT Server (used as a client or a member server) or NT Workstation have a similar interface to that of the domain controller computer running NT Server. NT machines can control their own resources with their own User Manager and by granting permissions to local files and directories. Further, NT machines can connect easily to the server, and to each other, using the Network Neighborhood, Explorer, and/or the My Computer window. Loading protocols and services, configuring the workstations, and other procedures are nearly the same in NT Workstation computers as in NT Server computers. You can use NT versions 3.51 and/or 4.0 for workstations that are compatible with NT Server 4.0. Windows 95, which has an interface similar to NT 4, also works well with NT Server 4; Windows 95 procedures are also similar to those used in any NT 4 software.

Windows for Workgroups 3.1 integrates well into the NT network; although you'll lose many of the NT security features and benefits. Similarly, MS-DOS workstations can access NT networks, but you lose a lot of the NT innovations. NT Server provides a client you'll need to install for MS-DOS workstations. See Chapter 12, "Client Considerations," for more information.

You may decide to upgrade some or all of your client computers to enable the Windows 95 or Windows NT Workstation operating systems. Make sure the workstation machines have enough power to run the software—generally 486-based or higher processor, 8 to 16M RAM, VGA or higher resolution monitor, and 90 to 130M disk space is required for either operating system.

One important feature of NT Server is that the NT CD contains files for creating an installation startup disk and the installation and setup files to install Win-

Preparing for the Migration **123**

dows 95 to a client computer. All you have to do is purchase the license for the client from Microsoft. For information about installing Windows 95 from the NT Server distribution files, see Chapter 12.

Note: As far as preparing your users for the migration, very little front-end work on your part is necessary. The users will, of course, need to understand how to browse the server and access resources; this information is covered in Chapter 12 because you won't need to address this until after the migration is complete. The only major change for the user will be in the client software, if you choose to upgrade an MS-DOS client, for example, to a Windows NT Workstation client. When upgrading a client, I suggest you purchase any of the third-party "quick" or "easy" books on the software for your users to read to familiarize themselves with the operating system.

Peripheral Factors

Before migrating from NetWare to NT Server, be sure to appraise the peripherals attached to the network and make sure you have all of the software you need to switch them to the NT system. First, check all of your peripherals with Microsoft's Hardware Compatibility List. If your devices are listed in the HCL, you can proceed.

Next consider, for example, peripherals attached to the NetWare network that use NLMs (NetWare Loadable Modules). Make sure you have the correct drivers you need to run those same peripherals on the NT system.

NT supplies many drivers for peripherals, but verify that you have the drivers and software you need to run all of your hardware attached to the network. If NT doesn't supply the appropriate software, contact the peripherals' manufacturers to see if they have developed and distributed NT drivers for that specific device. Consider the software for the following peripherals:

- UPS (Uninterrupted Power Source)
- backup tape drives
- CD-ROM drives and/or towers
- sound cards
- optical disk drives
- modems and/or modem servers
- print devices

> **TIP:** For more information about print devices, see Chapter 5, "Managing Print Services." For more information about installing drivers, configuring devices, and so on, see Chapter 13, "Tying Up Loose Ends."

Application Considerations

Another factor to consider is the applications you use and how they'll work with NT's clients. Some applications may not be suited to running on a Microsoft network at all while others may need only a simple upgrade.

One important consideration is in vertical market software—specialized applications created to perform services specifically for your business, such as real estate, insurance, and so on. Verify with the application's manufacturer that the program will work with NT. The manufacturer may have developed an upgrade for NT or may be in the process.

Another thing to consider is any application that uses NLMs, such as faxing or database programs you use with NetWare. Make sure you can get an appropriate replacement or upgrade for those applications, as well.

Research other applications, such as your virus protection software and/or dial-in programs. Most likely, any Windows programs you've used on NetWare clients will work fine with NT; but check for any application that requires a NetWare component added to the workstation to run. You may need a substitute for that component. Again, check with the manufacturer of the product to confirm it will work with Windows NT.

Backing Up before Migration

Make a complete backup of your NetWare server information before migrating to NT, just in case some catastrophe occurs. Also back up files and directories of data and user and group account information, including the bindery database or Directory Services.

Following is a handy method of backing up your bindery in NetWare version 3.1x:

1. On a workstation connected to the NetWare server, log in as Supervisor, and at the DOS-prompt, change to the SYSTEM directory.

2. Type **bindfix** and press Enter. This utility cleans up the database by deleting users that no longer exist and related data about those users. This command

Preparing for the Migration **125**

also backs up the bindery. (I always run bindfix a second time to guarantee a clean copy of the database.)

3. Bindfix creates three files: NET$OBJ.OLD (objects), NET$PROP.OLD (properties), and NET$VAL.OLD (values) in the SYSTEM directory. Copy these three files to diskette as your bindery backup.

4. To restore the bindery at any time, copy the three files to the SYSTEM directory and at the prompt, type **bindrest** and press Enter. The bindery is restored to the system.

For NetWare 4.x, you can back up your NDS database using a utility available on the Internet: http://www./sentex.net/avax/avaxnetw.html, the Palindrome™ Backup Director. There are also other utilities available on the Net, on CompuServe, and so on.

Preparing for Migrating a NetWare 4.x Server

Thus far, most of what I've said about NetWare works for both versions, except where I've specified either version 3.1x or 4.x. From this point through the migration chapters, you'll notice some variations in procedures where NetWare version 4.x is concerned. Generally, the steps are the same, but as you might imagine, NetWare 4.x requires a few modifications to the planning and the migration.

The biggest deterrent for migrating from a NetWare 4.x server is NDS. NT's Migration Tool cannot see NetWare NDS structures; therefore, you must set the bindery context for those containers you want to migrate (explained in Chapter 10). After you set the bindery context, however, the files, directories, groups, and users in any container migrate perfectly.

When planning for the migration, you might want to consider this: The major concern is that NT does not see NDS containers. If you have stored users in various containers, the Migration Tool will migrate all users and groups within your various NetWare 4.x containers on the same level, flat. When you view your groups and users in NT User Manager for Domains, all users will be mixed together with no definitions as to which belonged to what container.

To alleviate this problem, you can create a group representing each container and place the users in that container in the group. If you have 10 containers to migrate, and each has users, you'll have 10 different groups. The Migration Tool will transfer the groups and users.

On the other hand, if you choose to migrate to multiple domains, you can migrate each container to a domain. Users and groups, therefore, will be separated by domain but can be joined by NT's trust relationships. I suggest you read Chapter 15, "Managing Multiple Domains," before planning your migration.

7   Planning the Migration

When you migrate from NetWare to NT Server, NT's Migration Tool transfers certain user account information, rights, and file and directory permissions already set in NetWare, but some of these settings do not transfer. This chapter covers some of these issues so you can make changes to your NetWare settings before migrating, if necessary. Specifically, this chapter covers the following topics:

- Comparisons of NetWare and NT rights
- Comparisons of administrative accounts between the two networks
- File and directory permissions that transfer during the migration

User Account Comparisons

User accounts, whether on NetWare or NT, perform the same function: they distinguish the user from others on the network. A user account contains a user name, password, the user's full name, and group membership information. With both NetWare and NT, each user's account has restrictions that apply to the user and/or the group(s) to which the user belongs.

With NetWare, you set individual user account restrictions using the Supervisor Options. With NT Server, you can set both individual user account restrictions and account policies that affect the entire domain. When you migrate, you can choose to transfer the NetWare restrictions from the Supervisor account, or not transfer and use the existing NT Server account policies; transferring the NetWare settings is the default. In NT, you can change the following rights in the User Manager for Domains on the NT Server primary controller. Figure 7.1 shows the Account Policy dialog box in which you set default account policies for all users in the User Manager for Domains (**P**olicies, **A**ccount).

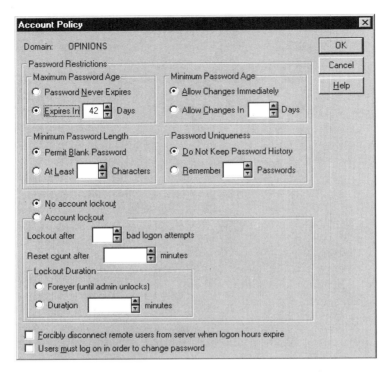

Figure 7.1 In the Account Policy dialog box, you set NT default account policies for user accounts.

Note: For more information about NT users accounts and groups, see Chapter 3, "Working with Users and Groups." For more information about user rights, abilities, and permissions, see Chapter 4, "Managing Security Policies."

Table 7.1 shows you the NetWare account restrictions with the NT equivalents. The following sections explain each restriction in detail. You set the NT restrictions in the User Manager for Domains on the NT server that is the primary domain controller.

Note: Even though some NT equivalents sound like the opposite of the NetWare restriction, the NT option is one you can select to activate or deselect to deactivate. For example, Password Never Expires, when selected, means the user's password never expires; when this option is deselected, however, the user's password does expire at a date set by the administrator.

Table 7.1 NetWare to NT Account Restrictions

NETWARE	NT
Expiration Date	Expiration Date
Account Disabled	Account Disabled
Force Periodic Password Changes	Password Never Expires (see following note)
Allow User to Change Password	User Cannot Change Password (see following note)
Time Restrictions	Logon Hours
Require Password	Permit Blank Password (see following note)
Minimum Password Length	Minimum Password Length
Days between Forced Changes	Maximum Password Age
Require Unique Passwords	Password Uniqueness
Intruder Detection/Lockout	Account Lockout
Limit Concurrent Connections	Not transferred
Grace Logins	Not transferred
Station Restrictions	Not transferred

Rights Transferred by Individual User Account

During the migration, certain NetWare rights assigned to users transfer to those same users on the NT server. Some rights have NT equivalents that perform the same, or nearly the same, functions. Individual rights are controlled in the User Properties dialog box in the User Manager for Domains (see Figure 7.2). Select the user and then choose **U**ser, **U**ser Properties.

The following list of NetWare account restrictions are transferred to Windows NT by individual user account:

Expiration Date. In NT, the equivalent is also called Expiration Date. Both NetWare and NT support the date the user can no longer access the account. In NetWare, the date listed is the day the account is expired, whereas in NT, the date listed is the last day the account is valid.

Account Disabled. The same wording is used in NT for this restriction. The user cannot access the disabled account until and unless the administrator enables the account again.

Force Periodic Password Changes. In NT, this option is called Password Never Expires; if the check box for this option is not checked, the administrator can set a time limit on the password and force the user to enter a new password at the end of that time. In NetWare, the user must change the password within 40 days, by

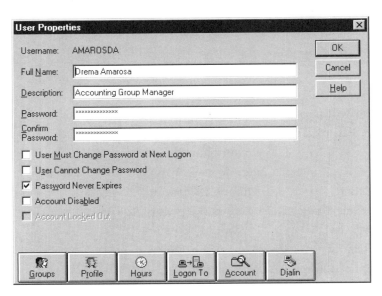

Figure 7.2 Set rights for specific users in NT in the User Properties dialog box.

default; in NT, the user must change the password in 42 days, by default. Naturally, the administrator can choose to change the time limit for a password limit.

Allow User to Change Password. In NT, this restriction is the User Cannot Change Password check box. A check mark in the check box means the user cannot change his or her password; a clear check box means the user can change the password.

Time Restrictions. NT's equivalent is Logon Hours. You can set the times of the day an individual user can access the network and limit both hours and full days. In NetWare, you set the time in half-hour blocks; in NT, the blocks are per hour. When you migrate, the times are adjusted to one-hour blocks. Figure 7.3 shows NT's Logon Hours dialog box (choose H**o**urs button in the User Properties dialog box, User Manager for Domains).

Rights Transferred by Policy for Entire Domain

Some NetWare rights transfer to NT as an account policy that affects everyone on the domain. Naturally, the administrator can modify the rights to any group or user after migration. You can control Account policies through the User Manager for Domains, **P**olicies menu, **A**ccount command.

NetWare account restrictions that transfer to Windows NT as an account policy for all accounts on the domain include:

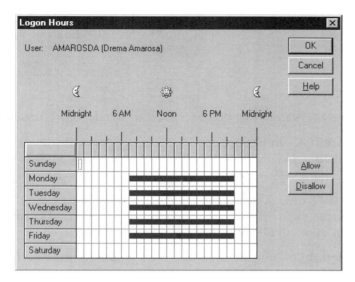

Figure 7.3 *Similar to NetWare's time restrictions, NT's Logon Hours enables you to set hours for individual users.*

Require Password. NT's equivalent is the Minimum Password Length area of the Account Policy dialog box. In this area, you must choose one of the following options: Permit Blank Password or At Least *n* Characters (where *n* is a number you enter).

Minimum Password Length. NT uses the same wording and meaning for this restriction. The user must enter a password that has the minimum number of characters that you specify; in NT, the value can range from 1 to 14 characters.

Days between Forced Changes. In NT, this option is the Maximum Password Age, and sets a time limit for the password, from 1 to 999 days. When the time limit has expired, the user must change to a new password.

Require Unique Passwords. The NT equivalent is Password Uniqueness. This option specifies the number of new passwords a user must use before an old password can be reinstated. In NetWare, the system requires eight different passwords; in NT, although the default is five, the administrator can set the number from one to eight.

Intruder Detection/Lockout. Account Lockout in NT applies to too many incorrect logon attempts by any user on the domain. When the account is locked out, the user cannot log on to the account. In NetWare, seven attempts is the default; in NT, five is the default. In NT, when you choose this option, you also choose the number of incorrect logon attempts (from 1 to 999), the number of minutes that must pass between an incorrect logon attempt and the next logon (from 1 to 99999), and whether to lock out the account until the administrator unlocks it.

Rights Not Transferred

NetWare account restrictions that do not transfer to Windows NT include:

Limit Concurrent Connections. NT does not transfer this information because unlike NetWare, NT does not limit the current connections for any user unless you're running FPNW for NT.

Grace Logins. NT doesn't support the number of logins a user can complete after the password has expired, so this information isn't transferred during a migration unless you're running FPNW for NT.

Station Restrictions. Limits set on which workstations a user can use to log in to the network apply only in NetWare. NT doesn't support this feature unless you're running FPNW for NT.

Note: If you use the add-on product FPNW for NT (File and Print services for NetWare), the NetWare account restrictions Limit Concurrent Connections and Grace Logins are transferred to NT by individual user account. You must purchase FPNW separately from Windows NT Server.

Administrative Account Comparisons

NetWare and NT use similar user or group accounts for the administration of the network. Both operating systems must designate someone who has complete control over the network and the users to manage people and resources. In NetWare, that person is a Supervisor or Admin; in NT, that same person is an Administrator. Both operating systems also include users who have special rights to administer limited elements of the network.

Supervisors/Admin

Whether you're using NT or NetWare, you must have full control rights to create and modify users and groups, assign rights and permissions, and otherwise administer the network. In NetWare 3.1x, the Supervisor has complete control over the

Planning the Migration **133**

network; in NetWare 4.x, it's the Admin; and in NT, any member of the Administrators group has full access rights and control over the network.

NetWare 3.1x's Supervisor and 4.x's Admin have all rights to all directories, and these rights cannot be revoked. As necessary, they can delegate system administration responsibilities to organization managers and operators. The same is true for NT's Administrator and Administrators group.

When you first set up NT Server, you use the Administrators group, which is a member of the administrator group. Using the Administrator account, you can create users and groups, assign permissions and rights, and otherwise administer the network. Additionally, any member of the Administrators group can perform all management tasks on a domain controller, member server, or workstation on the domain and on trusting domains.

Note: The NT Administrator account on NT cannot be deleted or disabled, whereas in NetWare 4.x, an Admin can be deleted after you've given someone else all administrative rights.

During migration, NT doesn't automatically add Supervisor accounts to the Administrators group, but you can choose to add those accounts in the User and Group Options dialog box as shown in Figure 7.4 (in the Migration Tool, choose the **U**ser Options button). You also can add any user to Administrators in the User Manager for Domains.

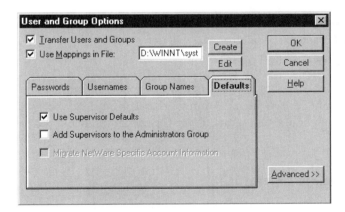

Figure 7.4 *Choose options for dealing with the Supervisor account in the User and Group Options dialog box before migrating.*

> **TIP:** You should set up an account for yourself, using your name instead of Administrator, and assign yourself to the Administrators group (see Chapter 3 for more information). This way you'll have the Administrator account as a backup to get into the server and administer the network.

Workgroup Managers and User Account Managers

NetWare 3.1x also includes the Workgroup Manager and User Account Manager accounts for delegating administration within the network. Workgroup Managers have rights to create and delete bindery objects (such as users and groups) and to manage user accounts; generally, Workgroup Managers supplement the network Supervisor.

The User Account Manager can delete managed users and groups, assign a managed user to a managed group, modify such options in SYSCON as Account Balance, Account Restrictions, Password, Login Script, Managers, Security Equivalences, and so on.

NT transfers these accounts to its Account Operators group. Members of NT's Account Operators have the following rights and abilities assigned to them by default:

- Log on to the server.
- Shut down the system.
- Add workstations to the domain.
- Create and manage user accounts.
- Create and manage global groups.
- Create and manage local groups.

Members of the Account Operators group cannot, however, modify the Administrators account, the Domain Admins global group, or the Administrators, Server Operators, Account Operators, Print Operators, or Backup Operators local groups.

File Server Console Operator

NetWare 3.1x's File Server Console Operator, a delegated manager, can broadcast messages to users, change file servers, access connection information, change the system date and time, and so on. The Windows NT Server Operators group is similar to NetWare's File Server Console Operator; however, since NT's Server Operators group has more power, the Migration Tool doesn't transfer the accounts during the move.

Members of the Server Operators group have the power to manage the primary and backup domain controllers, to perform such tasks as creating, deleting, and modifying printer shares, network shares, and so on. They also can log on to the server and shut down the system, change system time, back up and restore files and directories, lock and unlock the server, and create groups.

Finally, members of the Server Operators group have these rights and abilities for all servers in the domain, not just a single server like a file Server Console Operator. Consider carefully before assigning a File Server Console Operator to the NT Server Operator group.

TIP: You could create your own custom group to represent the File Server Console Operator and assign only the rights and abilities you want. See Chapter 3 for more information.

Print Server Operator and Print Queue Operator

NetWare's Print Server Operator transfers to Windows NT Print Operators group during a migration. NT's Print Operators group members have the rights and abilities to log on to the server, change the system time, and share and stop sharing printers. Members of the Print Operators group can administer printers and print queues through the Printers folder (Control Panel); see Chapter 5 for information about print queues and print servers.

The Migration Tool does not, however, automatically replace NetWare's Print Queue Operator (who can create, manage, disable, and enable print queues) because NT's Print Operators group has more authority than the Print Queue Operator. You could, of course, assign any user to the Print Operators group after migration.

File and Directory Permissions

You use file and directory permissions to control the access that a group or user can have to the resource. NT Server offers a set of permissions, but only for NTFS file systems. NTFS (New Technology File System) is NT's native file system. When installing NT Server (see Appendix A), you can choose to format the drive as either NTFS or FAT. FAT doesn't support file permissions, although you can apply directory permissions and, through those, keep files secure.

NT's standard permissions are combinations of the individual permissions, which enable specific types of access to files and/or directories. For more information about NT permissions, see Chapter 4. NT's individual permissions, and their abbreviations are as follows:

Read (R)
Delete
Write (W)
Change Permissions (P)
Execute (X)
Take Ownership (O)

When migrating, NetWare files and directories to NT files and directories (folders), many of your attributes and rights will also transfer if you're using the NTFS file system with NT.

File Rights

When you migrate to NT, all files that are transferred are owned by the Administrators group. Naturally, any user on the network who creates a file after the migration becomes the owner of that file, but all transferred files automatically belong to the Administrators group. NT Server doesn't support the NetWare rights: Create and File Scan (F) so these rights are not transferred (see sidebar).

Figure 7.5 shows the File Permissions dialog box in which you set file rights in NT. To open this dialog box, in the Explorer, select the file and choose **F**ile, **P**rop-

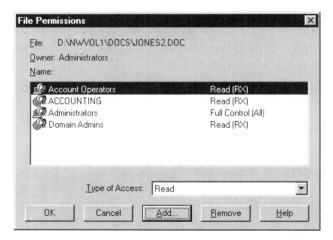

Figure 7.5 NT's file rights correspond with many NetWare file rights.

Planning the Migration

Table 7.2 NetWare to NT File Rights

NETWARE	NT
Supervisory (S)	Full Control (All)
Read (R)	Read, Execute (RX)
Write (W)	Read, Write, Execute, Delete (RWXD)
Erase (E)	Read, Write, Execute, Delete (RWXD)
Modify (M)	Read, Write, Execute, Delete (RWXD)
Access Control	Change Permissions (P)

erties. Choose the Security tab and then the **P**ermissions button. Table 7.2 describes the NetWare file access rights and the corresponding NT file permissions.

Directory Rights

NT's Migration Tool transfers NetWare directory rights to NT folder permissions using combinations of the individual rights as previously described. Table 7.3

File Scan

NetWare includes the File Scan file system right that enables users to see the directory and files with the DIR or NDIR directory command. You might attach this right to a directory containing files such as time cards or other data files. Users cannot see, and therefore cannot open, any file in the specified directory unless they know the exact file name.

NT doesn't have File Scan or even a comparable right or permission. If you want to limit user access to files in a directory, you can use the No Access file attribute, but this takes some time and effort to accomplish. Another solution is to store each user's file in a directory that only the user can access; again, this will take considerable time and effort (not to mention disk space).

Another use for the File Scan right is to prevent users from seeing files (and then viewing contents) just by scanning the directory, such as data files in a payroll or accounting program. You cannot assign NT's No Access file attribute to these files or use the hidden file attribute because the file is needed by an application that all users must access. In this case, there is nothing you can do to protect that file in NT. Unfortunately, NT's lack of the File Scan right may cause you some consternation; you'll have to find a way to work around it if you want to migrate to NT.

CHAPTER 7

Table 7.3 NetWare to NT Directory Rights

NETWARE RIGHTS	NT PERMISSIONS	NT PERMISSIONS FOR NEW FILES
Supervisory (S)	Full Control (All)	Full Control (All)
Read (R)	Read, Execute (RX)	Read, Execute (RX)
Write (W)	Read, Write, Execute, Delete (RWXD)	Read, Write, Execute, Delete (RWXD)
Create (C)	Write, Execute (WX)	Not specified
Erase (E)	Read, Write, Execute, Delete (RWXD)	Read, Write, Execute, Delete (RWXD)
Modify (M)	Read, Write, Execute, Delete (RWXD)	Read, Write, Execute, Delete (RWXD)
File Scan	Read, Execute (RX)	Not specified
Access Control	Change Permissions (P)	Change Permissions (P)

shows the NetWare directory rights and NT folder permissions. The first set of NT permissions refer to the directory itself; the second set of permissions refer to permissions assigned to any new files created in the directory. Figure 7.6 shows the Directory Permission dialog box in which you set NT directory rights.

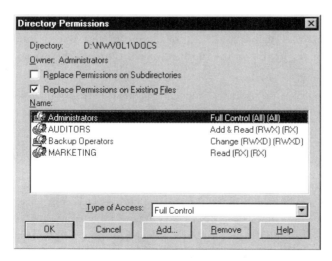

Figure 7.6 Set directory rights to protect directories and their contents in the Directory Permissions dialog box.

Planning the Migration

To open the dialog box, in the Explorer, select the directory and choose **F**ile, **Pr**operties. Select the Security tab and choose the **P**ermissions button. Use the **T**ype of Access drop-down list to choose a permission.

File Attributes

Both NetWare and NT use file attributes to protect files in the system, and the Migration Tool transfers many of NetWare's attributes during the move. Table 7.4 lists the NetWare file attributes with the corresponding NT attributes. Figure 7.7 shows a file's Properties dialog box, in which you set file attributes.

To open the dialog box, in the Explorer, select the file and choose **F**ile, **Pr**operties. In the file's Properties dialog box, choose the General tab. The Migration Tool doesn't transfer hidden or system files unless you direct it to do so. See Chapter 10 for information.

NT does not support, and therefore ignores, the following NetWare file attributes:

Copy Inhibit
Delete Inhibit
Execute Only (X)
Indexed (I)
Purge (P)
Rename Inhibit (R)
Read Audit (Ra)
Shareable (Sh)
Transactional (T)
Write Audit (Wa)

Table 7.4 NetWare to NT File Attributes

NETWARE ATTRIBUTES	NT ATTRIBUTES
Read Only (Ro)	Read Only (R)
Archive Needed	Archive
System (SY)	System (S)
Hidden (H)	Hidden (H)
Read Write (Rw)	Files without the R attribute, in NT, can be read and written to

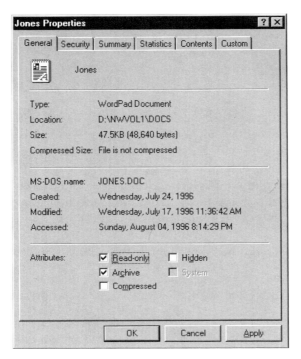

Figure 7.7 *File attributes protect individual files from being modified, read, or deleted.*

Next Steps

Now that you understand how NetWare security, user information, and other data compares to NT, you can review your NetWare setup and make any changes to permissions or user accounts before the migration. Of course, you also can make changes to the accounts after the migration in NT. Planning is the key. Review your list of users, groups, and permissions, and decide what you want to do with them once you get to NT.

Your next step is to install the Gateway Service for NetWare to the NT Server. You'll need the Gateway Service to use the Migration Tool. Additionally, you'll need to install NWLink, a protocol for communication between NetWare and NT servers. Chapter 8, "Considerations for Using a Gateway Service," and Chapter 9, "Using the Gateway Service for NetWare," explain the Gateway Service for NetWare and how to install it.

PART IV

Gateway Service for NetWare

8 Considerations for Using a Gateway Service

Novell NetWare has always held the majority of the networking market; Novell states that 55 percent of the small business networks in place today are based on NetWare version 3.1x or 4.x (according to Novell's Web site). Even though NT is taking over the networking market by offering many advantages—such as ease of administration, improved accessibility to the Internet, easy client use and access, and so on—you may not be convinced to change your system over to Windows NT.

If you prefer to keep your NetWare server and use it in conjunction with Windows NT Server, or if you want to use the two systems simultaneously for a while before performing a migration, then the Gateway Service for NetWare is for you. The Gateway Service for NetWare enables Windows NT clients to share and access resources on the NetWare server without supplying the clients with NetWare client software. In this chapter, you will:

- Learn to understand the Gateway Service for NetWare.
- Consider client issues when using the Gateway.
- Appraise security issues when using the two systems together.
- Become aware of potential problems with using the Gateway Service.
- Set bindery context for NetWare 4.x servers.

Understanding the Gateway Service

Microsoft supplies the Gateway Service for NetWare with the Windows NT Server 4.0 software to enable your NT clients to access NetWare print and file resources. You might want to try running the two servers at the same time until your clients get used to NT, and/or you may find you prefer running the two networking operating systems together. But if you want to perform a migration from NetWare to NT, you must install the Gateway Service before doing so.

Note: You must install both the NetWare Link IPX/SPX Compatible Transport (NWLink) and the Gateway Service for NetWare to the computer running the NT Server software before you can migrate from NetWare to NT. The protocol and the Gateway Service enable the two networks to communicate and transfer data. See Chapter 10, "Using the Migration Tool with NetWare," for more information.

Core Protocols

A core protocol is a set of procedures that a server's operating system follows to accept and respond to workstation requests, including routines for manipulating directories and files, opening semaphores (a signal that indicates the status of a shared resource), printing, and creating and destroying connections.

In Windows NT, the core protocol is the server message block (SMB) protocol, and in NetWare, it's the NetWare core protocol (NCP). The Gateway Service for NetWare translates requests between the SMB and the NCP, thus enabling NT clients to access NetWare file and printer services without running NetWare client software.

Network Redirector

The Gateway Service is an NT-based 32-bit NetWare redirector. The Gateway Service works in a similar manner to redirector software modules normally loaded onto workstations to enable communication between the workstation and the server. Installed only on the NT server, the Gateway enables any users to access NetWare resources from their workstations, without installing NetWare client software to each computer. The NT server acts as a gateway to the NetWare services; all workstations connected to the NT Server can see the NetWare drives and access its resources, including files and printers.

With the Gateway Service, the NT server redirects one of its drives to the NetWare volume and shares that drive with the NT clients. You map the NetWare volumes as shares when you set up the Gateway, as explained in the next chapter.

Sharing Resources

Using the Gateway Service for NetWare enables shared remote access services and shared backup services for all clients on the network—NT and/or NetWare. Addi-

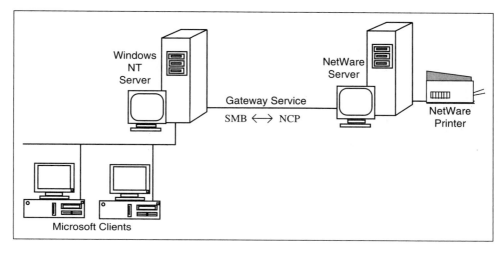

Figure 8.1 *Connect NT clients and servers to the NetWare resources through a gateway.*

tionally, all accounts become integrated so that the NT Server computer handles login validation and permissions for both NT users and NetWare clients. The NT server computer running the Gateway Service can access files, directories, printers, NetWare utilities, NLMs, and so on, from the NetWare server, as well. Figure 8.1 shows an example of a Gateway configuration. The gateway on the NT Server acts as the redirector for NetWare files and printers.

Why Use a Gateway?

The Gateway Service for NetWare enables Microsoft networking clients to access NetWare file and print resources. Say you use a NetWare network but you've been contemplating the NT Server operating system and its features and benefits. So, you set up a computer to run Windows NT Server, for any of multiple reasons:

- You're thinking of migrating to NT but are not really sure you want to move all users and data from NetWare to NT Server.
- You want to use NT Server with the Internet (set up a Web site, WINS, or DNS server, and so on). See Appendix E for TCP/IP information.
- You want to set up a Remote Access Server for your mobile users.
- You want the advantages of Windows 32-bit operating system.
- You want the benefits of using domains in your network.
- You need to attach to other NT domains in your corporation.

Next, you set up a few workstations to run on the NT network, such as computers running Windows NT Workstation, Windows 95, or Windows for Workgroups. As you're trying out the new system, things seem to go well, but you're still not convinced you want to migrate all of your users and files to NT. You would like to test the waters further. You need your Windows clients to be able to access the NetWare server and its resources. Your best bet is to load the Gateway Service for NetWare so you can share the NetWare resources with your Windows workstations.

Note: Before you can install the Gateway Service, you must remove any existing NetWare redirectors from the NT Server. You may have installed, for example, the NetWare Services for Windows NT redirector from Novell. See Chapter 9, "Using the Gateway Service for NetWare," for more information.

Client Issues

When using the Gateway Service for NetWare, your NT clients can access available NetWare resources using the NT server as a gateway, or bridge. As long as the users have permissions and rights to the NT server and to the NetWare resources, they can use NetWare files, directories, and printers. For more information about permissions and rights in NT, see Chapter 4, "Managing Security Policies."

Any client computer running MS-DOS, Windows for Workgroups, Windows 95, Windows NT Workstation 3.51 or 4.0, or Windows NT Server 3.51 or 4.0 can access resources through the Gateway. You do not need to install the NetWare client software on the workstations; however, you must install the IPX/SPX-compatible protocol and NWLink to each workstation that will access the Gateway.

To install the protocol to Windows 95 and Windows NT client computers, double-click the Network icon in the Control Panel. Add the IPX/SPX-compatible protocol and choose OK. You may need the Windows CD or diskettes to complete installation. You'll need to restart the workstation for the changes to take effect.

To install the protocol to a Windows for Workgroups computer, open the Network Setup icon from the Network group. Select the **D**rivers button and choose to Add **P**rotocol. From the list of protocols, choose the IPX/SPX-compatible and choose OK. Choose OK again to close out the remaining dialog boxes; again, you may need the Windows diskettes to complete the installation.

Note: Using the Gateway Service may be frustrating for clients on the NT network because Gateway access is slower than if they had the NetWare client software installed to their computers. If the workstations have enough memory and space, you can load the NetWare client supplied with Windows NT Workstation 3.51 and 4.0 and Windows 95 to help speed up the access. And yes, that eliminates the need for the Gateway.

One other point to mention is the use of login scripts. When configuring the Gateway Service (use the Gateway Service for NetWare—GSNW—dialog box), you can choose whether you want to run NetWare login scripts. If you choose to do so, the script file runs just after the user logs on to the network.

Security Considerations

The NetWare administrator has complete control over file, directory, and printer access to the NetWare server. The administrator controls membership to the group (NTGATEWAY) that can access the NetWare Server through the NT server. Additionally, the administrator controls which NT Server computers are gateways and which files, directories, and printers on the NetWare network are available to the gateways.

The NetWare file attributes also restrict access to certain files opened through the Gateway Service for NetWare. Following is a list of the NetWare file attributes that transfer to Windows NT, along with their abbreviations and attributes in NT:

NetWare	NT
Ro	R (Read Only)
A	A (Archive)
Sy	S (System)
H	H (Hidden)

These NetWare file attributes do not transfer to NT: RW (Read Write), S (Shareable), T (Transactional), P (Purge), Ra (Read Audit), Wa (Write Audit), and Ci (Copy Inhibit).

NT also enables you to assign permissions, or access rights to the files, through the Permissions button in the Configure Gateway dialog box (explained in Chapter 9). You can select certain groups and/or individuals and limit access to the NetWare files; you might, for example, assign one group Read and Execute permissions to the files and another group Full Control. Following is a list of file permissions in NT; for more information about NT permissions, see Chapter 4, "Managing Security Policies."

No Access	Cannot access the file in any way.
Read (RX)	**R**ead file contents and run (**ex**ecute) application files.
Change (RWXD)	**R**ead, **w**rite, **ex**ecute, and **d**elete the file.
Full Control (all)	**R**ead, **w**rite, **ex**ecute, **d**elete, set **p**ermissions for, and take ownership of the file.

NetWare Support for Utilities and Applications

When running the Gateway Service for NetWare, certain NetWare utilities and NetWare-aware applications can also be used with the NT Server. You can run the following MS-DOS-based NetWare utilities from a command prompt on a computer running Windows NT Server or NT Workstation:

chkvol	colorpal	dspace	flag
flagdir	fconsole	filer	grant
help	listdir	map	ncopy
ndir	pconsole	psc	pstat
rconsole	remove	revoke	rights
security	send	session	setpass
settts	slist	syscon	tlist
userlist	volinfo	whoami	

As for NetWare-aware applications, such as Attachmate Extra! for connectivity with mainframes or NetWare 3270 LAN Workstation for Windows for UNIX connectivity, the applications may work with Windows NT Server 4.0. To find out for sure, contact the product's manufacturer for updated software and/or requirements for running the application with NT Server.

To run the NetWare utilities, and some NetWare-aware applications, you may need to install and configure the following files; the application will specify which file(s) it needs in a message box when you're installing it:

NWIPXSPX.DLL Required by many applications written for 16-bit Windows that are also NetWare-aware. This file must be located in the *\SYSTEMROOT\SYSTEM32* directory on the NT server; after copying the file, log off and then log back on to activate the changes.

NETWARE.DRV Sometimes required by NetWare-aware applications that use the API to send and receive NCP packets. Install the file to the *\SYSTEMROOT\SYSTEM32* directory. This file installs with the Gateway Service; however, some NetWare-aware applications may need the file supplied by Novell, dated 10/27/92

> with a file size of 126,144 bytes. If your NetWare-aware application will not run, replace the existing NETWARE.DRV with the file supplied by Novell.
>
> **NWNETAPI.DLL or NWCALLS.DLL** One of these files may be required along with NETWARE.DRV. NECALLS.DLL is used with more recent version (4.x) of NetWare. Install either of these files to the *\SYSTEMROOT\SYSTEM32* directory.
>
> These are all Novell files. You might find the file you need on the Server; use the Find Files command (Start, **F**ind, Find Files). You may find the files on a computer running Windows 3.1 or Windows for Workgroups 3.11, as well. If the files are not on the NT Server, search the NetWare client disk (for NT, Windows 95, and so on) using the Windows NT Find feature; or check out Novell's Web site on the Internet (http://www/novell.com); or try CompuServe (type Go NetWire and choose the File Updates icon).

Printing through the Gateway

You can add any NetWare printer to your NT print server for use by the clients on your network. Adding the NetWare printer is similar to adding any printer to the server: establish a printer name for users to identify the printer, install the driver, and configure the printer. After adding a NetWare printer, you can administer the print queue for that printer and control print jobs sent to the printer.

Note: If you're installing the Gateway Service as a first step to migration, you do not need to worry about installing or configuring NetWare printers through the Gateway. Instead, perform the migration and then physically connect the printers to the NT network. You can install printer drivers to the NT server, as described in Chapter 5.

After installing the printer to the server, you'll want to share it. You can install various printer drivers to the NT server—such as those Windows 95 or Windows NT Workstation would use—so your clients can access the printer without installing drivers to their workstations. With the drivers installed to the server, NT determines the client sending a print request and uses the appropriate driver automatically.

Additionally, you can set permissions for the NetWare printer similarly to setting permissions for any network printer. You can choose groups and/or users and assign the following access types:

No Access. User or group does not have permission to print or otherwise use the printer.

Print. Grants permission to print to the printer.

Manage Documents. Grants permission to open the print queue and re-arrange printing order, delete or pause printing, and otherwise manage the printing of the documents in the queue.

Full Control. Grants permission to print, manage print jobs in the queue, and to manage the printer.

For more information about permissions, see Chapter 4, "Managing Security Policies." For more information about installing a Gateway printer, see Chapter 9, "Using the Gateway Service for NetWare."

You also can choose various print options (in the Gateway Service for NetWare dialog box). You can add an additional page at the end of the print job to separate jobs, notify the user when the job has printed, and/or print a banner page at the beginning of each job to identify that job. See Chapter 9 for more information about GSNW and configuring printing.

NetWare Version Issues

If you're using NetWare 3.1x, you don't have to modify the NetWare server before using the Gateway. NT's Gateway Service for NetWare connects to the 3.1x server and displays all available resources.

If, however, you're using NetWare 4.x, you'll need to set the bindery context on the container in which the server is located. And when you add yourself as a user and the NTGATEWAY group to the NetWare 4.x server, do so in the same container in which the server is located; otherwise, the Gateway will not be able to see you, the NTGATEWAY group, or the NetWare server.

Understanding Bindery Context

As you know, NetWare 4.x uses NDS (NetWare Directory Services) in place of the bindery database to provide global access to all network resources to which you have rights. NT Server 4.0 doesn't recognize NetWare's NDS structure and therefore cannot access items on the NetWare server unless you set the bindery context. NetWare 4.x networks have backward compatibility to previous versions for use with bindery services.

Objects in a bindery exist in a flat database instead of the NDS hierarchical database. Bindery services create a flat structure for the objects within an Organization object or Organizational Unit object. Therefore, all objects (users and groups) within that container object can then be accessed by bindery clients and servers, and NT.

The bindery context is the container object in which Bindery Services is set. You can change the bindery context by using the SET command, and you can set multiple bindery contexts—up to 16 per server.

Using the Bindery Context Path

The bindery context path is a path statement that allows bindery context to be set; setting the bindery context allows bindery objects on the NetWare 4.x server to be located in multiple containers. For NT, the bindery context path enables the Gateway services to see the leaf objects within containers.

You must take care, however, when setting bindery contexts; since you can have objects with the same names in different containers, you must be careful when setting context for multiple containers. For the Gateway Service, you need to set only the bindery context for the container in which the server resides. For migration, however, you'll want to set the bindery context to any container in which users and groups that you want to migrate exist. Therefore, you must check each container carefully for duplicate user and group names before setting multiple bindery contexts and before migration.

Figure 8.2 shows the root and containers on a NetWare 4.1 server in the NetWare Administrator (from a Windows for Workgroups 3.11 client). The Humble Organization includes three containers, or Organizational Units: Administration, Marketing, and Oakhill. The Oakhill container includes the server, a couple of groups, print queues, and users.

Generally, the bindery context is set for the container in which the server resides, but you'll want to verify this. However, if you need to set the context, you must do so at the NetWare server, not at a workstation.

To set the bindery context for the container in which the server resides, enter the following at the prompt on the NetWare server:

```
SET BINDERY CONTEXT = OU=OAKHILL.O=HUMBLE
```

Oakhill is the Organizational Unit and Humble is the Organization.

When you're ready for migration, you'll need to set the bindery context for multiple containers, if you want to migrate users and/or groups within those containers. To set the bindery context for multiple containers, separate the OU and O labels with a semicolon, all on the same line, as follows:

```
SET BINDERY CONTEXT = OU=OAKHILL.O=HUMBLE;OU=ADMINISTRATION.O=
HUMBLE;OU=MARKETING.O=HUMBLE
```

152   CHAPTER 8

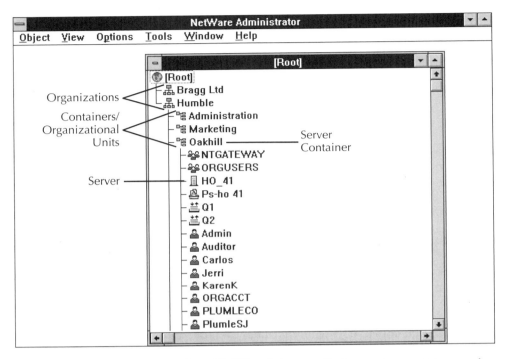

Figure 8.2 The Directory tree for a NetWare 4.1 server displays various containers and objects.

Files within a NetWare 4.1 server aren't affected by these containers or the bindery; only users and groups are influenced.

Problems with the Gateway Service

The major problem with the Gateway Service is that it slows data transfer. If you have a lot of users gaining access to the NetWare server via the Gateway, you may want to install the client software to those workstations instead of using the Gateway.

Another possible problem is that clients, if their NT password is different from the Novell password, often get a message asking for the NetWare password. When this happens, instruct clients to use the NetWare SETPASS command to change the password so the two match.

If you have trouble starting the Gateway Service, check your network adapter card to make sure it is properly installed and configured. In NT Server, open the Control Panel and double-click the Network icon. Choose the Adapters tab, select

Considerations for Using a Gateway Service

the adapter, and click the **P**roperties button for information about configuration. See Appendix A for more information about installing and configuring network services and protocols.

Also, if you have trouble starting the Gateway Service, check that you removed any other network redirector on the NT server. If, for example, a Novell redirector was installed previously to the Gateway Service, the Gateway Service won't work.

If the Gateway Service still doesn't start, open the Event Viewer (Start, **P**rograms, Administrative Tools) and look for the following sources for errors: Service Control Manager, NWLinksys. If the error reads that the system could not find a specified file, the Service may have been installed improperly; open the Network dialog box (Control Panel, Network icon) and remove the Gateway Service, then install it again. Next, turn to the Protocols tab of the Network dialog box and remove the **NWLink IPX/SPX** Compatible Transport Protocol; then reinstall it. If the error states there's a problem binding to the adapter card, check your adapter card settings in the Network dialog box; pay special attention to the frame type used for your adapter card. For more information about installing the Gateway Service, see Chapter 9; for more information about installing protocols, see Appendix A.

If the Gateway Service works but you don't see a server or you're denied access to the server, make sure your user account is a member of the **NTGATEWAY** group and that you have sufficient trustee rights. See Chapter 9. If you have other problems with printing, applications, or the network, see Appendix D, "Common Problems and Solutions."

9 Using the Gateway Service for NetWare

The Gateway Service is a link between the NT and NetWare core protocols. It enables NT clients to access and use NetWare resources, including files and printers, depending on permissions and file attributes. Advantages of the service are many, including conserved client memory and disk space, integrated backup and remote access services, and linked security features. Unfortunately, you'll also notice that Gateway Service provides slow connections and slow access to NetWare resources.

This chapter shows you how to install and configure the Gateway Service. Specifically, you learn to do the following:

- Remove unnecessary redirectors.
- Install the Gateway Service and the NWLink transport protocol.
- Set the preferred server, print options, and login script options.
- Enable the Service.
- Configure the Service.
- Set permissions and restrictions.
- Set up print services.

Installing the Gateway Service

You install the Gateway Service for NetWare from a computer running NT Server 4.0. You must have Supervisor or Admin rights to the NetWare server, and you must have administrative rights to the NT server to install and configure the Gateway Service.

Note: If you're running NetWare 4.x, you'll need to set the bindey context for the container in which the server resides. See Chapter 8 for instructions.

When you install the Service, NT automatically installs NWLink, a transport protocol that is IPX/SPX-compatible. NWLink supports the sockets application program interface (API); some NetWare-based applications servers (NLMs) use sockets to communicate with client computers. Therefore, you can use NWLink to help the NT computers act as clients in the NetWare-based environment.

Installing the Gateway Service involves several steps, as explained in the following sections. After the Service is installed, you can configure it to use with your NT network.

Removing Unnecessary Redirectors

Since the Gateway acts as a redirector between the NT and NetWare servers, you must remove any existing NetWare redirectors from the NT Server before you can install the Gateway Service. You may have installed, for example, the NetWare Services for Windows NT redirector from Novell or a similar product.

To remove a redirector or NetWare service, follow these steps:

1. Double-click the Network icon in the Control Panel to display the Network dialog box.

2. Choose the Services tab. In the list of installed services, select the existing NetWare redirector and choose the **R**emove button; confirm the deletion by choosing **Y**es in the Confirmation message dialog box.

3. Choose OK to close the dialog box. You must restart the computer for the changes to take effect.

Creating the NT User

You must be logged on to the NT Server as a member of the NT Administrators group to install the Gateway Service. Before you install the service, however, create a user specifically for implementation with the Gateway Service (I'll call it the Gateway User throughout this chapter to avoid confusion). In NT, you create users in the User Manager for Domains; see Chapter 3 for more information. Then add the new user to the Administrators group so you'll have full control over the network and network services.

Now log off NT and log back on as the Gateway User you created. To log off, choose Start, Shut Down, and select the option for closing all programs and logging on as a different user. When NT prompt you, press Ctrl+Alt+Del and enter the user name and password of the Gateway User. Be sure to make note of the exact user name and password to duplicate later on the NetWare server. Now you're ready to add the Gateway Service.

Adding the Gateway Service

You add the Service in the Network dialog box, much as you would a protocol, adapter, or other service in NT. You'll need the Windows NT Server CD-ROM; or you can enter a path to the NT installation files on the NT network. Before rebooting your computer as NT suggests, check for the NWLink protocol as explained in the following steps; you cannot use the Gateway Service without it.

1. Open the Control Panel (Start, **S**ettings, **C**ontrol Panel) and double-click the Network icon. The Network dialog box appears.
2. In the Services tab, choose the **A**dd button. The Select Network Service dialog box appears.
3. Choose the Gateway [and Client] Service for NetWare, as shown in Figure 9.1, and then choose OK.
4. NT prompts you for the path of the Windows NT files; enter the path to the CD-ROM drive or to the drive on which the distribution files reside and choose OK. NT copies the files and adds the Gateway Service for NetWare to the list of **N**etwork Services in the Network dialog box (see Figure 9.2).

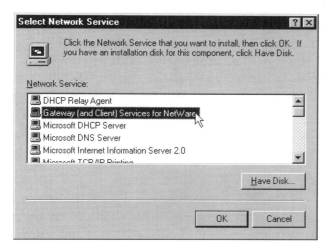

Figure 9.1 *NT displays the available services you can install to the network; choose the Gateway Service.*

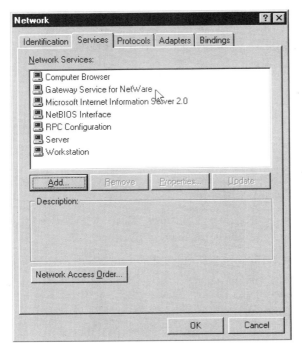

Figure 9.2 *The installed Gateway Service appears in the Network Services list.*

> **Note:** When you install the Gateway Service, NT also installs the NWLink transport protocol. It's a good idea to confirm the installation. Before closing the Network dialog box, choose the Protocols tab and check to see if NWLink NetBIOS is listed in the protocols. If by chance it is not, choose the **A**dd button and select the protocol; choose OK, insert the Windows NT installation CD-ROM if necessary, and then continue with step 5.

5. Choose OK to close the Network dialog box. NT notifies you to restart the computer for the changes to take effect. Choose **Y**es to restart.

Creating the NetWare User

Next, you must move to a workstation connected to the NetWare server so you can add a user and group for use with the Gateway Service. You can use SYSCON, NETADMIN, or NWADMIN to create the user, depending on the NetWare version of the server. It is important to use the same user name and password as the Gateway User you created for on the NT Server.

To create the user at the workstation attached to the NetWare server, follow these steps:

1. Start SYSCON, NETADMIN, or NWADMIN. You'll most likely be logged on as a Supervisor or Administrator; if you're not, log on to the NetWare server as such.
2. Create a user on the NetWare server with the same user name and password as the Gateway User on the NT Server. Give the user Supervisory or Admin rights.

> **Note:** If you're using NetWare 4.x, create the NTGATEWAY group and the Gateway User in the same container in which the server resides; see Chapter 8 for more information.

3. Create a NetWare group called NTGATEWAY and place the new user in that group.
4. Log off the NetWare server and log back on as the Gateway User.

Now you can go back to the NT server to complete the Gateway installation.

Completing the Gateway Installation

The NT server should have rebooted and be waiting for the logon. You must log on as the Gateway User. Again, this user must be a member of the Administrative group in NT and use the same password as the one created on the NetWare server.

After you log on, NT may display the Preferred Server dialog box, from which you can choose the NetWare server you want to connect to automatically when you log on. You can choose the NetWare server in this dialog box or you can choose Cancel and set the preferred server using the Gateway Service for NetWare dialog box, as described in the following steps. The only difference between the two is that using the Gateway Service for NetWare dialog box gives you more options about the service.

To complete the installation, follow these steps:

1. Open the Control Panel and double-click the GSNW (Gateway Service for NetWare) icon, as shown in Figure 9.3.
2. The Gateway Service for NetWare dialog box presents several options for the service. Choose any options you want and choose OK to close the dialog box; alternatively, you can choose the **G**ateway button to enable and configure the Service, as explained in the next section. Figure 9.4 shows the dialog box and Table 9.1 describes the options.

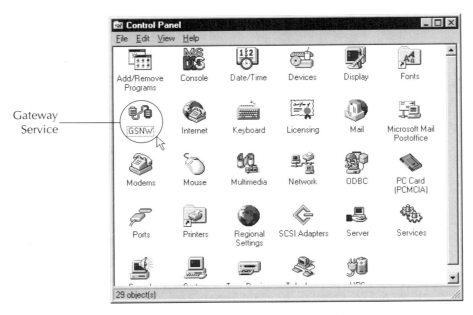

Figure 9.3 NT adds the GSNW icon to the Control Panel after you install the Gateway Service.

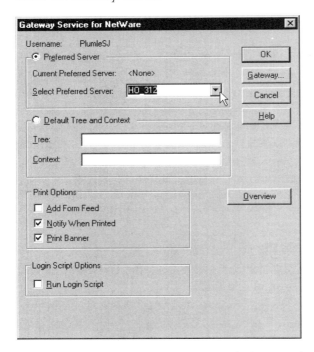

Figure 9.4 Set the preferred server or default tree and context for the Gateway Service.

Using the Gateway Service for NetWare

Table 9.1 GSNW Options

Option	Description
Preferred Server	Choose the NetWare server to which you connect when you log on to the network and share available NetWare resources; choose **S**elect Preferred Server drop-down list box and select the NetWare server.
Default Tree and Context	For NetWare 4.x, choose to define the name and position of the user on the network; enter the tree name in the **T**ree text box and enter the context name in the **C**ontext text box (label or label-less format accepted).
PRINT OPTIONS	
Add Form Feed	When checked, prints additional page at end of the print job.
Notify When Printed	Notifies the user when his or her print job is complete.
Print Banner	Prints a banner page before each document.
LOGIN SCRIPT OPTIONS	
Run Login Script	Runs the BAT, CMD, or other login script file when you log on to the network
Gateway	Click this button to enable and configure the Gateway Service.

Note: In NT, you can choose either the Preferred Server or the Default Tree and Context but you cannot choose both.

Enabling and Configuring the Gateway Service

After installing the Gateway Service, you must enable the service for it to run properly. You also can configure the service by mapping drives and assigning permissions for the NetWare resources. Only the NetWare drives you map are accessible to users, and only to users to whom you grant permissions.

Enabling the Service

To enable and configure the Gateway Service, follow these steps:

1. In the Gateway for NetWare dialog box, choose the **G**ateway button. The Configure Gateway dialog box appears.
2. Choose the **E**nable check box. The rest of the dialog box becomes available.

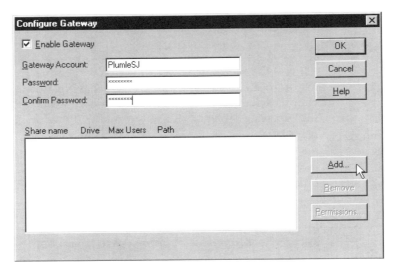

Figure 9.5 *To enable the Gateway, enter the user name as it appears in the NTGATEWAY group, and enter your password.*

3. In the **G**ateway Account text box, enter the user name (the one in the NT-GATEWAY group on the NetWare server).

4. In the Pass**w**ord text box, enter the user's password and then enter it again in the **C**onfirm Password text box. Figure 9.5 shows the Configure Gateway dialog box after it's enabled.

5. You'll create the shares for directories in the **S**hare name area of the dialog box. Choose the **A**dd button to display the New Share dialog box, as shown in Figure 9.6.

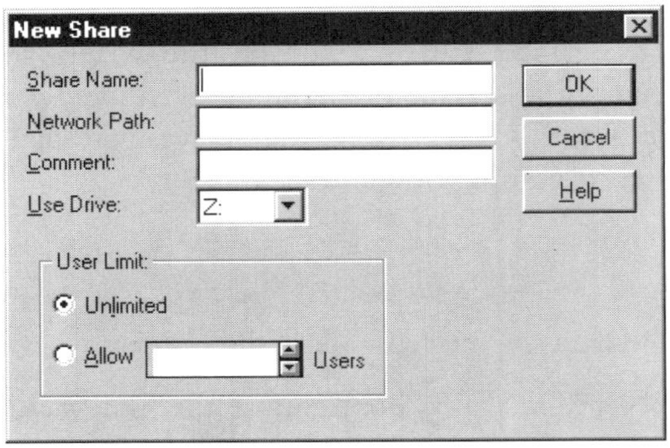

Figure 9.6 *Define the NetWare share in the New Share dialog box.*

6. Enter the name you want to use for the NetWare volume in the **S**hare Name text box; this is the name the clients will see and use.

> **TIP:** If you have any MS-DOS workstations (including Windows for Workgroups) on the network, use the 8.3 character-naming convention; if your clients consist of Windows NT and/or Windows 95 machines, you can use up to 12 characters for the share name.

7. Enter the path to the volume in the **N**etwork Path text box, using the following syntax: *nameserver*\sys\.
8. Optionally, enter a comment or description in the **C**omment text box.
9. In the **U**se Drive box, choose the drive letter to represent the NetWare volume on the local drive. Z is the default; however, you can select any letter you want.
10. The default limit on the number of users who can access the NetWare drive is set to Un**l**imited by default; you can change the limit by entering a maximum number in the **A**llow *n* Users text box, to correspond with your NetWare license.
11. You can choose OK to complete the drive mapping; or you can create more drive shares by following the previous steps. Add as many shares as you want and choose OK when done.

Setting Permissions

You can select users and/or groups and assign permissions to them that control their access to each NetWare resource. The permissions, or types of access, you can assign to a group or user are No Access, Read, Change, and Full Control. For more information about permissions, see Chapter 4, "Managing Security Policies."

To set permissions for any NetWare share, follow these steps:

1. Select the NetWare share in the Configure Gateway dialog box and choose the **P**ermissions button. The Access Through Share Permissions dialog box appears (see Figure 9.7).
2. To add users and/or groups to the permissions **N**ame list, choose the **A**dd button. The Add Users and Groups dialog box appears.
3. In the **L**ist Names From drop-down list box, select the domain from which you will choose users and groups.

164   Chapter 9

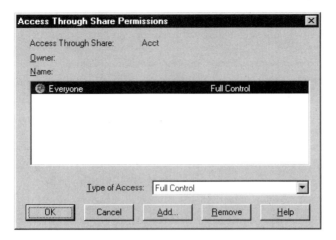

Figure 9.7 Assign permissions to groups and/or users for access to the NetWare resource.

4. In the **N**ames list, select any group to add to the permissions list and choose the **A**dd button (see Figure 9.8).

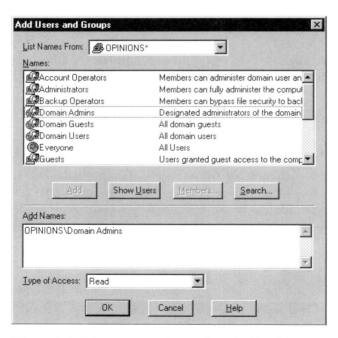

Figure 9.8 Select groups and users from the list of Names to add to the permissions list.

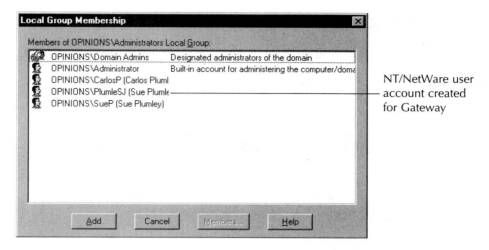

NT/NetWare user account created for Gateway

Figure 9.9 Review group memberships and choose specific members or the entire group.

5. You also can perform the following procedures in the Add Users and Groups dialog box:

   Select a group in the **N**ames list and choose the Show **U**sers button to display the users in that group at the bottom of the list box; select individual users to add to the permissions list.

   Choose the **M**embers button to show the local group membership in the domain and add those members to the permissions list (see Figure 9.9). The Members button will not be available unless you've selected a group from the names list.

   Choose the Search button to locate specific members and/or groups in the domain.

6. Select the **T**ype of Access to apply to each name as you select it in the **Add** Names list box; alternatively choose OK to return to the Access Through Share Permissions dialog box, from which you can select each group or user individually and assign a **T**ype of Access from the drop-down list in that dialog box (refer to Figure 9.7).

TIP: You should remove the Everyone group from the Permissions list or change the Full Control permission for the group to a more reasonable type of access.

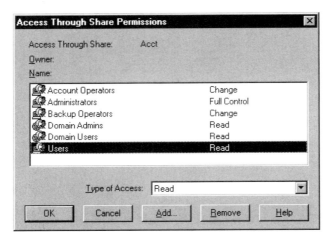

Figure 9.10 Select any group or users and change their type of access before choosing OK to close the dialog box.

7. When you're done choosing groups and users, choose OK to close the Add Users and Groups dialog box. Figure 9.10 shows the Access Through Share Permissions dialog box with groups added.

8. Change any permissions in the Access Through Share Permissions dialog box and choose OK to return to the Configure Gateway dialog box. Set permissions for all shared drivers by following the previous steps.

9. Choose OK to close the box and return to the Gateway Service for NetWare dialog box (refer to Figure 9.4).

10. Choose OK to complete the Gateway. The message dialog box in Figure 9.11 displays; choose OK.

11. Choose Start, Sh**u**t Down to display the Shut Down Windows dialog box.

12. Choose **C**lose All Programs and Log on as a Different User. Choose **Y**es. When Windows prompts you, press Ctrl+Alt+Del and enter the user name and password, using the same Gateway User name and password.

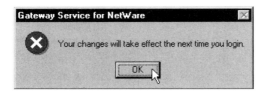

Figure 9.11 Choose OK to close the message dialog box.

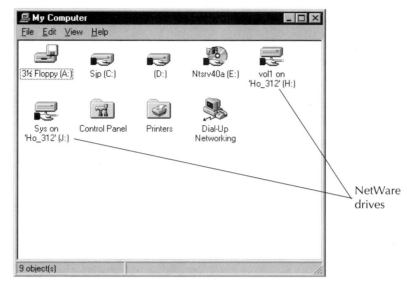

Figure 9.12 *NetWare drives mapped to the NT server using the Gateway Service are also available to NT's client workstations.*

You can view the shared NetWare drives in the My Computer window or Explorer. Figure 9.12 shows two NetWare drives in the My Computer window.

Figure 9.13 shows the two NetWare drives in the Windows NT Explorer; you can expand a folder in the Explorer by double-clicking it in the left pane of the window. For more information about using the NT Explorer, see Chapter 4.

Note: Even though the figures show the Gateway with a NetWare 3.12 server, the procedure and results are exactly the same for a NetWare 4.x server, as long as you set the bindery context for the container in which the NetWare server resides so the Gateway can see the NTGATEWAY group and the Gateway User.

Installing NetWare Printers for use with the Gateway Service

To use a NetWare printer with the NT server and network, you must install the printer to the NT server. Remember, the *print device* is the actual printer; whereas the *printer* is the interface between the operating system and the print device. When you install the printer to the NT server, you install the necessary drivers not only for the server but for clients as well. If you install Windows 95 and/or Win-

168 CHAPTER 9

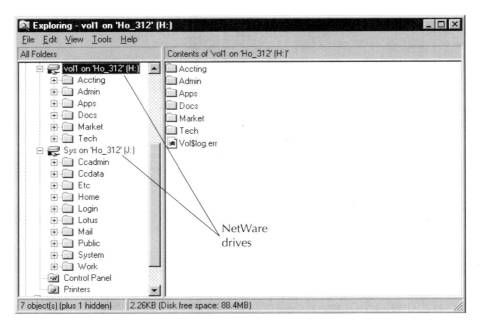

Figure 9.13 View and explore the NetWare drive to which you have rights.

dows NT client drivers to the server, NT automatically uses the appropriate driver for the client requesting the print job. For other clients, such as MS-DOS or Windows for workgroups, you'll need to install the individual driver directly on the workstation to enable printing to the NetWare printer.

TIP: You don't need to install the NetWare printer if you're planning to migrate to NT and leave your NetWare server behind.

After installing the NetWare printer to the server, you must designate the printer as shared. You can then set permissions for groups and users to access the printer. Additionally, you can control the NetWare printer's print queue as you would any network printer. For more information, see Chapter 5, "Managing Print Services."

Installing the NetWare Printer

You install the NetWare printer to the NT server only after you've enabled and configured the Gateway Service. Use the Printers folder to install the printer, as explained in the following steps:

Using the Gateway Service for NetWare

Figure 9.14 The Printers window displays printers already installed to the server, plus the Add Printer tool.

1. Choose Start, Settings, Printers. The Printers window appears (see Figure 9.14).
2. Double-click the Add Printer icon; the Add Printer Wizard dialog box appears, as shown in Figure 9.15.
3. Choose the Network printer server option and then select the Next button. The Connect to Printer dialog box appears (see Figure 9.16).
4. Double-click an item in the Shared Printers list, such as the NetWare or Compatible Network or the server name, to display its contents. Select a printer from the list; alternatively, enter the path and the printer name in the Printer text box using the syntax: *nameserver**nameprinter*.

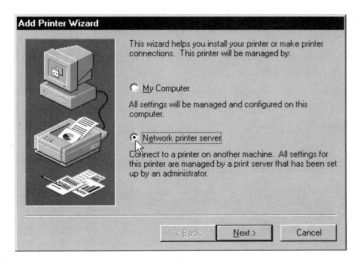

Figure 9.15 The Printer Wizard guides you, step by step, through adding a printer to the server.

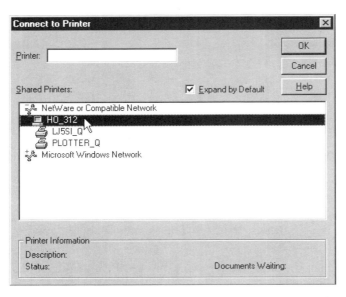

Figure 9.16 Expand the NetWare server to view printers that are available through the Gateway.

5. Choose OK. A message dialog box appears that says the server doesn't have a suitable printer driver (see Figure 9.17); choose OK to install the driver to the NT server.
6. The next Add Printer Wizard dialog box appears, as shown in Figure 9.18.
7. In the **M**anufacturer list, select the maker of the printer; in the **P**rinters list, choose the model. You can, alternatively, choose the **H**ave Disk button and use the manufacturer's floppy disk to install the driver; follow the instructions on screen to use a disk.
8. Choose OK. NT displays a dialog box prompting you to insert the NT Server CD-ROM. Insert the CD and choose OK. NT copies the appropriate files.

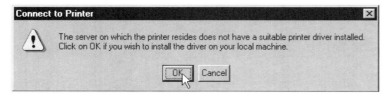

Figure 9.17 Choose OK to install the printer driver to the NT server.

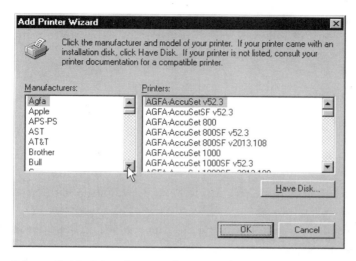

Figure 9.18 *Select the manufacturer and model of the NetWare printer to be installed.*

9. The Printer Properties dialog box appears; select device settings such as paper source, printer memory, font cartridges, and so on or accept the default selections (for more information, see Chapter 5). Choose OK.

10. The next Add Printer Wizard dialog box asks if you want to use the NetWare printer as a default printer for all Windows printing; most likely, you'll want to choose **N**o. Choose **N**ext.

11. The final Add Printer Wizard dialog box appears, stating the installation was successful; choose the Finish button. The NetWare printer is added to the Printers window (see Figure 9.19).

Figure 9.19 *The NetWare printer is captured to the NT server for use by NT's clients.*

You can add more printers from the NetWare server by following the preceding steps. Also, you can follow the previous steps for setting up a printer attached to a NetWare 3.1x or 4.x server.

Sharing a Printer

Before your NT clients can use the NetWare printer, you must designate it as shared. You can install drivers for your Windows NT and Windows 95 clients so they can use the printer without installing software to their own machines.

To share the NetWare printer, follow these steps:

1. Select the NetWare printer in the Printers window (Start, **S**ettings, **P**rinters).
2. Choose **F**ile, S**h**aring. The printer's Properties dialog box appears.
3. Choose the **S**hared option and the rest of the dialog box becomes available (see Figure 9.20).
4. Optionally, assign a new shared name for the printer; this is the name the clients will see on the network.

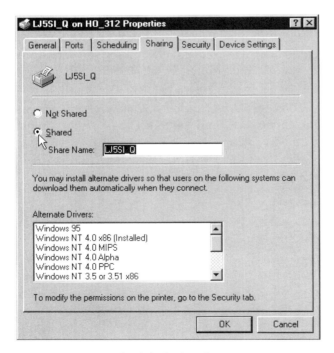

Figure 9.20 *Use the default shared name or enter a new one.*

5. Optionally, select additional drivers to install in the Alternate Drivers list. Install drivers for your Windows 95, Windows NT Workstation 3.5, 3.51, and 4.0 clients to access automatically from the NT server.

Before closing the dialog box, set permissions for the use of the printer, as described in the following section.

Setting Permissions

You can also set permissions for users and groups who access the NetWare printer; for example, you may want to assign one or more users to manage the documents in the print queue and assign the rest of the users only print access to the NetWare printer.

Printer permissions include: No Access, Print, Manage Documents, and Full Control; naturally, all permissions depend on the NetWare administrator and the rights he or she enables the users on the NT network. If you're both the administrator for NetWare and for NT, there is no need to worry.

Note: You also can set auditing and ownership in the Security tab of the printer's Properties dialog box; see Chapter 4 for more information about those features. Additionally, you can use the printer's Properties dialog box to adjust device settings, ports, and scheduling; see Chapter 5, "Managing Print Services," for more information.

To set permissions on the NetWare printer, follow these steps:

1. In the printer's Properties dialog box (from the Printers window, select the printer and choose **F**ile, **S**haring), choose the Security tab (see Figure 9.21).

   Note: You cannot set auditing options for a NetWare printer therefore you cannot track the use of the printer through NT's Auditing log.

2. Choose the **P**ermissions button; the Printer Permissions dialog box appears. As shown in Figure 9.22, the dialog box uses similar features and procedures to the Access Through Share Permissions dialog box described previously (refer to Figure 9.7).
3. Perform the following procedures to manage printer permissions:

   Select a name in the **N**ame list and change the user or group's permissions by selecting the permission from the **T**ype of Access drop-down list box.

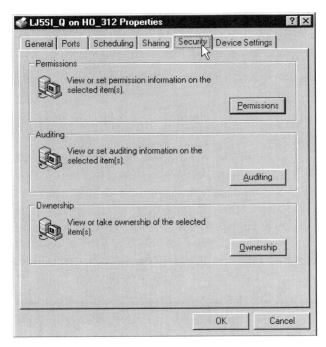

Figure 9.21 Set permissions in the printer's Properties dialog box.

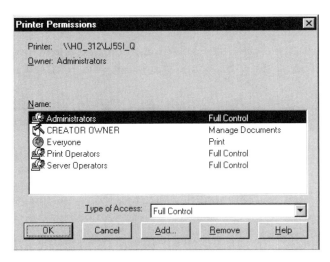

Figure 9.22 You can add to the default names that have access to the NetWare printer, remove names, or change access to the printer.

Using the Gateway Service for NetWare **175**

> Choose the **A**dd button to display the Add Users and Groups dialog box and add individuals or groups to the permissions list.
>
> Select a name in the **N**ame list and choose **R**emove to exclude that user or group from the permissions list.

4. Choose OK to close the Printer Permissions dialog box and return to the printer's Properties dialog box.
5. Choose OK to close the Properties dialog box. Clients can now access and use the NetWare printer through the Gateway Service. You can add more NetWare printers by following the previous steps to installing, sharing, and setting permissions for a printer over the Gateway.

For information about using and controlling the print queue, see Chapter 5, "Managing Print Services."

PART V

Migrating the Network

10 Using the Migration Tool with NetWare

NT's Migration Tool enables you to migrate, or transfer, data on your NetWare server to a computer running Windows NT Server 4.0. You can migrate one or more NetWare servers and their user and group accounts, files, directories, volumes, and so on.

This chapter leads you through the steps to migration using the Migration Tool; it is recommended that upon completing these steps, you run a trial migration as described in Chapter 11 before running the actual migration. The trial migration will give you a preview of possible problems you may experience, and thus the opportunity to resolve those problems before the actual migration.

In this chapter, you learn to do the following:

- Select servers for the migration.
- Set user and group options.
- Create mapping files for users.
- Keep your NetWare 4.x containers through a migration.
- Set file and directory options for the migration.
- Select logging options.

Last-Minute Checklist

Before you choose to migrate or perform a trial migration, review Chapters 6 and 7 and resolve any conflicts and clarify other issues mentioned in those chapters. Make sure you have a plan for a domain model, client software, account restrictions, and so on. The NT Server on which you've installed the Gateway Service is the server from which you'll run the Migration Tool.

And don't neglect the following details:

1. Install the Gateway Service and NWLink transport protocol to the computer running NT Server.
2. Enable the Gateway Service, and connect from the My Computer Window to confirm the connection.
3. Make sure you're logged on—to both the NetWare server and the NT server—as the user you created for the Gateway Service, and that you have Supervisor/Administrator rights on both servers.
4. No users are logged in to the network
5. You've set the bindery context for any containers from which you want to transfer user and/or groups on your NetWare 4.x server(s), or you're planning to migrate to multiple domains.
6. Use the Migration Tool from a computer running NT Server as a primary or backup domain controller.
7. Make sure you set permissions on the NT server root so that you can transfer NetWare volumes, directories, and files during the migration; you can go back and remove the permissions after the migration.

Note: You can copy the necessary Migration files to an NT Workstation (NWCONV.EXE, NWCONV.HLP, LOGVIEW.EXE, and LOGVIEW.HLP found in the server's SYSTEM32 folder) and use that computer to run the Migration tool from the NetWare server to an NT Server primary or backup domain controller. You also need to install the Gateway Service and NWLink protocol to the Workstation and to the server to which you're migrating. You might do this if the NT server computer was off-site; otherwise, you would run the Migration Tool from the NT server to which you're migrating.

One final point before proceeding: You may want to check your directory structure on the NetWare server to make sure you know to whom the files and directories belong. When you migrate, ownership of all files and directories transfers to the administrator of the NT server. If there are any files or directories on the NetWare server about which you have a question, now is the time to get the answer.

Starting the Migration Tool

The first steps to migrating include selecting the servers and starting the Migration Tool. If you do not select workable servers or do not have the appropriate rights to

Using the Migration Tool with NetWare **181**

> ### Retaining the NetWare 4.x NDS Structure through Migration
>
> If you're concerned about losing your NDS structure, you can migrate to multiple NT domains to retain the organizations and organizational units that comprise your network. You can accomplish this feat with multiple NT domains.
>
> NT enables you to set up multiple domains within your network. Each domain has a primary domain controller (PDC) that authenticates users and groups for access to the domain. Included in a domain can be backup domain servers, member servers that act as file and/or print servers, and multiple workstations. This one domain is equal, more or less, to one NetWare 4 container.
>
> When you migrate, you select one NetWare 4.x container to migrate to one NT Server domain. Set the bindery context for that one container. The users and groups migrate; the files and directories migrate. Now, if you have containers within the container you plan to migrate, you'll have to create groups in which to appoint the users in each container; this will keep the division lines between containers clear.
>
> Next, you'll need to set up a second domain, which will include a PDC, BDC, and any member servers and workstations you want to add. Set up the trust relationship (as described in Chapter 15) between the two NT domains and migrate the second container from NetWare to this new NT domain.
>
> NT's multiple domain structure is very similar to the NetWare 4.x NDS hierarchical structure. If you want to retain that NDS hierarchy, set up and migrate to multiple domains. In planning your migration, I suggest you reread the information in Chapter 2 about trust relationships, read Chapter 3 again for information about domain models, and, finally, read Chapter 15, "Managing Multiple Domains."

select the servers for migration, NT will not display the servers in the Migration Tool dialog box and you can go no further with the process.

To select the servers and start the Migration Tool, follow these steps:

1. Choose Start, **P**rograms, Administrative Tools, Migration Tool for NetWare. The Select Servers For Migration dialog box appears (see Figure 10.1).

2. In the **F**rom NetWare Server text box, enter the server name or click the browse button (designated by an ellipsis) to display the Select NetWare Server dialog box.

3. Select the first NetWare server to migrate and choose OK, as shown in Figure 10.2. NT returns to the Select Servers For Migration dialog box.

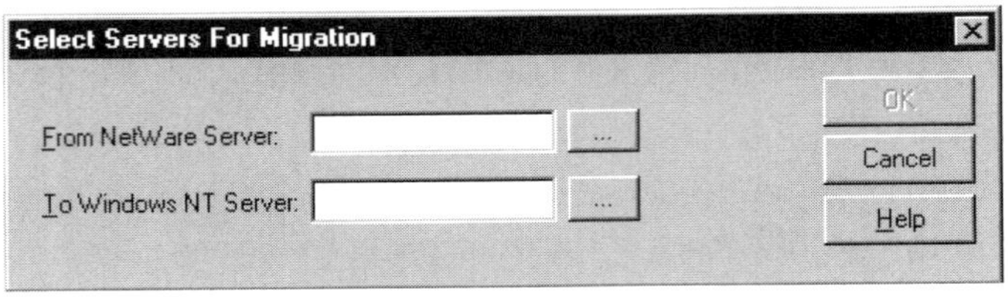

Figure 10.1 *You must designate the NetWare and NT servers before you can proceed with the migration.*

4. In the **T**o Windows NT Server text box, enter the NT server's name or click the browse button (an ellipsis) to display the Select Windows NT Server dialog box (see Figure 10.3).
5. If necessary, double-click the domain name to expand the servers in the list. Select the server and choose OK to return to the Select Servers For Migration dialog box.
6. Choose OK; the Migration Tool for NetWare dialog box appears, with the servers selected for migration as shown in Figure 10.4.

If you want to migrate additional servers, select the **A**dd button in the Migration Tool for NetWare dialog box. The Select Servers For Migration dialog box

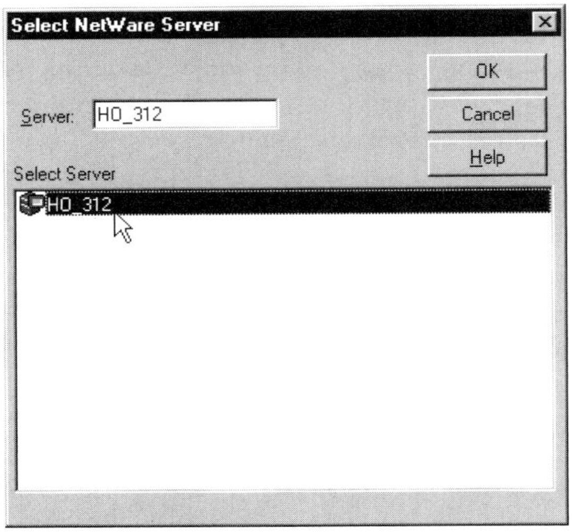

Figure 10.2 *All NetWare servers connected by the Gateway Service appear in the Select Server list.*

Using the Migration Tool with NetWare

Figure 10.3 *The domain appears in the Select Windows NT Server dialog box.*

displays (refer to Figure 10.1). Select the NetWare and NT servers following steps 2 through 5, clicking OK when you're done. To remove any server from the Server for Migration list in the Migration Tool, select that server and choose the **D**elete button.

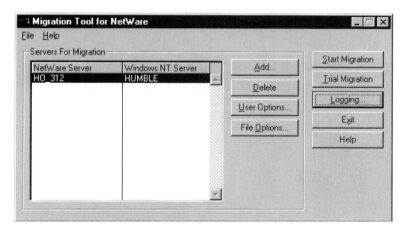

Figure 10.4 *The Migration Tool starts only after you select viable servers for the migration.*

Selecting User and Group Options

Within the user and group options for migration, you can choose to migrate all users and groups, specified users and groups, or no users and groups at all. By default, all user and group accounts are transferred to the domain of the NT Server computer. You implement the User Options to resolve possible conflicts with duplicated user and group names.

When you migrate the user accounts, the user name, password, time restrictions, expiration date, disabled status, password expiration, and other restrictions are migrated as well by default. You can control how the user passwords, user names, group names, and passwords are migrated, as described in this section.

Note: You can set the user and group options for each server you plan to migrate; select the server in the Migration Tool and then choose the User Options button.

Transferring Users and Groups

To select user and group options for any server in the Migration Tool dialog box, select the server and then choose the **U**ser Options button in the Migration Tool dialog box. The User and Group Options dialog box appears (see Figure 10.5).

To transfer users and groups, check the **T**ransfer Users and Groups box; a clear check box means users and groups will not be transferred. If you choose not to transfer users and groups, you can transfer files only, as described later in this chapter.

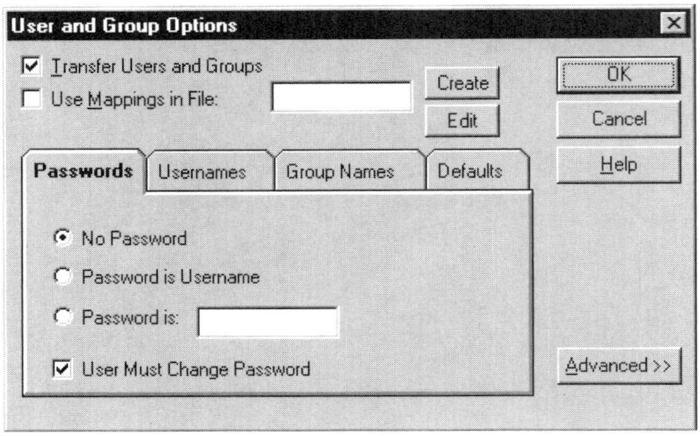

Figure 10.5 Choose whether to transfer users and groups during the migration.

Methods of Transferring Accounts

If you do choose to transfer users and groups, you can specify user accounts and passwords individually or set defaults for all accounts. When you specify users and groups individually, you have more control over the way the accounts transfer; you can change user names and passwords and group names. Alternatively, you can specify default passwords, user names, and group names that will apply to all users, and, optionally, make necessary changes after the migration.

Note: Remember that you can control the users' passwords by setting a time limit on them, having the user create a new password, and so on, in the User Manager for Domains; see Chapter 3 for more information about passwords.

Setting Specific User Options

A mappings file is one in which you specify the account information that will transfer during the migration. When you create the file, NT lists all users and groups on the NetWare server from which you'll migrate; you can create a mapping file before you open the Migration Tool or from within the User and Group Options dialog box.

If you create the mappings file before opening the Migration Tool, you should use NT's Notepad accessory and save the file in text format; however, use the MAP file extension in the DOS 8.3 file-naming convention. Make sure to include the required section headings such as [users] and [group]. It's easier to create the file in the Migration Tool because NT automatically adds the section headings and the names of all user and group accounts from the NetWare server. You can then open and edit the file by adding or removing users and/or groups and by adding a password for each account.

Note: User names must be unique on the server and in the domain. The limit for a user name is 20 characters. You can use upper- or lowercase characters in the user name; the name is case-sensitive. You cannot use the following characters in a user name: " / \ : ; , + = ? | < >, or spaces. Passwords can be up to 14 characters in NT, and they, too, are case-sensitive.

To create and edit a mappings file, follow these steps:

1. In the User and Group Options dialog box, check the User **M**appings in File box.

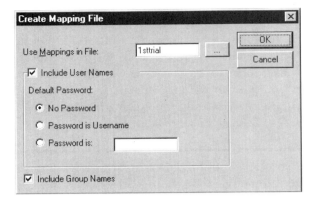

Figure 10.6 Select defaults for the mappings file in the Create Mappings File dialog box.

2. In the text box beside the option, enter a name for the file (follow the 8.3 character-naming convention; NT automatically adds the MAP extension).

3. Choose the Create button; NT displays the Create Mapping File dialog box (see Figure 10.6). The browse (...) button beside the User Mappings in File text box enables you to open a file you've created from the NT drive; MAP files are normally saved in the SYSTEM32 directory.

4. Choose to Include User Names by selecting the check box; if you leave the check box blank, only group accounts will be included.

5. Select one of the following Default Password options:

    No Password. All users can log on to the network without a password.

    Password is Username. The user's name will be used as a password; all letters are uppercase.

    Password is (and enter password). Enter one password for all users to use.

Note: If you choose No Password, you can enter a different password for each user in the mappings file, as explained later. Users can change the password after logging in to the network, if they want.

---

6. Check the Include Group Names box to transfer the groups; a blank check box means no group names will be included in the migration.

7. Choose OK. The Migration Tool creates the file and displays the message box shown in Figure 10.7.

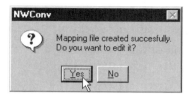

Figure 10.7 In the NWConv message box, choose to edit the mappings file to control which users and groups are transferred.

8. Choose **Y**es to edit the file; choose **N**o to close the message box. You can edit the file at any time from within the Migration tool by selecting the Edit button next to the Use **M**apping in File text box.
9. When you choose to edit the file, NT's Notepad accessory appears with the file in its window (see Figure 10.8).
10. Making sure you retain the format of the file as you edit, you can add, remove, or edit any user or group name in the file using the following guidelines in the [user] section:

The first name on the line of text is the original NetWare name.

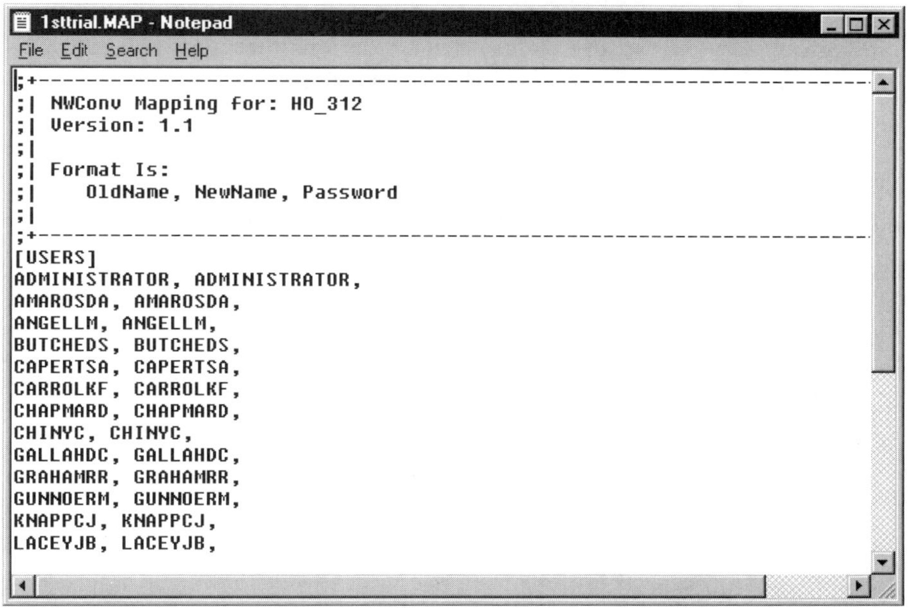

Figure 10.8 Review the user and group names and make modifications to the file.

The second name on the line, separated from the first by a comma, is the name that will be assigned in NT; you can change this name or leave it as is.

You can add a third item to the line of text by entering a password for the user. Separate the password from the new user name with a comma and enclose the password in brackets.

For the [group], the format is as follows:

The first name is the group name as in NetWare.

The second name, separated from the first with a comma, is the new group name that will be used in NT.

11. When you're done, choose **F**ile, **S**ave to save the file and then select **F**ile, E**x**it to return to the User and Group Options dialog box.

When you create a mappings file, three tabs of the User and Group Options dialog box become grayed and thus unavailable to you: Passwords, Usernames, and Group Names; you can still change options in the Default tab, as described later in this chapter.

Setting Default User Options

If you do not choose the Use **M**appings in File option, you can set all users and groups to transfer and choose default options that govern the transfer. Clear the User **M**appings in File check box to set default options in the User and Group Options dialog box.

I suggest trying the mappings file method with one trial migration, and in the second trial, use the defaults. After the trial migrations, read the log files to see which method transferred the users and groups the way you wanted. See Chapter 11 for information about log files.

Passwords Passwords in NetWare are encrypted; therefore, they are not transferred in a migration. You can assign a specific password to each user by way of a mapping file, as described previously, or you can assign general password guidelines for the transfer. In the Passwords tab (refer to Figure 10.5), choose one option from the following:

No Password. All users can log on to the network without a password.

Password is Username. The user's name will be used as a password; all letters are uppercase.

Password is (and enter password). Enter one password for all users to use.

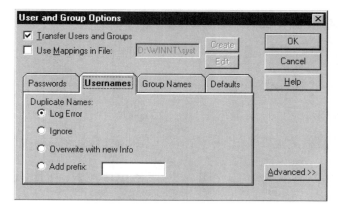

Figure 10.9 *Access the Usernames tab in the User and Group Options dialog box to specify how you want to deal with duplicate names during the migration.*

Additionally, you can choose the User Must Change Password check box so that the first time the user logs on to the network after the migration, he or she must enter a new password (an excellent idea).

User Names Choose the Usernames tab in the User and Group Options dialog box to set default options, as shown in Figure 10.9. These options govern how NT handles identical accounts for a user in NT when you transfer the NetWare accounts. By default, users with names that already exist on the NT domain are not transferred; conflicts are recorded in the log file. You can change this setting, if you want.

Choose one of the following options in the Duplicate Names list:

Log Error. Records the error in the log file but does not transfer the account.

Ignore. Doesn't transfer the information; doesn't record the error.

Overwrite with new info. NetWare account information overwrites the NT information for duplicate accounts and the occurrence is recorded in the log file.

Add prefix. Creates a new account with prefixes you enter in the text box; records the occurrence in the Error.log file.

The Error.log file is covered in detail in Chapter 11.

Group Names By default, when the Migration Tool transfers a group name that already exists on the NT domain, it adds the listed user accounts from Net-

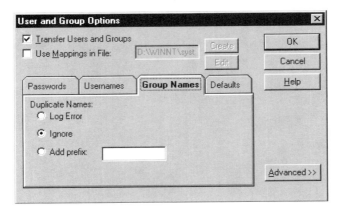

Figure 10.10 Set defaults for duplicate group names via the Group Names tab.

Ware to NT without logging an error. You can change the default by accessing the Group Names tab from the User and Group Options dialog box to choose the action the Migration Tool should take in case of duplicate group names. Figure 10.10 shows the Group Names tab.

Choose one of the following options:

Log Error. Records the conflict in the Error.log file but does not overwrite the group name.

Ignore. Conflicts are not logged or transferred.

Add prefix. Creates a new group using the prefix you specify and records the occurrence in the log file. Use this option when you're transferring accounts from several NetWare servers to one NT domain and you don't want to merge identical groups into one.

Setting Options in the Default Tab

By default, users and groups with Supervisor rights are transferred to NT without administration privileges. The Defaults tab (see Figure 10.11) is available whether you use the default transfer of users and groups or the mappings to a file method of transfer. Use the Defaults tab to set any or all of the following options:

Use Supervisor Defaults. If checked, the restrictions for the Supervisor are transferred; if the check box is clear, the NT Account Policy settings are used instead.

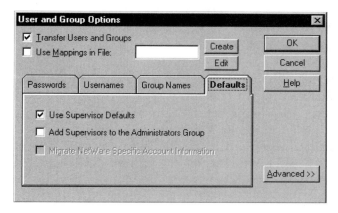

Figure 10.11 Set Supervisor defaults via the Defaults tab in the User and Group Options dialog box.

Add Supervisor to Administrators Group. Choose this check box to supply any user with Supervisory rights with Administrators rights in NT.

Note: Chapter 7 has more information about how restrictions, such as password length, periodic password change, and account lockouts, are transferred during a migration.

Advanced Option

The single master domain model consists of a master domain and one or more resource domains. The master domain contains all user and group accounts, and the resource domains share their resources—such as printers and file servers—with the users and groups in the master domain. All users log on to the master domain. All resources are located in other domains. The resource domains establish a one-way trust with the master domain, which enables the users access to the resources.

You can, during migration, transfer all user accounts and groups to the domain controller of the master domain, and transfer all files and directories to a resource server. The resource server must be added to the Servers For Migration list in the Migration Tool.

The **A**dvanced button in the User and Group Options dialog box enables you to transfer users to trusted domains when you're using Master domains. Check the Trusted **D**omains box and enter the domain name. For more information about master domains, see Chapter 6, "Preparing for the Migration."

Setting File Options

File options enable you to choose how NetWare volumes, directories, and files transfer to NT. You can choose to transfer files or not; if you choose not to transfer files, the Migration Tool transfers only users and groups. By default, all NetWare volumes are transferred.

Additionally, you can choose which of the volumes, directories, and files you want to transfer to NT and specify a directory and share name for those volumes. You can, for example, select VOL1 on the NetWare server and place it in a specific directory of the NT server. When setting the path for the volume, you can designate its share name.

Transferring Files

You can choose to transfer files in the File Options dialog box for each server you migrate. To choose whether to transfer files, follow these steps:

1. Select the server and then choose the File **O**ptions button in the Migration Tool. Figure 10.12 shows the File Options dialog box.
2. To transfer files from the NetWare server to NT, choose the Transfer Files check box.
3. To add volumes not listed, choose the **A**dd button in the File Options dialog box.

To delete any volume from the list, select the volume in the Source Files list box and choose the **D**elete button.

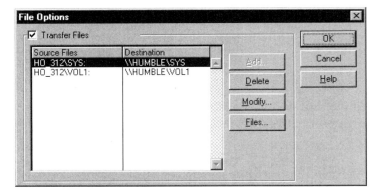

Figure 10.12 *Choose whether to transfer files in the File Options dialog box.*

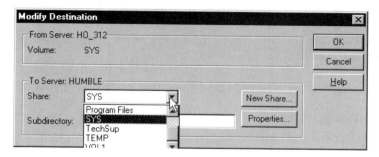

Figure 10.13 *Access the Modify Destination box to change the destination of the volume and its contents.*

Setting the Destination of the Volumes

The Migration Tool transfers the contents of each volume to an NT shared folder of the same name; you can specify a different folder as a destination. You might want to set a new destination, for example, when you're transferring the volumes of multiple NetWare computers and some of those volumes have the same name. If you do not change the destination of one or more of the volumes, all volumes with the same name are merged into one folder on the NT server.

You can direct the destination of any NetWare volume and assign a share name to the volume in the File Options dialog box. To set options for specific volumes, follow these steps:

1. Select the volume in the Source Files list box of the File Options dialog box and choose the **M**odify button. The Modify Destination dialog box appears (see Figure 10.13).

2. In the To Server area, use the Share drop-down list to select an existing drive or directory (folder) to which you will transfer the volume. Enter a name in the Subdirectory text box to create a subdirectory within the share directory. Use the Properties button to enter a path to the share and subdirectory. Alternatively, choose the New Share button to display the New Share dialog box. Enter the share name in the appropriate text box, and enter the path and the name of the folder to the share in the **P**ath text box (see Figure 10.14); NT creates the new folder on the NT server. Choose OK to close the dialog box and return to the Modify Destination dialog box. Choose OK again to close the dialog box and return to the File Options dialog box. Figure 10.15 shows the File Options dialog box with the destinations for both NetWare volumes changed to new shares on the NT server.

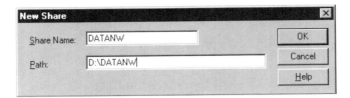

Figure 10.14 In the New Share box, create a new share and enter its path for the NetWare volume.

Selecting Files to Transfer

By default, all files and directories are transferred except for the files on the NetWare administrative directories—\SYSTEM, \LOGIN, \MAIL, \ETC—and any hidden and system files. You can choose which directories and designate files within the directories of any NetWare volume to transfer with the migration.

You might want to check the PUBLIC and the LOGIN directories for any utilities you added for easy user access. Normally, you wouldn't to transfer either of these directories during the migration, but you may have placed other files or utilities in them to save time and energy mapping users to another directory.

Note: During migration, only the selected folder structure is transferred; so, if you have not selected a first level folder for transfer, it will not be transferred.

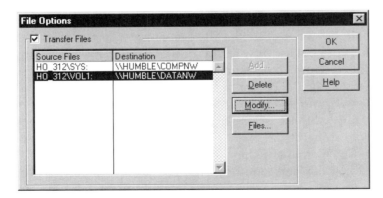

Figure 10.15 The File Options box shows where the NetWare volumes transfer on the NT server.

Using the Migration Tool with NetWare

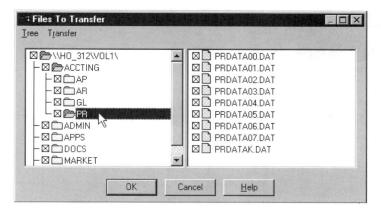

Figure 10.16 *Double-click folders in the Files To Transfer box to display their contents.*

To select the files you want to transfer, follow these steps:

1. In the File Options dialog box, choose the **F**iles button. The Files To Transfer dialog box appears.

2. To view more of the structure, double-click the volume or folder in the left window pane. Files stored in the directory in the left pane are displayed in the right pane of the dialog box (see Figure 10.16). You also can use the **T**ree menu to display branches in the left window pane of the Files To Transfer dialog box. Select one of the following commands; E**x**pand One Level, Expand **B**ranch, Expand **A**ll, or **C**ollapse Branch.

TIP: Select **H**idden files and/or **S**ystem files from the **T**ransfer menu to display those file types.

---

3. Any volume or directory with an X in the check box is selected and will transfer during the migration, as will its contents. Any file with an X in its check box is also selected. To deselect any volume, directory, or file, click the check box to remove the X. Items with a cleared check box will not be transferred. Figure 10.17 shows the SYS drive on the NetWare server with some directories deselected; by default, the Migration Tool doesn't transfer NetWare administration files, unless you select them to be transferred.

4. Choose OK when you're finished selecting files for the transfer. NT returns to the File Options dialog box. Choose OK again to return to the Migration Tool.

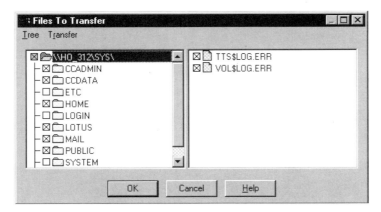

Figure 10.17 When marked with an X, the folder and/or file transfers; when the check box is cleared, the file or folder does not transfer.

Recording the Migration in a Log

NT records the migration or trial migration in a log you can view to determine how files and users were transferred, detect possible problem areas, and otherwise observe the migration process. You can set logging options in the Migration Tool by choosing the **L**ogging button. The Logging dialog box displays, as shown in Figure 10.18. Choose one or all of the following options:

Popup on errors. Displays a message box telling you of errors as they occur.

Verbose User/Group Logging. Lists the maximum amount of information recorded for the transfer of users and groups.

Verbose File Logging. Lists the maximum amount of recorded information about the file transfers.

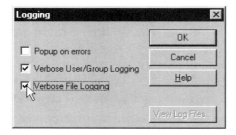

Figure 10.18 Set logging options before the migration.

> **FPNW and Login Scripts**
>
> FPNW (File and Print Services for NetWare) is a separate Microsoft product that enables an NT Server computer to provide file and print services directly to NetWare client computers. The NT server appears just like a NetWare server to the NetWare clients. Clients can access volumes, files, and printers from the NT server. You do not have to make any changes to the client computers to use FPNW; just install it to the computer running NT Server.
>
> If your NT server is running FPNW, you can use the Migration Tool to migrate users' login scripts. Make sure you transfer the NetWare server's MAIL folder. After the migration, the logon scripts run for those users who log on to the server from a NetWare client.

Choose the View Log Files button to view any current files in the log viewer; if you've never migrated, there are no files in the log and the button is dimmed. You may want to perform several trial migrations, however, and view the log files for each before performing the final migration.

11 Running a Migration

NT provides a method of testing the waters for a migration so you can make sure users and groups, files and directories flow correctly before you take the final plunge. A trial migration is a test of the settings, options, and events that will take place in the final migration.

During the trial migration, NT tracks and records information, problems, and other data you can review. You use this information to correct any problems before you actually run the migration. When you're comfortable with the results of the trial migrations, you can run a migration and check transferred group, user, and file information in NT.

In this chapter, you will learn how to:

- Run the trial migration.
- View the log files.
- Problem-solve NetWare 3.1x trials.
- Problem-solve NetWare 4.x trials.
- Perform the final migration.
- Check the transferred data.

Why Run a Trial Migration?

In Chapter 10, "Using the Migration Tool with NetWare," you learned about the options and defaults to set to run the migration. For the trial migration, you must prepare as if you were running the real thing; so start the Migration Tool and set up options as explained in Chapter 10.

You may want to run several trial migrations before performing the real migration, so you can test different setups and see which is the best for your system. You might, for example, try using the user and group defaults for passwords, user names, and group names for the first trial. If you don't like the results, you can assign users new user names and/or individual passwords in a mapping file for the second trial migration.

If you're running NetWare 4.x, you may want to set the bindery context on only a few containers to see how the transfer is made. You can always come back and transfer other containers after the migration or after the trial.

You'll want to experiment with your file system, as well. Transfer several volumes using the defaults on the first trial, and then try assigning specific share names and locations to your volumes and directories.

Indeed, if you are migrating multiple NetWare servers, you must perform trial migrations to confirm transfers before executing the final migration. All systems are different, and for every system, there are different problems that can occur when you migrate. Hopefully, however, you'll learn valuable solutions from each trial migration that will help you during the real thing.

Running a Trial Migration

To run a trial migration, open the Migration Tool and set options for users, groups, and files. Refer to Chapter 10 to refresh your memory regarding these issues, if necessary.

TIP: When setting options in the Migration Tool, set the Logging options to Verbose User/Group Logging and Verbose File Logging so NT records all possible information about the transfer.

Choose the **T**rial Migration button when you're ready. The Migration Tool displays the Converting dialog box as it transfers data. When it is finished, it displays the Transfer Completed dialog box (see Figure 11.1).

At this point, nothing from the NetWare server has been transferred to the NT server; if you cancel the operation, everything remains the same as it was before you started the Migration Tool. This was only a test so it doesn't take very long to run a trial; when you run the real migration, it will take much longer to actually transfer all files, users, and groups. Choose the View Log Files button to see the three log files created during the transfer.

Running a Migration

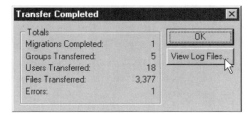

Figure 11.1 The Transfer Completed dialog box summarizes the total users, files, and groups transferred.

Using the LogView Utility

When you choose to view the logs created during a trial migration (or a real migration), NT displays the LogView utility, as shown in Figure 11.2, with the current log files displaying. You can click on the title bar of any of the log windows to view the information in that file; alternatively, you might prefer to maximize one log window so you can view more information at one time. To maximize the window, click the Maximize button.

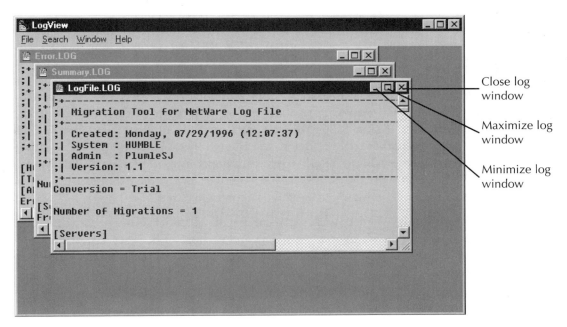

Figure 11.2 The LogView utility enables you to browse various information about the transfer of groups, individuals, and files.

You may also prefer to print the contents of a log file so you can study it on paper instead of on-screen. To print a log file, select the log file window and choose **F**ile, **P**rint. You also can use the **F**ile menu to exit the LogView program (choose **F**ile, E**x**it) or to open a log file not displayed in the application window. To open a log file, choose **F**ile, **O**pen. Log files are stored on the root directory of the NT server drive, and they have LOG extensions.

After you perform a couple of trial migrations, you may want to search through a log file to find a particular piece of information. You can search for a user name or group name, for example, or for a specific file to see if it transferred. To search for text in a log file, select the Log File window and choose the **S**earch menu, **F**ind command. Enter the text for which you're searching and choose OK.

Note: Get help by choosing the **H**elp menu and then **C**ontents or **S**earch; then enter a word or phrase. The Help file in the LogView program was designed specifically to aid you in using the application.

Finally, to switch between the three open logs without minimizing or closing the windows, choose the **W**indow command and select the log you want to view.

Trial Migration Log Files

When you run the trial migration, the Migration Tool creates a set of three log files that record problems, information, and track progress of the transfer; the extension for these files is LOG. You can view each of the files after the trial. Each time you run another trial migration, the Migration Tool creates another set of log files without overwriting the other sets from previous trial migrations. The Migration Tool renames the previous set using a number for the file extension.

The three files created during the trial migration are:

LogFile.log. The LogFile.log records general information, such as the date and time of the migration, the names and versions of both servers, original and new user and group defaults, and file information on each file and directory transferred.

Error.log. The Error.log records errors that occur during the transfer, such as duplicated user and group names, network errors, and system errors.

Summary.log. The Summary.log registers the total users and groups transferred, number of files and bytes involved in the migration, and so on.

Running a Migration **203**

Note: When you perform a trial migration, the log files show you what will happen if you migrate using the settings you just used for the trial; none of the users, directories, or files listed in the log file has actually been transferred.

LogFile.log

The LogFile.log includes information about users, groups, and files about the transfer and about the data existing on NetWare server. Both successful and failed transfers are recorded in the LogFile.log. Figure 11.3 shows the first page of the LogFile.log, which describes the NT Server's drives and shares; the next page reviews the NetWare shares.

When viewing the NT Server's shares, you can see how the NetWare volumes and their contents have transferred. If you're not happy with the structure, you can change it in the Modify Destination dialog box in the Migration Tool when you're preparing for the migration.

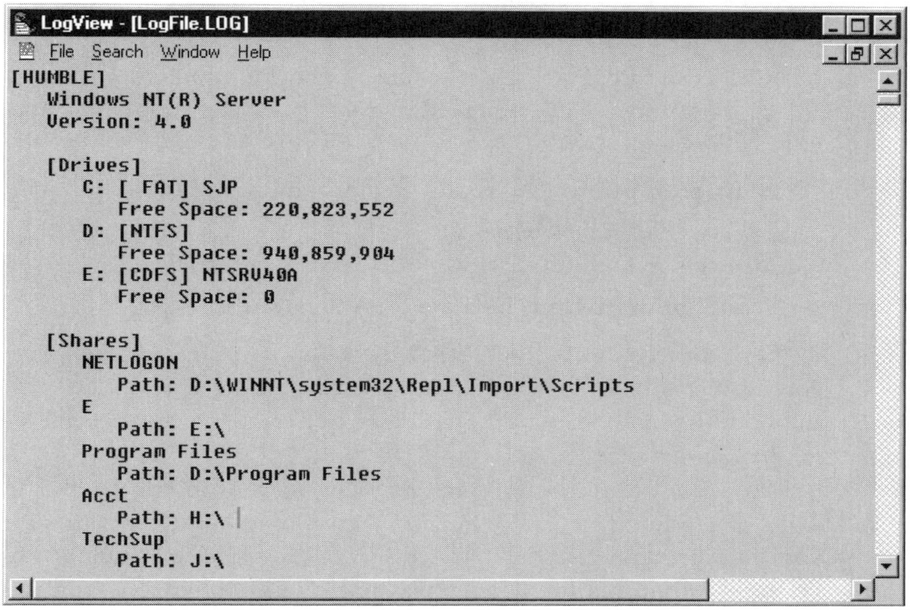

```
LogView - [LogFile.LOG]
File  Search  Window  Help
[HUMBLE]
    Windows NT(R) Server
    Version: 4.0

    [Drives]
        C: [ FAT] SJP
            Free Space: 220,823,552
        D: [NTFS]
            Free Space: 940,859,904
        E: [CDFS] NTSRV40A
            Free Space: 0

    [Shares]
        NETLOGON
            Path: D:\WINNT\system32\Repl\Import\Scripts
        E
            Path: E:\
        Program Files
            Path: D:\Program Files
        Acct
            Path: H:\
        TechSup
            Path: J:\
```

Figure 11.3 Examine basic drive and directory information after the trial migration on the first page of the LogFile log.

204   CHAPTER 11

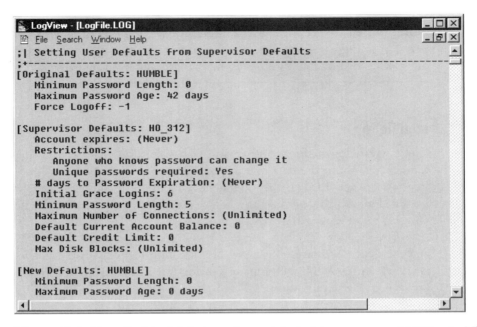

Figure 11.4 Lists of original defaults and new defaults let you compare NetWare to NT.

Next in the LogFile.log is a record of general information about the transfer, including both successful and failed transfers (see Figure 11.4). Included in the log are the following:

Transfer Options. A record of the settings and options you set for users, groups, and file transfers.

Supervisor Defaults. A list of the defaults for NetWare's Supervisor account.

Group Information. Lists the NetWare groups.

This information transfers from the options you set in the User and Group Options dialog box. If the results are not what you want, you can change the default options you marked in the dialog box or create a mappings file to better control the transfer of accounts.

The record of file options and any new shares you created also appear in the LogFile.log (see Figure 11.5). The number of users and their names are also listed. Notice in the figure that a duplicated account for the Administrator was found; the NetWare Administrator account was not transferred to NT and this error was recorded in the Error.log, discussed later in this section.

Figure 11.6 shows original user account information, which is recorded for each added user from NetWare to the NT server. If you see (Added) to the right of a user, you know that user was successfully assigned to the NT server. In addition

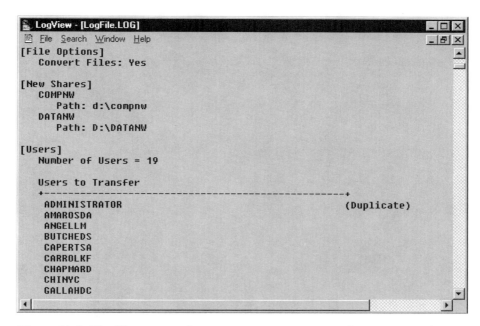

Figure 11.5 The file presents information you can use as a record to compare trial migrations.

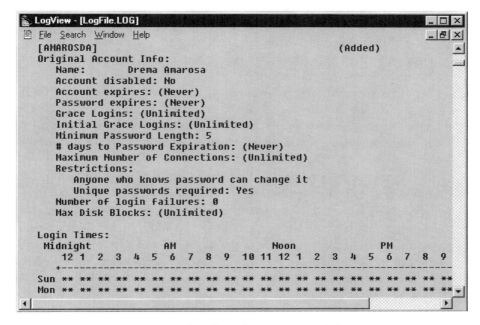

Figure 11.6 NetWare account facts for each user are recorded.

206 CHAPTER 11

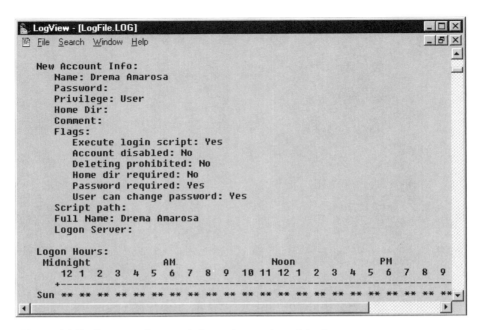

Figure 11.7 Compare the new information to the original.

to data about password restrictions, you'll see login hours, account expiration information, and the user's full name.

Directly following the original account information for a user is the new account information on the NT server, listed in the same way, so you can review and compare the two accounts (see Figure 11.7).

If you need to make adjustments to any user's account, it may be easier for you to do so in NetWare, since you're familiar with the procedures. On the other hand, many user restrictions can be controlled in the User Manager for Domains after the migration, if you prefer. For now, you should make note of the changes so you can deal with them later.

As you progress through the LogFile.log, you'll notice listings of groups that transferred with the members of the group listed below. In Figure 11.8, a list of the Security Equivalences for certain users and groups appears. These users were assigned as Managers of various groups in NetWare; since NT does not have "Managers," the Migration Tool lists the accounts and groups but doesn't assign any specific rights to the users. After the migration, you can create a Managers group in the User Manager for Domains and allocate rights to that group; then you can assign these users to the Managers group.

Running a Migration **207**

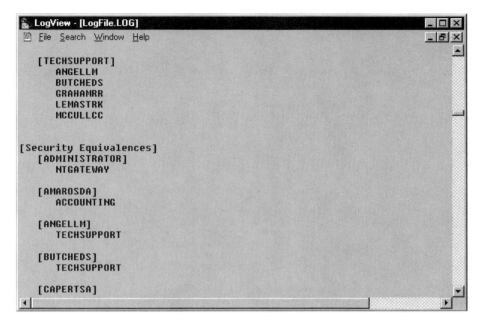

Figure 11.8 *Check to make sure users are transferred to the correct groups during migration.*

The rest of the LogFile.log deals with files and directories that have been transferred. For each directory, the file lists the source directory and the destination directory, the files contained in the directory, file size, and any transferred attributes (see Figure 11.9).

If you choose to transfer the login directory (MAIL), the LogFile.log also lists these transfers as source directory and destination directory. The access rights for the user of the directory are also listed (see Figure 11.10). Additionally, you'll want to transfer the users' home directories since they will likely have files saved that they will need later.

Note: You might want to transfer the MAIL directory so you can have a copy of each user's login script handy when you're ready to re-create either a login script or a user's profile; you can open and print the login script for each user from the NotePad accessory in Windows NT since they're stored in text files. Chapter 14 discusses both of these subjects.

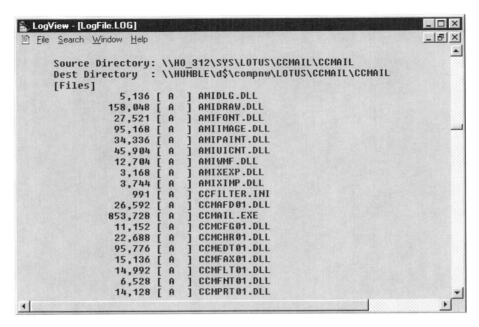

Figure 11.9 A cc:Mail directory transferred from NetWare to NT.

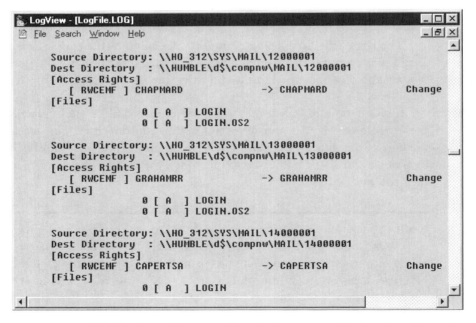

Figure 11.10 The log lists information from the login script files found in the NetWare MAIL directory and transferred to NT.

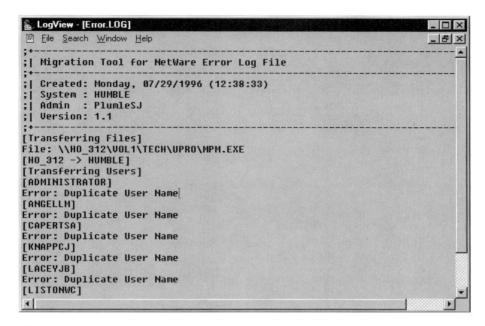

Figure 11.11 Duplicate name errors are recorded in this log for easy reference.

Error.log

The Error.log records any errors during the migration occurring from duplicate user or group names, system problems, or failure to locate a server for the transfer. The user and group names in the Error.log were recorded, depending on your selection in the Logging dialog box when you set up the Migration options, if one of the following occurred:

> You chose to record the error in the log file but not transfer the account.
>
> You chose to overwrite the NT account information with NetWare data for duplicate accounts.
>
> You created a new account with prefixes.

See Chapter 10 for more information about the Logging dialog box. Figure 11.11 shows the Error.log with several duplicate user names found during the trial migration.

Summary.log

General information, such as the server names, number of users and groups, number of files, and so on, is contained in the Summary.log. I print out the

210 CHAPTER 11

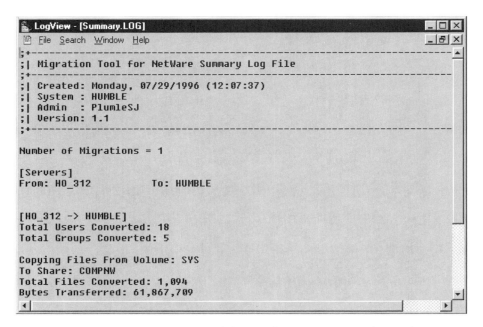

Figure 11.12 Print out a summary of the transfer to compare to other trial migrations.

Summary.log for each trial migration and carefully compare the numbers for Total Files Converted and Bytes Transferred. If there is any shift in the numbers from one trial to the next, I try to locate the problem before migrating to avoid possible problems with transferring my files. Figure 11.12 shows the Summary.log.

Note: You can view the log files at any time, whether you've just performed a trial migration or not, by opening the Migration Tool. Cancel the Select Servers for Migration dialog box and choose the **L**ogging button. From the Logging dialog box, choose the View Log Files button.

Problem-Solving the Trials

The reason for running the trial migration is so you can prepare for problems before you actually run the migration. If you study the log files created during the trial, you may be able to spot problem areas. The Migration Tool logs errors such as no server connection, not enough disk space, and duplicate user and/or group names. These are the easy problems to handle.

The more difficult problems may be hidden within the log files and take some time and effort to discover. I suggest running several trial migrations and printing the LogFile.logs from each trial. Then study the logs carefully, checking the transfer of users, groups, and files with a fine-toothed comb. I can't predict problems you may have since I don't know your setup; however, I can tell you to concentrate on such things as the successful and accurate transfer of user names and directory and file structure.

You can take care of user passwords, group memberships, adding groups, and so on in NT's User Manager for Domains at any time after the migration; although it may be time-consuming, at least you can correct most problems occurring in these areas. Uncertainty about file integrity and problems with directory transfers may be a bit harder to detect and to fix; the best prevention is to plan ahead.

Checklist for General Problems

If you're having trouble attaching to the server, or have duplicate user names, limited disk space, and so on, you can check some of the following items to help alleviate the problems. The list is divided into specific problem areas.

Trouble Connecting Servers or System Errors during Migration Trial

- Check the list of hardware requirements for the computer running the NT Server software for memory and disk space (see Appendix A).
- Make sure you can attach to the NetWare server using the Gateway Service before you try migrating.
- Check that you've added the NTGATEWAY account on the NetWare server and that your new user is a member of the group.
- Make sure you're logged on—to both the NetWare server and the NT server—as the user you created for the Gateway Service and that you have Supervisor/Administrator rights on both servers.
- Check that you're using the Migration Tool from a computer running NT Server as a primary or backup domain controller, not a member server; you cannot run it from an NT Workstation.
- Make sure you set permissions on the NT server root so that you can transfer NetWare volumes, directories, and files during the migration.
- Check files carefully so you do not transfer nonessential files that take up disk space.

Problems with Users and/or Groups

- Check for duplicate user and group accounts on the NT server before the trial migration.

- In Chapter 7, review the list of user rights that do and do not transfer.
- Use the mappings file to transfer users and groups so you can view, add, or delete duplicate names, names you no longer need, and so on.
- If you do use the default Username options, use a prefix to identify duplicate user and group names.
- Use the Verbose User/Group Logging option for any migration to record as much data about the process as possible.

File and Directory Transfer Problems

- Review the list of file rights and attributes in Chapter 7.
- Create a new share when setting the destination of the NetWare volumes instead of choosing an existing share on the NT server; or create a subdirectory within an existing destination share, to maintain file and directory organization.
- Double-check the files and directories you've marked for transfer, deselecting any that are not necessary for the NT network and selecting any that the users might need.
- Use the Verbose File Logging option for any migration to record as much data about the process as possible.

NetWare Versions and Migration

There really is no difference between migrating versions 3.1x and 4.x that I haven't already covered. Your biggest task in NetWare 4.x is to check all containers that you plan to migrate and confirm that there are no duplicate user names or groups. Duplicate names, once migrated, will mean you lose some users and their data.

When using NetWare 4.x, don't forget to place all users in any one container in a group to avoid a flat transfer of accounts and data. And set the bindery context for all containers you want to transfer. Other than that, the transfer should proceed similarly to a NetWare 3.1x migration.

Performing the Migration

When you're satisfied that you've done all you can in preparation for the migration, you can begin the migration. Depending on the number of users, groups, and files you plan to migrate, the migration could take one hour or several. You can watch the progress in the Converting dialog box that displays during the migration. The dialog box lists the number of users and groups as they transfer, the number of files as they transfer, and the number of errors that occur during the transfer.

Running a Migration

To start the migration, open the Migration Tool and set the options as described in Chapter 10, using your trial migration successes as a guide. Choose the **S**tart Migration button. When the migration is complete, a message box displays and you can view the view the log files just as you did with the trial migration.

Migration Log Files

The migration log files are similar to those you viewed with the trial migration. You'll see a LogFile.log, an Error.log, and a Summary.log, all with the same type of information you are now familiar with.

No matter how many trial migrations or how much problem-solving you do, there may still be errors that appear during the migration that didn't appear during the trial. This is normal, and most likely, the errors will not be devastating. Figure 11.13 shows a list of errors that resulted from a duplicate group account that did not show up, for some reason, in the trial migrations.

Figure 11.14 shows the Error.log file for the same duplicate name problem; one duplicate name can affect other groups and users being transferred. This problem, however, is easily fixed in the User Manager for Domains. You can quickly add the users to the existing group, as shown later in this section.

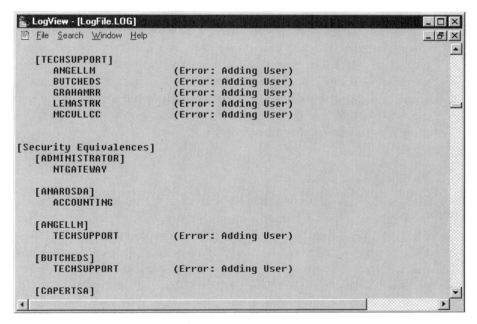

Figure 11.13 One duplicate group affects many users in the transfer.

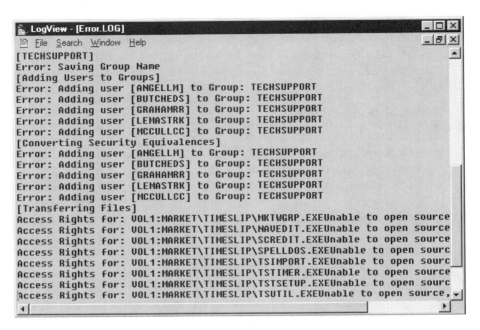

Figure 11.14 This Error.log file lists problems with duplicate group names.

Another error that appears in Figure 11.14 deals with access rights for some executable files. This problem is caused by NetWare's Execute attribute. NT doesn't transfer the Execute attribute and ignores the NetWare files assigned with that attribute. Since NT couldn't transfer the files, it lists them in the Error.log. This problem did not show up in the trial migration; but fortunately, it's easily fixed. I can remove the Execute attribute from the files on the NetWare server and select those files to transfer during a second migration.

Viewing User Transfers

You can view, and modify, the NetWare users that transferred in the User Manager for Domains (Start, **P**rograms, Administrative Tools, User Manager for Domains). Figure 11.15 shows the NetWare users and groups added to the NT server in the User Manager for Domains. NetWare users and groups are represented in all uppercase letters, whereas the existing NT users are in upper- and lowercase (unless you used all uppercase characters to enter your NT users).

If you check the group memberships for any transferred user, you'll see the transferred NetWare groups as well as any automatic NT memberships (see Figure 11.16). If you find the group memberships have not transferred the way you thought they should, see Chapter 7 for information about equivalent groups.

Running a Migration

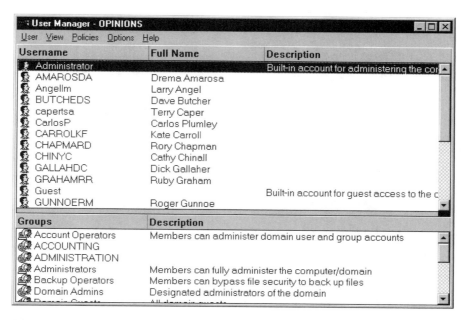

Figure 11.15 *You can modify the users transferred from NetWare in the User Manager for Domains.*

You can assign group memberships to your users in the User Manager for Domains. You can also set password restrictions, account lockout options, security policies, and so on. Chapter 3 explains how to use the User Manager for Domains to create users and groups; Chapter 4 explains how to assign rights and permissions to individuals, groups, and objects.

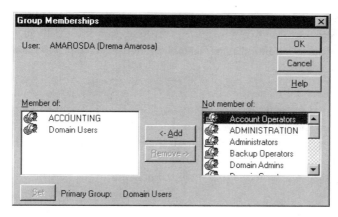

Figure 11.16 *The user is still a member of the ACCOUNTING group.*

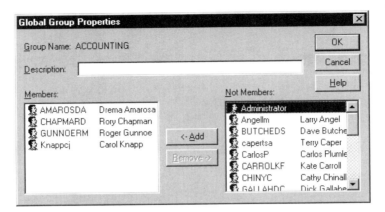

Figure 11.17 Members of the group, as well as users who are not members, are displayed in the Properties dialog box.

Viewing Group Transfers

You also use the User Manager for Domains to view and modify groups in NT. You can view the properties for any group by double-clicking the group name in the User Manager window. Figure 11.17 shows the Properties dialog box for the ACCOUNTING group transferred during the migration.

> ### Domain Users Global Group
>
> Notice the transferred users are moved into the global group Domain Users, as opposed to limiting their membership to the local group Users. You can grant rights and permissions to global groups for accessing their own domain, other workstations or member servers in their own domain, and trusting domains and their related resources. Local groups, on the other hand, are limited to receiving rights and permissions for only one domain.
>
> All transferred users are made members of the Domain Users global group. By default in NT, all new accounts created in the domain are added to the Domain Users group unless you choose to remove them. Members of the Domain Users global group are members of the Users local group for the domain; therefore these users have normal access to the domain, the computers in the domain, and resources in the domain. They also have access to any trusted domains in the network.

> For easiest administration, leave the transferred users in the Domain Users global group. Global groups can be put into local groups for assigning rights and permissions to a domain quickly and easily. Additionally, global groups can be granted permissions directly in other domains. Finally, global groups can be given permission to access Windows NT Workstation and/or member servers, whereas local groups cannot. For more information about global and local groups, see Chapter 3.

Viewing Transferred File and Directories

You can use the NT Explorer to view the file and directory transfers (Start, **P**rograms, NT Explorer). Figure 11.18 shows two migrated volumes in the Explorer. For information about how to use the Explorer, see Chapter 4.

In the Explorer, you can do the following:

- Expand directories (folders) and view subdirectories (subfolders) and files.
- View floppy, hard, CD, and network drives.

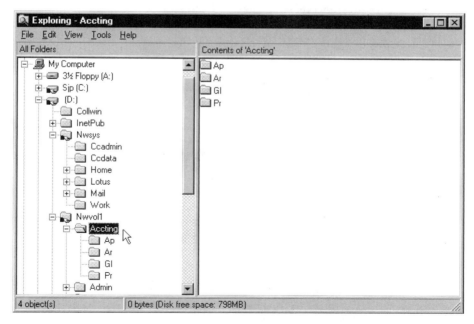

Figure 11.18 View the transferred NetWare directories and files in the NT Explorer.

- View mapped network drives and their contents.
- View file details about any file to see its size.
- Open, copy, move, delete, and rename files.
- Create directories (folders) and files.
- View file and directory properties, such as attributes, size, and security options.
- Share files and directories.
- Assign permissions to files and directories.
- Find specific files or directories.
- Map Network drives.

Using the Explorer, you can rearrange the transferred files and directories to any structure you want. Use the Explorer to manage and organize the server and the network drives and then to administer the files and directories on the server.

Part of administering files and directories deals with file permissions. Figure 11.19 shows the permissions for a file transferred in the migration. Notice that the rights of two NetWare groups—ACCOUNTING and MARKETING—have also been transferred with the file. The Administrators group is an NT group. Remember, all transferred NetWare files and directories become the property of the Administrators group after the migration, so members of the Administrators group automatically have Full Control over the files and directories.

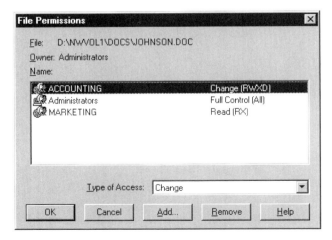

Figure 11.19 File attributes transfer to file permissions on NT.

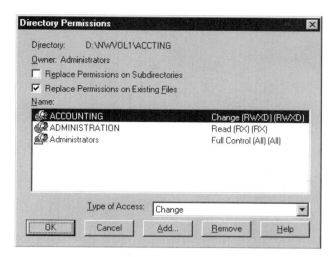

Figure 11.20 NetWare directory attributes become NT permissions.

Figure 11.20 shows the Directory Permissions dialog box for one of the transferred directories. Again, attributes for two of the transferred NetWare groups have transferred to NT permissions. Members of the Administrators group own the directory and therefore have full control access.

12 *Client Considerations*

The next step in migrating from NetWare to NT is to connect the client computers to the NT server. Before connecting clients, you'll need to install NT client software to each workstation. NT helps with this process by making various clients available to you through the NT server and the NT installation CD-ROM.

After installing client software, you can connect the clients to the server. This chapter also shows you how to connect to the server from the workstation and to the workstation from the server. Specifically in this chapter, you learn to do the following:

- Create client software.
- Install client software to MS-DOS and Windows for Workgroups.
- Configure network components in Windows NT Workstation computers.
- Configure network components in Windows 95 computers.
- Connect clients to the NT server.

Client Software Overview

NT provides a method by which you can create startup disks or installation disks for installing various clients. An installation startup disk enables you to start a client computer and connect to the NT server. From an installation directory created on the server, then, you can install the client software. You could, alternatively, create a network installation disk set that contains all of the files needed to install the client software. You use the Network Client Administrator tool to create the client software.

Note: Remember that your Windows NT Server software license requires you purchase a valid software license prior to installing additional copies of the Server software or of any client software.

Using NT's Network Client Administrator, you can create a network installation startup disk for Windows for Workgroups 3.11 (TCP/IP version) and/or for a Network Client version 3.0 for MS-DOS. Users can attach to the NT server and access resources using this client software.

Windows NT Server versions 3.5, 3.51, and 4.0; Windows NT Workstation versions 3.5, 3.51, and 4.0; and Windows 95 computers can connect to the NT server without special client software, if you install the appropriate protocol (generally NetBEUI, but either IPX or TCP/IP will work). Windows for Workgroups computers also can connect to the NT server using NetBEUI, if you're not set up to run TCP/IP.

If you prefer, you can create a set of installation disks for the following clients, instead of using the startup installation disks:

Network Client version 3.0 for MS-DOS

LAN Manager 2.2c for MS-DOS clients

LAN Manager 2.2c for MS OS/2 clients

Remote Access Service client 1.1 for MS-DOS

TCP/IP-32 for Windows for Workgroups 3.11

Starting the Network Client Administrator

Before you can create the client software, you must create a directory on the root of the NT server to hold it. Call this directory CLIENTS and make sure you designate the directory as shared (**F**ile, S**h**aring).

To start the Network Client Administrator, choose Start, **P**rograms, Administrative Tools, and Network Client Administrator. The dialog box shown in Figure 12.1 appears. The options in the dialog box are as follows:

Make Network Installation Startup Disk. Create a startup disk you can use to install the MS-DOS client software or the Windows for Workgroups TCP/IP client software.

Make Installation Disk Set. Create a set of disks you can use to install the client software to the workstation before connecting to the network.

Copy Client-Based Network Administrative Tools. You can copy the User Manager for Domains, Server Manager, and the Event Viewer to a com-

Client Considerations

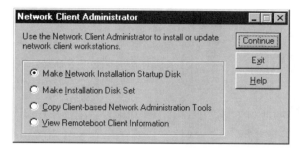

Figure 12.1 *Create client software using the Network Client Administrator.*

puter running NT Workstation or Windows 95 for remote access to the server from a workstation. For more information, see your Windows NT on-line help or documentation (see "Copying Client-Based Administration Tools" later in chapter).

View Remoteboot Client Information. If you're using NT's remoteboot service, you can view the computers attached with this option. The remoteboot service is a way of starting MS-DOS and Windows workstations over the network using software on the server, rather than on the client. For more information, see NT on-line help or NT documentation.

Copying the Installation Files

Before you can create the clients, you'll need to copy files to your hard disk from the NT CD-ROM. When you choose either of the first two options in the Network Client Administrator dialog box, the Share Network Client Installation Files dialog box appears (see Figure 12.2).

You can create subdirectories in the CLIENTS directory and copy the files yourself from the NT CD-ROM disk, or you can let the Network Client Administrator do it for you. The difference is that if you let the Network Client Administrator copy the files for you, it copies all of the files for all clients, the network administrator tools, and the remoteboot files to the server; you may not want or need all of these files on the server. You can copy the files yourself so you'll have only the client files you need and thus save space on your hard drive (refer to "Copying Installation Files to the Server").

In the Share Network Client Installation Files dialog box, the default path is to the CD-ROM drive; this is the source of the files you want to copy. You can choose the browse (...) button to view a network drive, if you've copied the NT distribution files to the network. Next, choose from one of the following options:

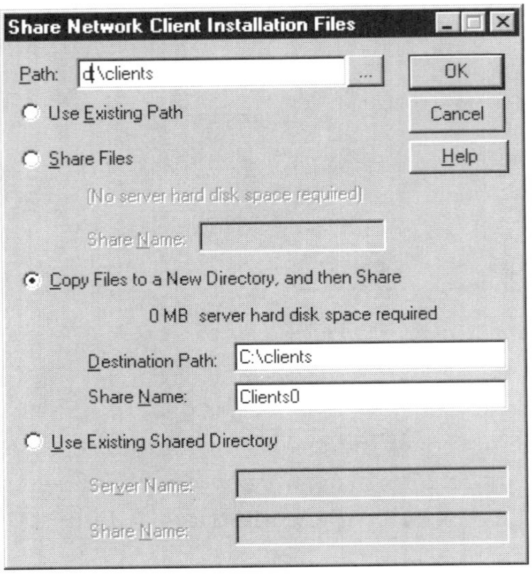

Figure 12.2 Choose how to copy the files to the server's hard drive in this dialog box.

> ### Copying Installation Files to the Server
>
> If you want to copy the files for specific clients to the NT server instead of letting the Network Client Administrator do a blind copy of all of the files, you can easily do so in the NT Explorer. Within the CLIENTS directory you created on the server, create any or all of the following subdirectories: MSCLIENT, WFW, LANMAN, LANMAN.OS2. Or, if you want to copy the client-based administration tools to the server, create these subdirectories in the CLIENTS directory: WINNT.SRV or WIN95.SRV.
>
> From the Windows NT CD-ROM, open any of the following directories and copy the NETSETUP folder to the appropriate directory on the NT server:
>
> | Client | Directory | Space Req. |
> | --- | --- | --- |
> | MS-DOS Client | MSCLIENT | 4M |
> | Windows for Workgroups | TCP32WFW | 25M |
> | LAN Manager for DOS | LANMAN | 3.5M |
> | LAN Manager for OS/2 | LANMAN.OS2 | 3.5M |
> | Administration Tools for NT | SRVTOOLS\WINNT | 11M |
> | Administration Tools for 95 | SRVTOOLS\WIN95 | 25M |

Use Existing Path. Choose this option if you previously copied the NT distribution files to the hard drive and that path displays in the **P**ath text box.

Share Files. Choose this option to use the files directly from the CD. Enter a name for the share. I don't recommend this method because you'll need to keep the CD in the drive until all clients have been installed; plus, I like to keep the CD as a backup of the files, just in case.

Copy Files to New Directory and then Share. This option copies the files (all client, remoteboot, and administration tools files) to the CLIENTS directory for you. Enter the destination path and the share name you want to use.

Use Existing Shared Directory. If you copied files from the CD to selected directories within the CLIENTS directory, use this option.

After you copy the files, you're ready to create the client, as described in the following sections.

Creating the DOS Client

You can create the client software (Microsoft Network Client version 3.0 for MS-DOS) for an MS-DOS computer by creating installation disks or by using a startup disk. The method you choose depends on how many DOS workstations you'll need to configure. If you only have one or two DOS clients, create the installation disks and save the server disk space for other things; however, if you have several DOS clients, you'll save time and effort by creating the startup disk and letting the clients attach to the server to copy the installation files.

Creating a Startup Disk

Using the startup disk to install the client is quick and easy. You'll need one floppy disk, high-density and formatted as a system disk. Format the system disk on a DOS workstation as opposed to within Windows NT or 95 or even Windows for Workgroups.

When clients use the network installation startup disk, they boot the computer with the disk inserted in the drive. The disk directs the computer to connect to the server that contains the installation files, and the disk initiates the installation process. Users follow directions to complete installation, enter their password, and the client software does the rest.

You must create one installation startup disk per workstation, since you use a unique computer name and user name when creating the startup disk. To create the startup disk, follow these steps:

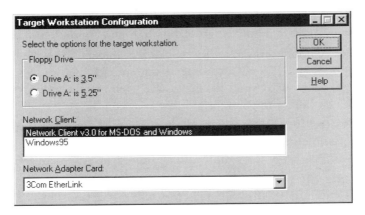

Figure 12.3 *In the Target Workstation Configuration dialog box, choose options for the floppy disk, client, and adapter card.*

1. Start the Network Client Administrator tool and choose Make **N**etwork Installation Startup Disk. The Share Network Client Installation Files dialog box appears (refer to Figure 12.2).
2. Choose the method you want to use to copy the files and choose OK. The Target Workstation Configuration dialog box appears (see Figure 12.3).
3. Choose the size of the floppy disk drive of the client computer, choose the MS-DOS client, and select the network adapter card installed to the client.

Note: Make sure you select the correct NIC driver when creating the installation startup disks. The client software doesn't automatically detect the network interface card so you must already have selected it.

4. Choose OK. The Network Startup Disk Configuration dialog box appears (see Figure 12.4).
5. Enter a unique name for the computer, the user's name as it appears on the server, and the domain name. The only protocols listed in the box are those installed to the server that can support an installation over the network.

Note: If you're using TCP/IP, choose the DHCP server to automatically configure the addresses; or you can enter the IP Address, Subnet Mask, and Default Gateway yourself. For more information about TCP/IP, see Appendix E.

Client Considerations

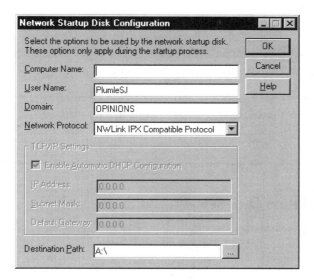

Figure 12.4 *Configure the client name, domain, and computer name in this dialog box.*

6. In the Destination **P**ath, enter the drive letter of the floppy disk to which you'll copy the client startup files and choose OK. The Confirm Network Disk Configuration dialog box appears (see Figure 12.5).
7. Choose OK to confirm. The tool begins copying files and then displays a message box telling the files have been copied; choose OK.

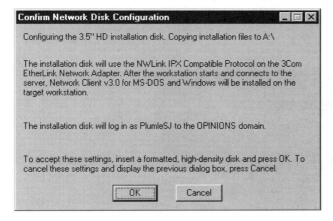

Figure 12.5 *Confirm your selections before creating the disk.*

You can use the startup disk to install the MS-DOS client to any workstation using the DOS operating system. The workstation can also use Windows 3.1 or Windows 3.11; however, the DOS client only enables you to connect to the network through DOS (see the section "Installing the DOS Client").

Note: When you close the Network Client Administrator tool, it displays a dialog box of items you should check before installing the client. Choose OK to close the box.

Creating an Installation Disk Set

You can, alternatively, create a set of installation disks for installing the client to an MS-DOS workstation. The disk set consists of two disks and guides the user to install and configure the client, as described later in this chapter. After the user installs the client, he or she can then connect to the NT server and the network. You can use the installation disk set to install multiple client computers, as opposed to the startup installation disks, which are created for a specific client computer.

You'll need two high-density, formatted disks to create the DOS installation disk set. To create a set of installation disks, follow these steps:

1. Start the Network Client Administrator tool and choose **N**etwork Installation Startup Disk. The Share Network Client Installation Files dialog box appears (refer to Figure 12.2).
2. Choose the method you want to use to copy the files and choose OK. The Make Installation Disk Set dialog box appears (see Figure 12.6).
3. Choose the Network Client for DOS and Windows client.

Figure 12.6 Choose options for the installation disk set in the Make Installation Disk Set dialog box.

Client Considerations **229**

4. Choose the **D**estination Drive: A or B; and, optionally, you can choose to **F**ormat the disks, if you haven't already formatted them.

5. Insert the first disk and choose OK. The tool copies the files. Insert the second disk when prompted. When the Network Client Administrative tool is finished, you're ready to install the client software to the client computers.

Installing the DOS Client

Whether you're installing the DOS client by using a startup installation disk or with installation disks, the software uses the same Setup program. The difference between the two is in the information the user must enter.

Using Installation Disks

To install the DOS client using an installation disk, start the computer, then insert the disk. Type **A:** and press Enter and then type **setup** and press Enter. The client software examines the network configuration and confirms the directory of the Network Client files. You'll be prompted to choose a directory for the Network Client; the default is \NET. You can accept the default or enter a new directory. Next, the software copies the files to the hard disk.

During setup, you must enter and/or confirm setup options and configuration of the hardware. You'll be asked to confirm or enter new names for the user, computer, and workgroup or domain. The user name should remain the same as you entered on the installation disk when creating it; otherwise you could have trouble logging in to the network.

Choose to Run Network Client if you want the network to start each time the user starts the computer. Choose Logon Validation for the user to enter a password and user name each time the computer starts.

Next, you must choose between the basic and the full redirector. The basic redirector provides all standard network configurations, such as connecting, disconnecting, and browsing the server. The basic redirector uses less memory and disk space. The full redirector, on the other hand, enables you to log on to Windows NT and get more use from the server and resources. Unless the client computer is short on memory and/or disk space, use the full redirector.

You should also check the adapter and protocol configuration. You can choose the adapter and then the Settings option to set the interrupt and I/O port for the adapter or to add or remove an adapter. Choose the Protocol option to add or change the protocol; depending on your system, you can choose IPX or TCP/IP.

The software finishes copying and configuring the network drive. Remove the disk and reboot the computer. You can change configuration at any time by switching to the client directory (NET) and typing **setup**. You'll need at least 429K of conventional memory to run the Setup program at any time.

Using the Startup Disk

The MS-DOS client is easy to install using the startup disk created with the Network Client Administrator. With the computer off, insert the diskette and start the computer or reboot. The startup disk initializes, loads the NWLink protocol, and starts the NET commands needed to access the server.

The user enters his or her name, or presses Enter to accept the default name, and enters the passwords for the workstation and for the domain. After connecting, the client software copies files to the NET directory on the client and continues to set up the client. Using the same Setup program as described in the previous section, you can change user, domain, or computer names; configure adapters and protocols; and otherwise change options in the Setup program.

You also can start the Setup program on the client by changing to the NET, or other client directory you specified, and typing **setup** and pressing Enter.

Attaching to the Network

When the DOS client computer boots, the user enters his or her name (or presses Enter to confirm the listed name) and enters his or her password. The first time the user logs on, he or she will have to enter a password for the client and then confirm it; this password should be the same as the user's password for the network, for ease and efficiency. Then the user enters the password for the network. After the first login, the user enters only one password.

To attach to the network, the user types **net** at the DOS prompt, and the Disk Connections dialog box appears; you could add the command to the computer's AUTOEXEC.BAT if you want. The user can use the following commands, pressing the Tab key or using the Alt+boldfaced key to select the command in the dialog box to connect and browse the network:

Dri**v**e. Enter the drive letter to represent the connection (mapping the drive).

Path. Enter the path to the network using the double slash and server name.

Connect. Choose to connect to the path specified using the drive letter specified.

Browse. View available resources on the network drive.

Disconnect. Disconnect from the network.

Note: The Net command is very similar to the Net command (located in the AUTOEXEC.BAT) used in the Windows for Workgroups network client.

Creating a Windows for Workgroups Client

You can attach a Windows for Workgroups computer to the NT Server as a member of a workgroup, using the NetBEUI protocol and a normal network connection. You can, alternatively, create a client for the Windows for Workgroups client to use if you're already using the TCP/IP protocol on your NT network.

You should remove all NetWare client software from the Windows for Workgroups workstation before installing the NT client. In addition to removing the DOS files that load the VLMs or IPX—such as STARTNET.BAT and related files—you should also remove references to the NetWare client in the WIN.INI and SYSTEM.INI files.

In the WIN.INI file, remove nwpopup.exe from the load=nwpopup.exe in the [windows] section. In the SYSTEM.INI file, remove the following:

Section	Statement:	Change Statement to Read:
[boot]	network.drv=netware.drv	network.drv=
[boot.description]	network.drv=Novell NetWare (v4.0)	network.drv=No Network Installed
[386Enh]	network=*vnetbios, vipx.386,vnetware.386	network=*dosnet,*vnetbios
[386Enh]	TimerCriticalSection=1000	(remove statement)
	ReflectDOSSln2A=TRUE	(remove statement)
	OverlappedIO-OFF	(remove statement)
	UniqueDOSPSP=TRUE	(remove statement)
	PSPIncrement=5	(remove statement)
[Network]	winnet=Novell/000400000	winnet=nonet

Creating the Client Disks

You can create installation disks for installing only the TCP/IP-32 Windows for Workgroups client. You'll need one high-density, formatted floppy disk. The process is similar to creating an installation disk for the MS-DOS client; refer to that previous section for more information.

To create the TCP/IP-32 Windows for Workgroups client, follow these steps:

1. Start the Network Client Administrator tool and choose Make **I**nstallation Disk Set. The share Network Client Installation Files dialog box appears (refer to Figure 12.2).

2. Choose the method you want to use to copy the files and choose OK. The Make Installation Disk Set dialog box appears (refer to Figure 12.6).
3. Choose the TCP/IP 32 for Windows for Workgroups 3.11 client.
4. Choose the **D**estination Drive: A or B; and, optionally, you can choose to **F**ormat the disk, if you haven't already formatted it.
5. Insert the disk and choose OK. The tool copies the files. Insert the second disk when prompted. When the Network Client Administrative tool is finished, you're ready to install the client software to the client computers.

Installing the Client to Windows for Workgroups

You install the client for Windows for Workgroups from the Network Setup dialog box in the Windows program on the client. The procedure is the same, whether you're using the installation disks you created for the TCP/IP-32 client or you're going to use the Microsoft Networks connection; naturally, there's more setup to the TCP/IP-32 option.

Note: To prevent trouble with Microsoft's TCP/IP-32 and connecting to the network, you should remove any previously installed, third-party TCP/IP protocols from the workstation before installing the NT client.

To install the client, follow these steps:

1. In the Program Manager Network group, double-click the Network icon. The Network Setup dialog box appears (see Figure 12.7).
2. Choose the **N**etworks button; the Networks dialog box appears (see Figure 12.8).
3. Choose the option **I**nstall Microsoft Windows Network. You can, alternatively, choose to support another network in addition to the MS Windows network.
4. Choose OK; Windows returns to the Network Setup dialog box.
5. Optionally, choose the **S**haring button to indicate whether to share files and/or printers with the rest of the network; choose OK to return to the Network Setup dialog box.
6. Choose the **D**rivers button. The Network Drivers dialog box appears (see Figure 12.9).

Client Considerations

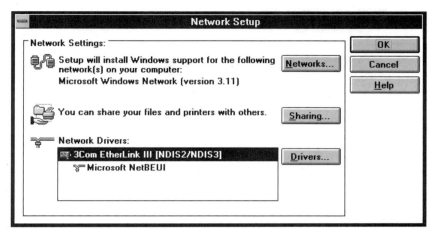

Figure 12.7 Use the Network Setup dialog box to choose network options, sharing choices, and drivers for the client.

7. Choose the Add **A**dapter button to install a different or additional adapter. Confirm the I/O port settings and choose OK. If you're adding a new adapter, you may be prompted for one of the Windows for Workgroups installation disks. Insert the disk and choose OK.

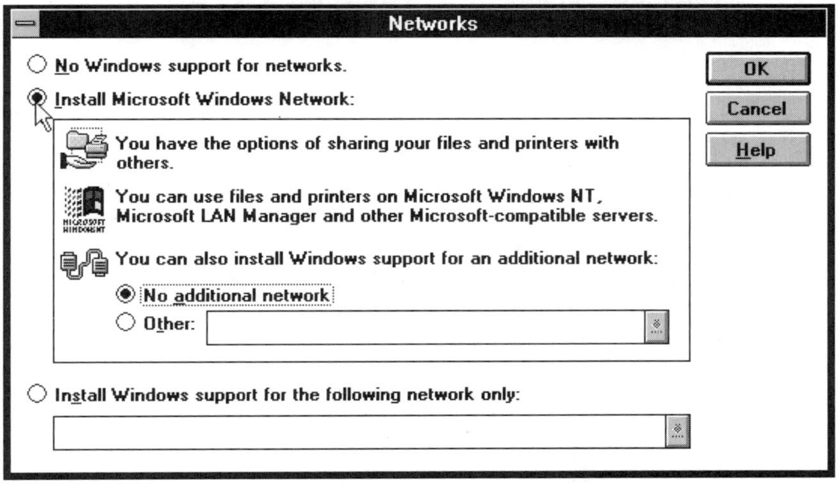

Figure 12.8 Choose to install the Microsoft Windows Network.

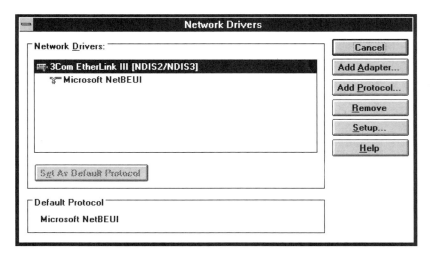

Figure 12.9 In the Network Drivers dialog box, install additional adapters and/or protocols to the client.

8. In the Network Drivers dialog box, choose the Add **P**rotocol button. From the list, select the NetBEUI or the MS TCP/IP-32 3.11b protocol and choose OK. If you choose to install the TCP/IP-32 protocol, the Install Driver dialog box appears. Enter the letter for the disk drive containing the Windows for Workgroups client and press Enter. The software copies the appropriate files to the hard drive. If you're installing the NetBEUI or other protocol, you may be prompted for one of the Windows for Workgroups installation disks. Insert the disk and choose OK.

TIP: If you are prompted to replace any files while the software is installing, choose **Y**es to replace older files with the newer versions.

9. Windows returns to the Network Drivers dialog box. Choose C**l**ose to return to the Program Manager.
10. If you installed NetBEUI, remove the disk from the floppy drive and restart the computer. If you installed the TCP/IP-32 client for Windows for Workgroups, you have a few more steps to complete the installation. The MS Windows Network Names dialog box appears; enter the user name, workgroup name, and so on. You'll be prompted to enter configuration information for the TCP/IP protocol, such as the default gateway, WINS server, IP address, Subnet mask, and so on. Remove the disk and restart the computer.

Client Considerations 235

Accessing the Network

You can use the File Manager to connect to the network drive and to map drives for your connections. Open the File Manager and choose **D**isk, Connect **N**etwork drive. The Connect Network Drive dialog box appears.

In the **D**rive drop-down list box, select the drive letter to represent this connection. Enter the path in the **P**ath text box or select the path from the Show Shared Directories on list box (see Figure 12.10). Double-click any item in the Show Shared Directories list to expand its contents.

You can map as many drives to the server as you like. Also, choose the Reconnec**t** at Startup check box to automatically reconnect the mapped drives whenever you start Windows.

Using Windows 95 Clients

If you have Windows 95 installed to workstations, you do not need to install a client to make the program work with the NT server; all you need to do is configure the network settings, as explained in the following section.

If you do not have Windows 95 installed on a workstation but have purchased an additional license for each workstation on which you want to use the software,

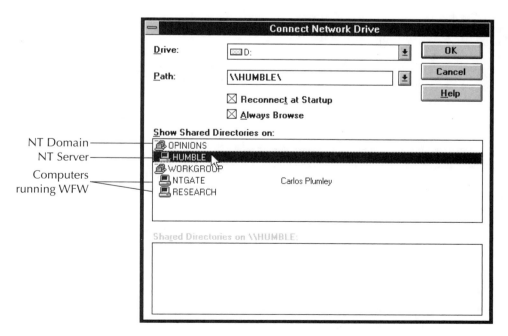

Figure 12.10 Connect to the NT server in the Connect Network Drive dialog box.

you can create an installation startup disk using the Network Client Administrator that enables you to install Windows 95. Microsoft requires that you have a license for each installation of Windows 95 that you perform. Using the startup installation disk to install the Windows 95 client from NT's distribution files configures the client to view and access the NT server.

Creating the Windows 95 Client Installation Startup Disk

The NT Server software includes a client service for the installation of Windows 95. You create an installation startup disk that boots the workstation and then accesses the server. The files necessary to install Windows 95 reside on the NT CD-ROM or on the server itself, if you've copied them. You'll need one high-density floppy disk formatted as a system disk.

Note: To install Windows 95, the workstation should be a 386DX or higher processor running MS-DOS version 3.31 or later, Windows 3.0 or later, or OS/2 version 2.0 or later; 8M RAM is recommended and the workstation needs about 40M disk space for the program files. A VGA or higher resolution graphics card is also required, and a mouse is optional but definitely recommended.

To create the installation startup disk to create Windows 95 clients, follow these steps:

1. In the Network Client Administrator dialog box (Start, **P**rograms, Administrative Tools, Network Client Administrator), choose Make **N**etwork Installation Startup Disk, and choose Continue.

2. In the Share Network Client Installation Files dialog box, choose the source for the NT distribution files. Choose OK.

3. In the Target Workstation Configuration dialog box, choose Win 95 from the Network **C**lient list box. Make sure you also select the appropriate adapter card for the client to which you're installing.

4. A message dialog box appears, stating you must purchase a license before you can install and use Windows 95. Choose **Y**es if you've purchased a license for the software.

5. The Network Client Administrator copies the necessary files to the startup disk and notifies you when it's done.

When you're ready to install Windows 95, insert the installation startup disk in the client's floppy drive and reboot the computer. Follow directions on-screen to

Client Considerations **237**

enter the user name and password. The disk connects to the server and initiates the Windows 95 Setup program. After checking the system for errors and running Scandisk, the program copies files to your hard drive and begins the Windows 95 Setup.

Follow directions on-screen to install the operating system. The disk and NT pretty much configure the workstation for you; however, if you need to configure any of the network components after the installation, see the next section.

Configuring Windows 95 Network Components

You'll be prompted for the Windows 95 CD-ROM disk during the network setup. Insert the disk when prompted so that Windows can copy the necessary files. To configure the network in Windows 95, follow these steps:

1. Choose Start, **S**ettings, **C**ontrol Panel. In the Control Panel, double-click the Network icon to open the Network dialog box, as shown in Figure 12.11.

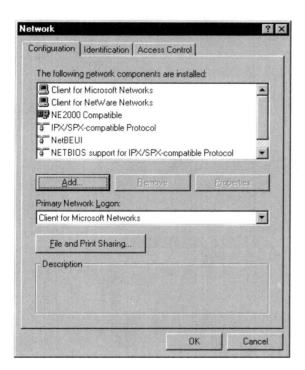

Figure 12.11 *Use the Network dialog box to add, remove, and configure adapters, protocols, and so on.*

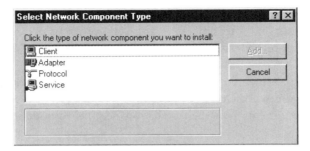

Figure 12.12 Select the network component you want to install.

2. In the Configuration tab, you can choose **A**dd to add a client, service, protocol, or adapter to the network configuration (see Figure 12.12).
3. Choose Client and select the **A**dd button. The Select Network Client dialog box appears. Choose Microsoft in the **M**anufacturers list and choose Client for Microsoft Networks in the Network Client list (see Figure 12.13).
4. Choose OK to return to the Select Network Component Type dialog box.
5. To add an adapter, select Adapter in the list and choose the **A**dd button. Windows displays a list of Manufacturers and the adapters they make. Select the manufacturer and the adapter type and choose OK to return to the Select Network Component Type dialog box.
6. Select Protocol and choose the **A**dd button. The Select Network Protocol dialog box appears (see Figure 12.14).

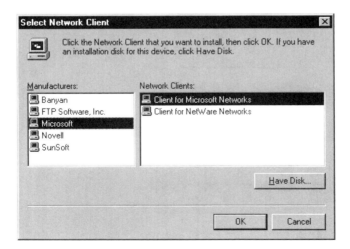

Figure 12.13 Install the Microsoft client if not already installed to the Network dialog box.

Client Considerations

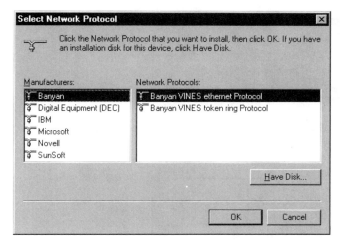

Figure 12.14 *Install the protocol you need to attach to the network.*

7. Choose Microsoft in the **M**anufacturers list and then choose NetBEUI or TCP/IP. Choose OK to close the dialog box and return to the Select Network Component Type dialog box.

8. Select Services and choose the **A**dd button. In the Select Network Service dialog box, select Microsoft from the Manufacturer list and choose File and Printer Sharing for Microsoft Networks.

9. Choose OK to return to the Select Network Component Type dialog box; choose OK to return to the Network dialog box.

10. To configure a service, adapter, or protocol, select the component in the Configuration tab and choose the **P**roperties button.

    Client properties include configuration includes logon validation, the domain name, and logon options.

    Adapter properties include driver type, bindings, and resources (IRQ and I/O address).

    Protocol properties include bindings and property values.

11. You can also configure the following in the Configuration tab:

    Remove any component in the list by selecting the component and choosing the **R**emove button.

    If the client attaches to multiple networks, you can select the Primary Network **L**ogon for the client. Select the network to log on to first from the drop-down list.

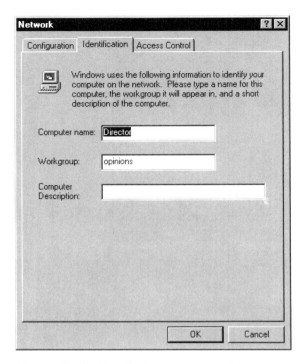

Figure 12.15 Identify the computer to the network.

Choose file and printer sharing options by selecting the **F**ile and Print Sharing button.
12. Use the Identification tab to assign the computer name and the workgroup name (see Figure 12.15). A description is optional.
13. Choose OK to close the Network dialog box and a message appears to restart the computer for the setting to take effect. Choose **Y**es.

Connecting to the Network

You can attach the NT network after configuring the network settings. When a user logs on to the network, he or she must type a user name and password that can be authenticated in the specified domain.

To connect to the network, the user double-clicks the Network Neighborhood icon on the desktop. The NT server appears in the dialog box, as shown in Figure 12.16. Double-clicking the server displays available resources the client can use.

Client Considerations

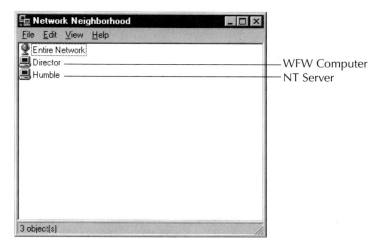

Figure 12.16 Use the Network Neighborhood to view the NT server.

The user can also access the server through the Windows 95 Explorer. In the Explorer, the user double-clicks the Network Neighborhood and then double-clicks the server to display the directories and printers to which he or she has access (see Figure 12.17).

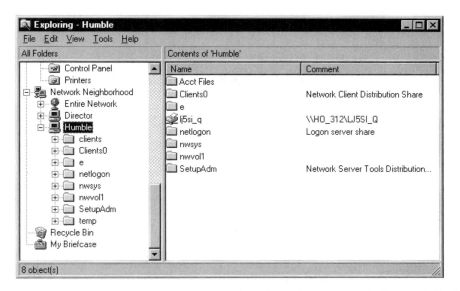

Figure 12.17 Double-click the server in the left window pane to display available folders and printers in the right pane.

> **Note:** In the Explorer, you can use the Tools command to map a network drive for quick and easy access.

For more information about Windows 95, refer to the program's on-line help or documentation.

Using Windows NT Workstation Clients

In addition to taking full advantage of NT security and auditing features, the NT client enables you to use certain administrative tools for remote management of the server (see "Copying Client-Based Administration Tools"). One problem you'll find with using the NT clients is that you may need to upgrade your workstations to run the NT software. After all, the NT Workstation software requires a 486 or higher processor, VGA monitor, 16M RAM, and at least 120M disk space for the operating system.

> **Note:** Using computers running Windows NT Server software is nearly the same as using NT Workstation clients; the only difference is the NT Server has the capability of performing more complex tasks. Changing network settings and connecting are the same.

Copying Client-Based Administration Tools

You may have need to administer the network from a computer other than the primary or backup domain controller. You can copy certain network administration tools to an NT Workstation computer or to a Windows 95 computer using the Network Client Administrator tool. You'll notice you have more choices and more control over the network if you install the client-based network administration tools to a computer running NT Workstation. You must be a member of the Administrators group to copy the necessary files.

To copy the administration tools, create the CLIENTS\WINNT.SRV or CLIENTS\WIN95. RV directory on the root of the NT Server computer and designate the folder as shared. Copy the files for the NT administration tools from the NT CD: \SRVTOOLS\WINNT and for the Windows 95 administration tools from the \SRVTOOLS\WIN95 directory on the CD.

> Alternatively, in the Network Client Administration tool, choose the option **C**opy Client-Based Network Administrative Tools and choose OK. Choose the appropriate option in the Share Network Client Installation Files dialog box; the tool copies the files for you to the CLIENTS directory. After the files are copied and the directory is designated as shared, clients can access the directory and install the tools to their Windows NT Workstation or Windows 95 computers.
>
> Windows NT Workstation tools include: DHCP Manager, Remote Access Admin, Remoteboot Manager, Server Manager, User Manager for Domains, and more. Windows 95 administration tools include only the Event Viewer, Server Manager, and User Manager for Domains.

Configuring the Network

NT workstations are ready to connect to an NT server without installation of a special client. You'll want to make sure you designate the same protocol, however, that you use on the NT server. You can install and configure adapter cards and protocols in the Network dialog box.

Note: You'll notice that configuring the network in an NT Workstation computer is similar to configuring the network in an NT Server computer. See Appendix A for information about the Network dialog box in the NT Server.

To open the Network dialog box, choose Start, **S**ettings, and **C**ontrol Panel. Double-click the Network icon. Figure 12.18 shows the NT Workstation Network dialog box. The Identification tab lists the computer's name and the domain or workgroup name. You can change a name by choosing the **C**hange button and entering the appropriate name.

Choose the Protocols tab to view installed protocols and add or remove protocols. In Figure 12.19, you see that all available NT protocols have been added. To add a protocol, choose the **A**dd button and select the protocol from the list. To remove a protocol, select it in the **N**etwork Protocols list and choose the **R**emove button. To view the properties of any protocol, select it and choose the **P**roperties button. Similar to the Protocol Properties in Windows 95, NT protocol properties present frame types for IPX/SPX. Additionally, the TCP/IP properties enable you to set the IP address, Subnet Mask, Default Gateway, DNS, and other options for the protocol.

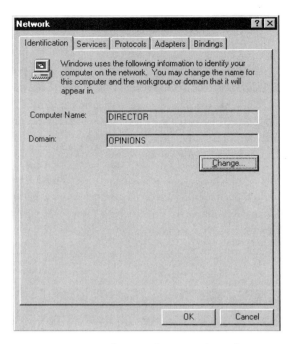

Figure 12.18 Make sure the network configuration is correct before attaching to the network.

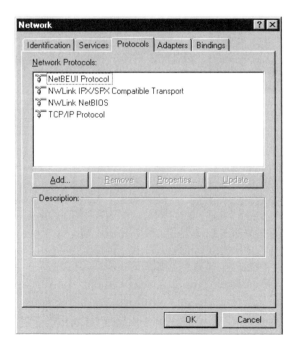

Figure 12.19 Add, remove, and/or configure protocols for the network.

Client Considerations

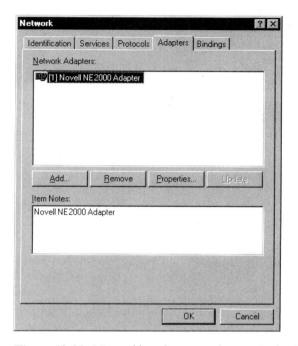

Figure 12.20 View, add, and remove adapters via the Adapters tab of the Network dialog box.

Note: The Services tab enables you to install such services as TCP/IP services, Remote Access Service, Client Service for NetWare, and so on.

The Adapters tab enables you to add or remove an adapter card, update drivers, and review properties of any adapter. Figure 12.20 shows the Adapters tab of the Network dialog box. To view an adapter's properties, select the adapter in the **N**etwork Adapters list and choose the **P**roperties button.

Figure 12.21 shows the selected adapter's Properties dialog box; change the IRQ or I/O port addresses for any adapter card by selecting the adapter and choosing the **P**roperties button.

Note: The Bindings tab displays all services and their bindings to protocols and adapters. You can enable or disable bindings via this tab.

When you're finished configuring the network in the client, choose OK to close the Network dialog box. You must restart the computer for the changes to take effect.

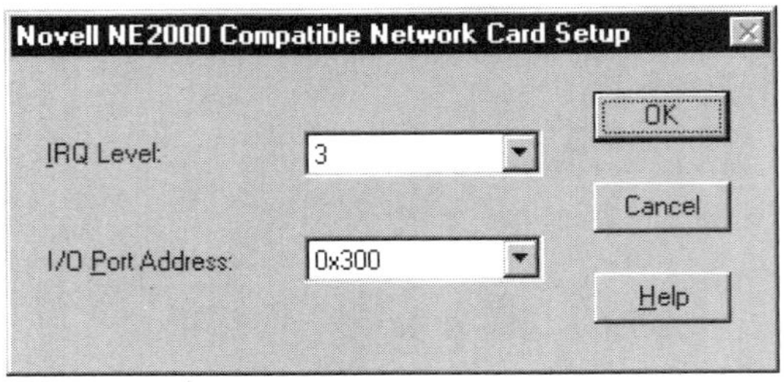

Figure 12.21 Configure the IRQ for an adapter to make sure the client can use the adapter card.

Connecting to the Network

When a user first starts the NT workstation, he or she must log in with a user name and password that can be authenticated on the designated domain. To connect to the server, the user must open the Network Neighborhood from the desktop by double-clicking it.

Figure 12.22 shows the Network Neighborhood with the NT server—Humble—displayed. Additionally, a Windows for Workgroups computer—Director—displays in the window. The client computer can attach to either of the computers and access any resources for which he or she has permissions and rights by double-clicking the computer.

The NT client can also use the NT Explorer to open the Network Neighborhood and view the server and available resources, as described previously in the Windows 95 section. For more information about Windows NT Workstation, refer to the program's on-line help or documentation.

Figure 12.22 Connect to the NT server and access its resources.

PART VI

Follow-Up to Migration

13   Tying Up Loose Ends

During the migration, you transferred your users, groups, directories, and files. Although you may have included program files and/or device drivers, you may experience problems after the migration. Most likely, you'll need to install new drivers for some of your devices and then configure them to work with NT.

There are other considerations after a migration. This chapter covers the following:

- Client clean-up
- Using the Control Panel
- Configuring devices: SCSI adapters, tape drives, UPS, and so on
- Information about using NT Backup
- Macintosh clients considerations

Client Clean-Up

After the migration, you'll need to clean up the system and check the clients. First, check to make sure all users have appropriate permissions to resources and rights assigned them. Next, load the client software and configure it to access the NT server. Following are a few points in particular to examine next.

Logon Scripts

If you're using the add-on product File and Print Services for NetWare (FPNW), your login scripts can be transferred during migration. FPNW enables the NT server to provide file and print services directly to NetWare clients. You'll want to check the scripts to make sure everything transferred as expected and that each client's script runs properly at login.

If you are not running the FPNW add-on, your NetWare login scripts do not transfer to NT. You can, however, simulate most of the items included in a login script in NT, including mapped drives, mapped false roots, and home directories. NT even enables you to create login scripts that run with when the user logs in. For more information on logon scripts and home directories, see Chapter 3, "Working with Users and Groups."

An additional tool NT enables you to use is the user profile. A user profile contains configuration information that includes such settings as network connections, printer connections, personal program groups, desktop arrangement, screen colors, screen savers, window size, and so on. You can create user profiles for one user, a group of users, or all users on the network. These profiles reside on the server and apply to a user each time he or she logs on to the network (similar to NetWare login scripts).

When creating the profiles, you can set up a default user profile and assign it to all users to identify network connections and printer connections; then you can let the user define the rest of the profile him- or herself, such as screen colors, window size, and so on. On the other hand, you can create a mandatory user profile that applies to all users, a group of users, or just one user. You set the configuration and the user has no choices in the matter. For information about creating user profiles, see Chapter 14, "Advanced Network Management."

Note: The NT logon script path is \WINNT\SYSTEM32\REPL\IMPORTS\SCRIPTS. The user profile path is \WINNT\PROFILES.

Mapping Drives

Another important issue is drive mapping. Since no previous drive maps transfer during the migration, you'll need to map drives on the workstations. In NT, you can create a drive mapping and save it to reconnect at login.

You map drives in the NT Explorer. Select **T**ools, **M**ap Network Drive. In the Map Network Drive dialog box, you choose the drive letter to represent the mapped drive, enter the path, and then enter the user name you want to connect as. You can choose to reconnect the drive at logon so you don't have to map the drive each time. Additionally, you can map drives and include those mappings in a user profile for specific users or groups of users. For more information about mapping drives, see Chapter 2, "Concepts Comparison."

Applications

You'll also want to check each client's applications to make sure they can start the programs and get to the data they need to complete their work. You may want all users to test this area for you and then make note of any problems they encounter.

If you run into problems, check drive mapping first. You may also find some applications do not transfer well in the migration and need to be reinstalled to the server. If you have problems with specific applications, contact the application's manufacturer or tech support for information about running the program with NT.

Configuring Peripherals

NT offers many device drivers you can use for installing and configuring your drivers; however, you may need to contact the manufacturers of some devices you use and ask for updated NT Server 4.0 drivers, if NT doesn't supply then. You'll need to install those drivers and configure the devices after the migration.

Before purchasing or installing any peripheral devices, check with the Hardware Compatibility List to make sure the device works with NT. See Chapter 5 for information about installing and configuring printers attached to the NT network.

Control Panel Overview

You configure most devices in the Control Panel in NT. Figure 13.1 shows the Control Panel, and the following list provides a brief explanation of each option, or icon, in the Panel. The upcoming sections explain the options you can use in configuring devices in more detail. To open any option in the Control Panel, double-click the icon.

The contents of the Control Panel are as follows:

Add/Remove Programs. Enables you to install and uninstall applications and run Windows NT Setup.

MS-DOS Console. Enables you to customize the command prompt window.

Date/Time. Set the date, time, and time zone of the server.

Devices. Start or stop devices, such as the network adapter, CD-ROM, and so on. See the following section for more information.

Display. Set wallpaper, screen saver, screen colors, and resolution. Be careful with screen savers and wallpaper on the server; those take precious memory away from the real tasks for which you need the server.

CHAPTER 13

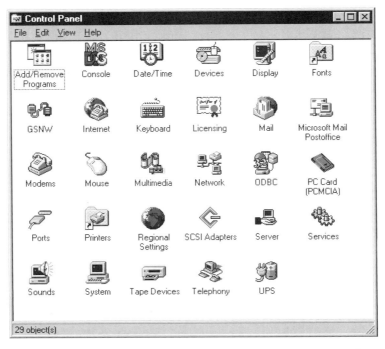

Figure 13.1 You can configure most server settings in the Control Panel.

Fonts. Install and remove fonts from the system.

GSNW. Gateway Service for NetWare.

Internet. Sets a proxy server to access the Internet and act as a security barrier between your network and the Internet.

Keyboard. Set options for the server's keyboard, such as language, repeat rate, cursor blink rate, and so on.

Licensing. Lists client licensing mode; see Appendix A for information about licensing.

Mail. Enables the setup for MS Exchange settings and properties.

Microsoft Mail Postoffice. Set up and configure a post office for the network, using MS Mail, Internet Mail, or another available program.

Modems. Install and configure a modem using the Wizard dialog boxes.

Mouse. Set button configuration, double-click speed, and so on.

Multimedia. Set audio, video, MIDI properties, and view multimedia device properties.

Network. Configure and install network components.

ODBC. Add, delete, and configure data sources, such as SQL Server databases or a directory of dBASE files.

PC Card. Applies only to the PCMCIA card and controller.

Ports. Specify communications settings for selected serial ports.

Printers. Use to install and configure printers; see Chapter 5 for more information.

Regional Settings. Set time zone, currency, numbering, language, and so on for your area of the world.

SCSI Adapters. View list of adapters and their properties; see the following section.

Server. Show the connected users, shared resources, network alerts, and so on.

Services. Displays the status of services, such as the Gateway Service, DHCP client, Event Log, and so on; see the following section.

Sounds. Change the sounds you hear when certain errors or tasks are performed on the server.

System. Check performance, environment information, user profiles, and so on.

Tape Devices. Lists tape devices, and enables you to add drivers; see the following section.

Telephony. Enter information about your area code, phone system, and so on, and add telephony drivers to use NT with dial out utilities.

UPS. Configure the UPS service; see the following section.

Setting Up Devices

You can control when many of the devices on the server start by using the Devices option in the Control Panel. The Devices dialog box lists available devices and their startup type (see Figure 13.2). Startup can be Boot, System, Automatic, Manual, or Disabled. You may want to configure a device to start when the system boots or to start only when you choose to start it. Additionally, you can disable certain devices for troubleshooting purposes.

To start or stop a device, select the device and choose either the **S**tart or St**o**p button. To configure startup types, select the device and choose the Sta**r**tup button. Select the startup type you want to use from the list.

254 CHAPTER 13

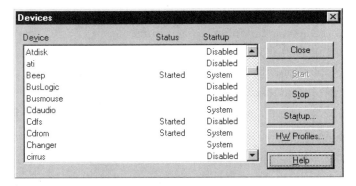

Figure 13.2 View device startup status in the Devices dialog box.

SCSI Adapters

Use the SCSI Adapters option in the Control Panel to view the properties of adapters and to add or remove drivers for SCSI adapters. Figure 13.3 shows the SCSI Adapters dialog box. The Devices tab lists the SCSI devices on the server.

In the Devices tab, select a driver and choose the **P**roperties button. You can configure the following properties:

Card Info includes the type, manufacturer, and status of the device.

Driver Info lists the name, file, and status of the driver.

Resources list the IRQ, I/O, memory range, and so on.

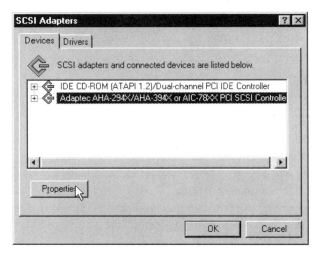

Figure 13.3 View a list of SCSI adapters on the server.

Tying Up Loose Ends

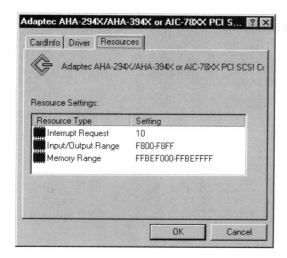

Figure 13.4 *View information about the device in the adapter's Properties dialog box.*

Figure 13.4 shows the Resources tab of the adapter's Properties dialog box. The Drivers tab enables you to add or remove drivers for the SCSI adapter.

Services

If you have problems with services or devices, you can check the status in the Services option of the Control Panel. Figure 13.5 shows the Services dialog box with the UPS service selected. If the UPS isn't functioning, make sure the service is configured to Automatic.

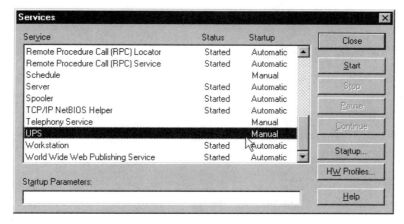

Figure 13.5 *View and configure services for certain devices in this dialog box.*

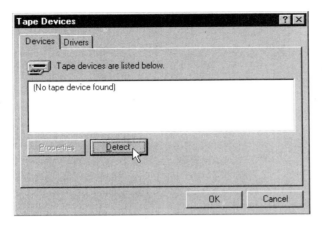

Figure 13.6 Let the Tape Devices option detect your tape device.

To change the service in question, select the service in the list and choose **S**tart to start it manually, **S**top to stop the service, **P**ause, or **C**ontinue. To change the startup type, select the service and click the Sta**r**tup button; choose Automatic, Manual, or Disabled.

Tape Devices

The Tape Devices option in the Control Panel enables you to view tape devices and install tape drivers. Figure 13.6 displays the Tape Devices dialog box. If no tape drives are listed, choose the **D**etect button. When the tape device appears in the list on the Devices tab, select it and view the properties by choosing the **P**roperties button.

Additionally, you can choose the Drivers tab to add or remove drivers. Figure 13.7 shows the list of NT's drivers; you can, alternately, insert a disk and choose **H**ave Disk to install the manufacturer's NT-designed driver for the device.

UPS

NT supplies a UPS service you can use to notify your users of power outages and actions that will result from the power failure. In NT during a power failure, the UPS service pauses the server service to prevent new connections. Additionally, the service sends a message to notify users of the power failure. The service then waits the amount of time you specify before warning the users of the impending shutdown. If power is restored before the shutdown, the UPS service sends a message to users that the power is restored.

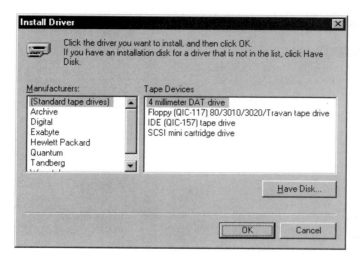

Figure 13.7 Choose the driver for the tape device.

Some of the UPS service configuration options may not be available with your UPS. And be aware that setting the UPS service incorrectly for your hardware can cause problems with the UPS operation. Check your documentation for the UPS device before setting the UPS service in NT.

You should use the following services in combination with a UPS device on the server: UPS, Alerter, Messenger, and Event Log. See the previous section on Services to enable these.

You can configure the UPS service using the UPS option in the Control Panel. Figure 13.8 shows the UPS dialog box and Table 13.1 describes the options.

Note: Make sure that both the UPS and the serial cable are NT-compatible by checking the Hardware Compatibility List.

Backing Up and Restoring Files

One important factor to your network is backing up data and files stored on the server, as well as files on other servers and workstations. You most likely have tape backup software you use to secure copies of your data. You can check with the HCL for compatibility of your tape drive or other media storage device. Additionally, check with the manufacturer of your software for updated programs to work with NT.

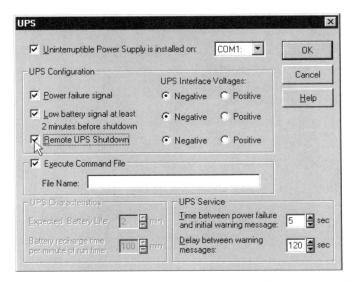

Figure 13.8 Configure an uninterruptable power supply installed to the server via the UPS dialog box.

Table 13.1 UPS Options

OPTION	DESCRIPTION
Uninterruptable Power Supply is installed on	Select this option to activate the UPS service on the server and select the serial port to which the UPS is installed.
Power failure signal	Indicate whether the UPS can send a message in case of a power failure (corresponds to CTS cable signal).
Low battery signal	Indicate whether the UPS can send a warning when the battery is low (corresponds to the DCD cable signal).
Remote UPS Shutdown	Enable or disable shutdown of the UPS (corresponds to the DTR cable signal).
UPS Interface Voltages	Select either Positive or Negative for each option.
E**x**ecute Command File	Select and enter a file name to execute immediately before the system shuts down (the file must be able to execute and complete within 30 seconds).
Expected Battery Life	Enter the time, in minutes from 2 to 720, that the battery will sustain the system.
Battery Recharge Time	Enter the time, in minutes from 1 to 250, it takes the battery to recharge.

Option	Description
Time between failure and initial warning messages	Enter a time, in seconds from 0 to 120, before the first warning message is sent to users.
Delay between warning messages	Enter the time, in seconds from 5 to 300, you want to delay between warning messages sent to the users.

Compatibility Issues

Basically, this sidebar lists some general compatibility issues for Windows NT Server. For specific information, see the HCL (Hardware Compatibility List) that came with your software. You might also check the Release Notes readme file on the NT CD for more information. For an updated HCL, you can download current lists from the Internet; see Microsoft's Web page at http:\www\microsoft.com. Note: Since I'm only discussing x86 processors in this book, I've left out such items as MIPS RISC, Digital Alpha AXP RISC, and so on, in the following list.

This list contains general information; for manufacturer's and specific models, see the HCL. Multiple manufacturers are represented for each device listed.

Processor	x86 architecture uniprocessor
	x86 architecture multiprocessor
	x86 PCMCIA (plus support for network adapters, add-in adapters, and modems, ISDN adapters, Serial and SCSI adapters for PCMCIA)
SCSI Adapters	CD-ROM, tape, scanners, fixed and removable drives
Non-SCSI	CD-ROM, tape drives
Display Adapters	640x480, 800x600, 1024x768, 1280x1024
Network Adapters	ISA, MCA, EISA, PCMCIA, PCI, VLB
Keyboards	102/102-key and IBM AT (84-key)
Pointing Devices	All versions Logitech and Microsoft and those 100 percent compatible with these.

Additionally, multiple manufacturers are listed for various UPS, Multimedia audio adapters, and multiple modems; plus, a few manufacturers and models are listed for hardware security hosts, ISDN adapters, multiport adapters, X.25 adapters, and third-party remote access servers. As for printers, NT includes many various drivers for nearly a thousand printer models.

Note: Windows NT includes many device drivers in the \DRVLIB directory on the Windows NT CD-ROM.

If you don't have a backup program but you do have a tape drive, NT includes a backup program you can use to back up and restore important files. Since I'm sure you're familiar with backing up your data, I'll just touch on NT's backup program briefly so you'll have an idea of what it can do. If you choose to use NT's Backup, you can find out more about it in on-line help and in the NT documentation.

With the NT Backup program, you can do the following:

- Back up and restore local and remote files.
- Back up and restore files on an NTFS or a FAT partition.
- Select files by volume, directory, or file name.
- View file information, such as size and modification date.
- Choose to verify the backup operation to ensure reliable backups and restorations.
- Perform Normal, Copy, Incremental, Differential, and Daily backups.
- Span multiple tapes with backup sets and files.
- Create a batch file to automate repeated backups.
- Control a restore's destination drive and directory.
- Save log information about the backup.

Figure 13.9 shows the Backup Program window; you can mark the entire drive to back up by clicking the check box.

To mark specific volumes, directories, or files, double-click the drive name. Figure 13.10 shows the open drive window. Select specific items to back up by clicking the check boxes.

Macintosh Considerations

If you've supported Macintoshes with your NetWare network, you'll want to attach and support them with the NT network as well. NT provides Services for Macintosh that you can install during the original installation, or use Setup to install at a later date.

With NT's Services for Macintosh, the Macs do not need any additional software, such as client software, to function as clients to the NT server. Using the Services, a Mac can share files and printers with the NT server, just as a PC client would. NT's Services for Macintosh offers these other advantages:

- Secured logon, providing added protection from network sniffers, which can detect cleartext passwords; a sniffer is a hardware and software diagnostic tool that can also be used to decipher passwords, resulting in unauthorized access to network accounts.

Tying Up Loose Ends **261**

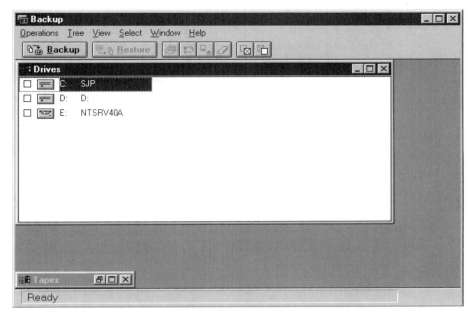

Figure 13.9 NT's Backup program enables you to back up any drive on the server and even remote drives.

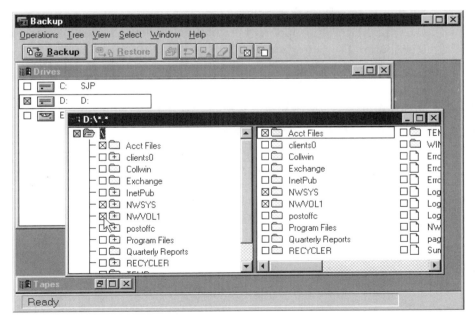

Figure 13.10 Double-click a drive or directory to display its contents.

- Printing to non-PostScript printers and printer sharing; thus all users on the network can send print jobs to all printers. Additionally, you can control all of the print queues from a single location.
- Compatibility with all computers on the NT network that run NT Server, for increased resource access.
- AppleTalk Phase 2 support enables NT server to provide routing and seed routing support. The AppleTalk router broadcasts routing information (network addresses, and so on) and keeps track of data packets on the AppleTalk network. Seed routers perform these functions and establish and initialize the network address information for that network. (Phase 1 is not supported.)
- If you're using applications that have both PC and Macintosh versions, such as Excel or Word, both PC and Macintosh users can work on the same data file.
- Simplified administration means you only have one set of users to maintain between PCs and Macintosh users; permissions are also translated between Macintosh and PCs.

To set up the Services for Macintosh, you need a computer running NT Server 4.0 software with an NTFS partition, so you can create directories that can be used by the Macintosh clients. The computer running NT Server will also need 2M extra hard disk space.

The Mac clients simply need to be able to use AppleShare and have version 6.0.7 or later of the Macintosh operating system (including System 7 or later). Services for Macintosh supports LocalTalk, ethernet, token right, and FDDI (Fiber Distribution Data Interface).

Note: Windows NT Services for Macintosh support version 6.x and later LaserWriter printer drivers as well as versions 2.0 and 2.1 of the AppleTalk Filing Protocol.

Setting up an AppleTalk network is beyond the scope of this book. For information about setting up your Macintosh clients, see the NT documentation and on-line help.

14 Advanced Network Management

Now that your users are connected to the network, you may want to fine-tune the way users work by creating user profiles. A user profile is one of NT's answers to login scripts. User profiles enable you to set working environments for your users, much as you would using login scripts.

You'll likely want to perform some administrative tasks to assess the network and resource use, find bottlenecks, and so on. Using the NT Server Manager, you can view any computer connected to the server and examine how resources are being used and by whom. The Server Manager also enables you to control workstations and other servers in the domain by supplying the tools for disconnecting users and resources, creating new shares, supervising services, and more.

One other task you may find a use for is directory replication. NT enables you to replicate not only directories but the files within those directories as well. You control replication in the Server Manager, as described in this chapter.

Finally, often you need information about your system's hardware, such as IRQs, I/O ports, memory specs, video driver version, and so on. Windows NT Diagnostics, an informational dialog box in NT Server, can give you the information you need.

Specifically, in this chapter, you learn to:

- Create roaming and mandatory user profiles.
- View users and resources connected to the server.
- View and create shared resources over the network.
- Remotely administer workstations and other servers.
- Replicate directories and files.
- View system, hardware, and other information about your computer.

Managing User Profiles

A user profile contains configuration information that includes such settings as network connections, printer connections, personal program groups, desktop arrangement, screen colors, screen savers, window size, and so on. You can create user profiles for one user, a group of users, or all users on the network. These profiles reside on the server and apply to a user each time he or she logs on to the network (similar to NetWare login scripts).

When creating the profiles, you can set up a default user profile and assign it to all users to identify network connections and printer connections; then you can let the user define the rest of the profile him- or herself, such as screen colors, window size, and so on. On the other hand, you can create a mandatory user profile that applies to all users, a group of users, or just one user; you set the configuration and the user has no choice in the matter.

Note: You can manage the user's work environment through user profiles on Windows NT and Windows 95 computers, if User Profiles is enabled (see "Enabling Windows 95 User Profiles" later in this chapter).

As soon as a user logs on to the workstation, NT creates a user profile for that person starting with the default user profile that's stored on every computer running Windows NT Workstation, Windows NT Server, and Windows 95. With each setting the user customizes, his or her profile changes. In NT, user profiles are made up of changes the user makes to the Explorer, Taskbar, Printer settings, Control Panel, Accessories, and in NT-based applications. Changes, or modifications, to these settings might include options for mouse and keyboard settings, network configurations, drive mappings, network printer settings, location of the Taskbar on-screen, and so on.

Default User Profile Folder

Generally, each user profile is located in the \WINNT\PROFILES directory. The default user profile folder and the all user profile folders are also located in this directory. The default user folder contains an NTuser.dat file and a directory of links to desktop items.

Within a user's profile folder are subfolders containing shortcuts to the desktop (Desktop folder), the Favorites folder, the Network Neighborhood (NetHood folder), most recently used items (Recent folder), templates (Templates folder), program items (Start Menu folder), and so on. Figure 14.1 shows a Windows 95

Login Scripts vs. User Profiles

As a NetWare administrator, you're used to using various logon scripts to set up defaults for users as well as specific connections and configurations. You can use logon scripts in NT to perform the same tasks: create network connections, start applications, and control the user's working environment. You also can control these things with the User Profiles; both perform similar functions, so use the tool that's most comfortable for you.

NT provides several special parameters you can use to specify the user's home directory, processor type, operating system, domain, user name, and so on. After creating the logon script in a text file, you enter the path to the file in the User Manager for Domains, User Environment Profile dialog box, on the server; the default path is \WINNT\SYSTEM32\REPL\IMPORT\SCRIPTS. You can name the text file with the user's user name. At logon, the domain controller authenticates the user and runs the logon script.

Additionally, you can replicate logon scripts to ensure that they are always available for the user. If you set up the primary domain controller as the export server, you can replicate the logon scripts to any backup domain controllers, as explained later in this chapter. For more information about logon script parameters, see Chapter 3.

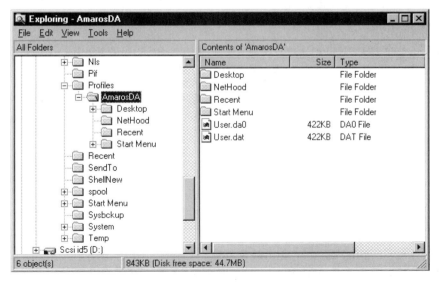

Figure 14.1 Open a user's profile folder in the Explorer to see the folders within.

user profile folder in the Explorer. Windows NT Workstation contains one extra folder that Windows 95 does not: the Application folder.

Note: Some folders, such as the NetHood, Recent, and Templates folders are hidden and therefore do not show up in the user's profile folder unless you choose to show all files in the Explorer (**V**iew, **O**ptions, Show All Files).

For each new user who logs on to a workstation, NT copies the default user profile folder as that user's profile, plus makes a copy of the NTuser.dat file (the Registry portion of the user profile) and the directory of links to add to the user's profile folder. When the user logs off, any configuration changes are saved to the user's profile folder.

Roaming User Profiles

You can enable a user to create his or her own user profiles; you can create a preconfigured user profile for each user account; or you create a mandatory user profile for each user. For users to create their own user profiles, you don't have to change a thing; each time the user logs off, the changes he or she made are saved to the profile, and that profile applies when the user logs on again.

Creating the Profile

The easiest method for creating a profile is to log on to an NT workstation as a new account and create the profile you want the users to implement. You might log on as Profile 1, for example, and set application, desktop, Network Neighborhood, and other settings the way you want them. Log off to save the settings and create the NTuser.dat file. Next, you can copy the file to the appropriate location on the server.

Note: User profiles can restore network connections at logon that were established prior to logging off; however, they cannot create new network connections at logon.

One thing to keep in mind when you're creating user profiles is the hardware on the various workstations. Differences in monitors, video cards, and so on may cause a problem from one machine to the next. You can avoid this dilemma by cre-

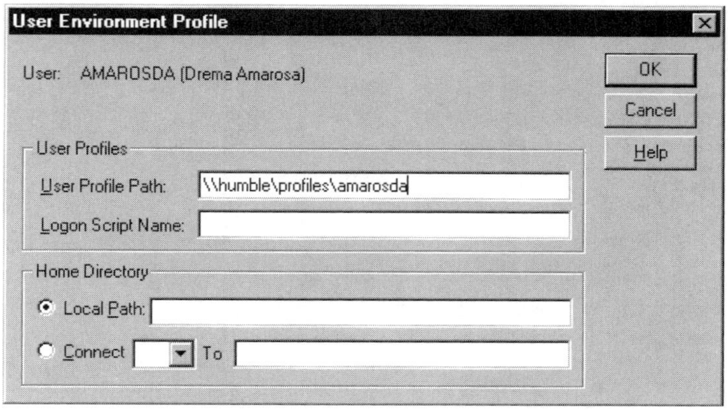

Advanced Network Management **267**

Figure 14.2 In this dialog box, you assign a specific user profile folder to the user.

ating one profile for a group of users who have the same hardware configurations; create the profile on one of the workstations for which you're designing the profile to be used.

Copying a Preconfigured Roaming Profile

To copy a preconfigured roaming profile, you save the user profile to a centralized location: the server. There are two steps to copying the roaming profile after you create it: assign the server location to the user's account from the server, and copy the file from the workstation on which you created it to the server location.

Assign server locations for specific user profiles in the User Manager for Domains (see Chapter 3). Figure 14.2 shows the User Environment Profile dialog box in the User Manager for Domains. The network path in the text box must be in the following format: *servername**profilesfoldername**username*, as shown in the figure.

After assigning a location on the server, open the System option in the Control Panel on the workstation (Start, **S**ettings, **C**ontrol Panel). In the System folder, choose the User Profiles tab (only in computers running NT, not those running Windows 95). Figure 14.3 shows the User Profiles tab of the NT Server; NT Workstation tabs look much the same. Select the Copy **T**o button and copy the preconfigured profile to the server.

Note: You cannot copy a user profile in the Explorer or My Computer. The only way you can copy a user profile is in the System option of the Control Panel in the User Profile tab.

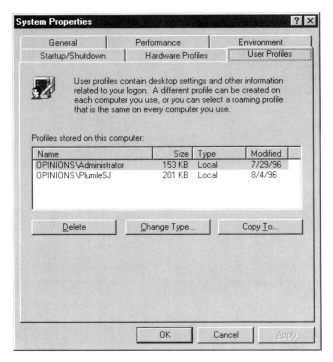

Figure 14.3 User profiles are listed in the System Properties dialog box.

This profile becomes the roaming user profile and is available wherever the user logs on. When the user logs off, the roaming user profile is saved to the local machine and a copy is saved to the server. Each time the user logs on, the roaming profile from the server is opened, providing the server is available. If the server isn't available, the local copy of the roaming user profile is used; or, if the user has never logged on to the computer before, a new local user profile is created.

Note: If the server is unavailable and the local copy is opened, the next time the user logs on, NT uses the most recent profile.

Making the User Profile Mandatory

To create a mandatory user profile, create the preconfigured roaming user profile as previously described and assign the location on the server. In NT Explorer, rename the NTuser.dat to NTuser.man by selecting the file and choosing **File**, **R**e-

Advanced Network Management

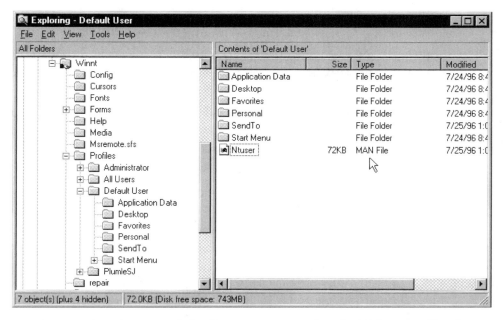

Figure 14.4 Any changes made by the user are not saved to the NTuser.man file when the user logs off.

name, then typing in the new name. When you press Enter to complete the renaming process, NT hides the extension but labels the file as a MAN file. Figure 14.4 shows a default NTuser.dat renamed as a mandatory file; the MAN extension makes the file read-only.

When you copy a user profile for use by another user or group, you must add the user or group to the permissions list so they have access to the file. In the System dialog box, User Profiles tab, choose the **C**hange Type button to add the user to the permissions list.

Don't assign a roaming user profile path to a group unless you make the user profiles mandatory. Each time a group member logs off, his or her profile overwrites the user profile on the server; thus the group's profile would constantly be changing.

Using the Server Manager

NT's Server Manager tool enables you to monitor the network, including shared resources, user access, and relationships between servers. Specifically, you can select

> ### Enabling Windows 95 User Profiles
>
> You can create and apply Windows 95 user profiles similar to those you create in Windows NT Workstation. The differences between Windows 95 and Windows NT user profiles are as follows; Windows 95:
>
> - User profiles do not contain all desktop items, only shortcuts and program information files.
> - Doesn't support the centralized default users profile.
> - The roaming path comes from the user's home directory instead of the server.
>
> In Windows 95, two files store the contents of the Registry file and folders containing the contents of the Start menu, Desktop, Network Neighborhood, and the Recent Documents list that you can choose to save with the user profiles: User.dat and System.dat.
>
> To enable user profiles in Windows 95, open the Passwords icon in the Control Panel and open the User Profiles tab. Choose Users Can Customize Their Preferences and Desktop Settings options. You can choose to include the desktop icons and Network Neighborhood contents and to include the Start menu and Program groups in the user settings. Choose OK. You must restart the computer to create the profiles folder (\WINDOWS\PROFILES).
>
> As in NT, Windows 95 user profiles are normally stored on the local drive. You can, however, store the profile on the network drive, in the user's home directory, to create roaming user profiles.
>
> Additionally, you can create and enforce mandatory user profiles in Windows 95. Create the user profile on a workstation and then logoff; then rename the User.dat file to User.man and copy the user profile folders to the home directories of all users on the primary domain controller. Once again, the MAN extension makes the file read-only.

the domain, workgroup, or computer and then view connected users, shared and open resources, and you can manage directory replication, administration alerts, services and shared directories. You can even send messages to connected users from the Server Manager.

You can add or remove servers from the domain, promote a backup domain controller, synchronize servers, and add and remove computers to a domain. Since you can use the Server Manager to manage domains and computers, this chapter

Advanced Network Management **271**

discusses managing computers; Chapter 15 discusses using Server Manager to manage domains.

Server Manager enables you to administer only those computers running NT Workstation and NT Server. Although you can see Windows 95 computers in the Server Manager, you cannot administrate them. You cannot see Windows for Workgroups or MS-DOS computers in the domain in Server Manager. You can, however, see NT computers from other domains that are active in the current domain.

Starting and Exiting the Server Manager

Only members of the following groups can open and administer the network from the Server Manager: Administrators, Domain Administrators, and Server Operators; Account Operators can add computers to the domain using the Server Manager but cannot perform any other tasks.

TIP: You cannot run the Server Manager remotely unless you expressly copy the needed files using the Network Client Administrator, as described in Chapter 12, and you have appropriate rights and permissions.

To start the Server Manager, on a domain controller choose Start, **P**rograms, Administrative Tools, and Server Manager. Figure 14.5 shows the Server Manager window with several computers listed.

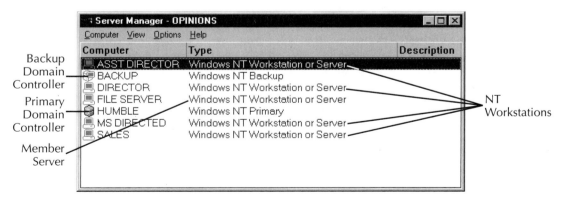

Figure 14.5 Only NT computers can be administered in the Server Manager.

> **TIP:** Icons located to the left of the computer's name in the Server Manager indicate the type of computer—server, workstation, and so on. Dimmed icons are not currently connected to the server.

In the Computer column, the computer's name appears as assigned to it in the domain. The domain name appears in the title bar of the Server Manager. The type of computer is assigned by Windows but you can always enter a description—such as the location of the computer, the user's name, or other designation—to display in the Description column.

You can view servers only, workstations only, or all computers in a domain by choosing the **V**iew menu and selecting one of the following: **S**ervers, **W**orkstations, or **A**ll. Additionally, you can choose **V**iew, Show **D**omain Members Only if you do not want to view computers that are visiting the current domain.

To exit the Server Manager, choose **C**omputer, E**x**it; alternatively, click the Close (X) button in the title bar of the Server Manager window.

Viewing Connections and Resource Usage on the Server

You can select any computer in the Server Manager Computer list to display more information about that computer's connection and resource information. Select the server, for example, and choose **C**omputer, **P**roperties. The computer's Properties dialog box appears, as shown in Figure 14.6.

In the Usage Summary area of the dialog box, you see the following selections:

Sessions. Displays the number of remote users currently connected.

Open Files. Displays the number of currently open files from the computer.

File Locks. Displays the current number of file locks on the computer by connected users. Files are normally locked to prevent replication; see the section later in this chapter.

Open Named Pipes. Displays the current number of pipes being used; a pipe enables communication between processes, both local and remote.

The **D**escription text box is optional, you can enter a description if you want; or there may already be a description of the computer. Use information such as the location, brand, speed, name of user, and so on for the descriptive text.

The buttons at the bottom of the dialog box each enable you to view more information about the selected computer. Following is a brief description of each button; the following sections describe each button in more detail.

Advanced Network Management

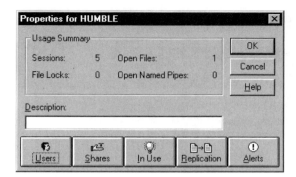

Figure 14.6 The Properties dialog box summarizes the usage for the selected computer.

Users. View the users connected to the server and the resources opened by a selected user; you can disconnect any or all of the users.

Shares. View shared resources and the users who are connected to the resource; you can disconnect any or all of the users.

In Use. View all open shared resources on server; you can close any or all of the resources.

Replication. Manage directory replication, as described later in this chapter.

Alerts. View the list of users and computers that are notified when administrative alerts occur.

Viewing User Sessions

In the computer's Properties dialog box, choose the **U**sers button to view all users connected over the network to the computer and the resources any selected user has opened. Figure 14.7 shows the user sessions on the selected server.

In the list of Connected Users, you see the user's name and the computer's name. The list of Opens is the number of resources currently open by that user; resources could be files, directories, printers, the CD-ROM drive, and so on. The Time column describes the hours and minutes since the beginning of the current session; Idle displays the hours and minutes that have elapsed since the user last initiated an action. The Guest columns states either Yes, the connected user is a guest, or No, the connected user is not a guest.

The Resource area of the dialog box lists the shared resources, such as directories, pipes, printers, and so on, that are currently being used. The IPC$ you see listed in the figure as a resource is a special share created by the system; see "Special Shares" for more information.

Figure 14.7 View the connected users and the shared resources currently being used.

To disconnect a user, open the User Sessions dialog box and choose the user you want to disconnect. Choose the **D**isconnect button to disconnect one user; choose the Disconnect **A**ll button to disconnect all users attached to the selected computer. Make sure you warn users before disconnecting them to prevent data loss; see "Sending a Message to a Computer" later in this chapter.

Special Shares

Normal shares are resources, such as directories or printers, that the user or the administrator has designated as shared. Special shares are those created by the system during installation, and each share has a specific use. Depending on the computer's configuration, all or only some of the following shares may appear on the computer.

Special shares cannot be deleted or modified. They are suffixed by a dollar sign ($) in the name so they can be easily identified. Following are a few of the special shares you'll see in the Server Manager. In an NT Workstation computer, only Administrators and Backup Operators can connect to a drive share; in NT Server computers, members of the Administrators, Backup Operators, and Server Operators can connect to a special share.

**IPC$** shares the named pipes that are essential for communication between programs. While you're remotely administering another computer, your user account is listed as a user connected to an IPC$ resource; you will not be disconnected if you disconnect all others.

Advanced Network Management

> **ADMIN$** is a share used by the system during remote administration. The path is always the path to the Windows NT system root, usually C:\WINNT.
>
> *driveletter$*, such as A$ or C$, is a share that enables the administrator to connect to the root directory of a computer or storage device.
>
> **NETLOGON$** is a share used by the NT Server computer to process logon requests.
>
> **PRINT$** supports the use of shared printers.
>
> **REPL$** is located on the replicator export server and supports replication, as described later in this chapter.

Viewing Shared Resources

In the computer's Properties dialog box, choose the **S**hares button to see available resources on the selected computer; and for any resource, see a list of connected users. Figure 14.8 shows the Shared Resources dialog box for the server.

The **S**harename lists the available resources. Uses list the number of connections to shared resources, and the Path shows the path to the resource. Select any resource in the Sharename list and view the connected users in the **C**onnected Users area of the dialog box. In addition to the name of the user, view the time in hours and minutes that the user has been connected and whether the resource is currently in use.

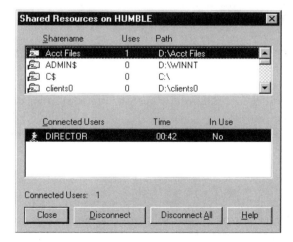

Figure 14.8 In the Shared Resources dialog box, view the list of users and the resources they're using.

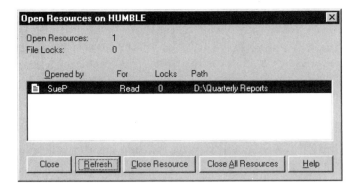

Figure 14.9 Check for open resources before shutting down the server, for example.

You can select a user and choose to **D**isconnect one or Disconnect **A**ll users connected to any resource; however, make sure you warn the users before disconnecting them so they do not lose data.

Viewing Resources in Use

Open resources describe those currently in use. To view these resources, choose the **I**n Use button in the computer's Properties dialog box. Figure 14.9 displays the currently open resources on the server.

The Open Resources dialog box for the selected computer lists the number of open resources, the number of locked files, the permissions granted the user, and the path to the open resources.

Note: Directory replication is a method by which shared files on the server are duplicated for easy access by many users and then updated to master files periodically so all files contain current information. Directory replication is covered completely in the following section.

Alerts

To view or set information about which computers are notified with Administrative alerts, choose the **A**lerts button in the selected computer's Properties dialog box. Administrative alerts are generated by the system and serve as warnings for the servers and resources; problems with security, access, user sessions, server shutdown, UPS services, and so on are included in alerts issued by the system.

Advanced Network Management

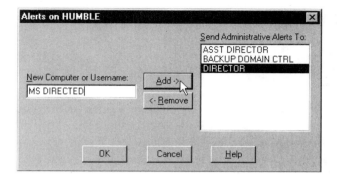

Figure 14.10 Consider listing all servers and workstations in the domain to receive administrative alerts.

TIP: To be able to send an administrative alert, the Messenger service and the Alerter service must be enabled. Check the services by choosing **C**omputer, **S**ervices for the server and for the computer in the Server Manager.

Figure 14.10 shows the Alerts dialog box, in which you can add the computer names (or user names) you want to alert. Enter a new name in the **N**ew Computer or Username text box and choose the **A**dd button. To remove a name from the **S**end Administrative Alerts To list box, select the name and choose the **R**emove button.

Viewing Resources and Users of Selected Computers

In addition to viewing resource usage and current users for the primary domain controller server in the domain, you also can view information about any connected computer on the domain in the Server Manager. You might want to check member servers, for example, to see if bottlenecks occur around any specific resource. You could also check workstations to see if others are accessing resources or causing problems with limited resources.

Properties

To view the properties information for any selected computer, follow these steps:

1. In the Server Manager, select the connected computer about which you want to view information.

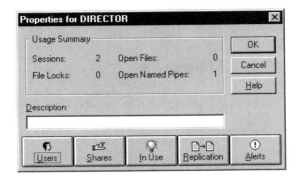

Figure 14.11 View currently open files, sessions, locks, and pipes for the selected computer.

2. Choose **C**omputer, **P**roperties. The computer's Properties dialog box appears, as shown in Figure 14.11.
3. Choose the **U**sers button to show connections to the selected computer. Naturally, the server would be on the list of connected users. Choose OK to return to the computer's Properties dialog box.
4. Choose the **S**hares button to display a list of available resources on the selected computer, as shown in Figure 14.12. Choose OK to return to the computer's Properties dialog box. Choose OK again to return to the Server Manager.

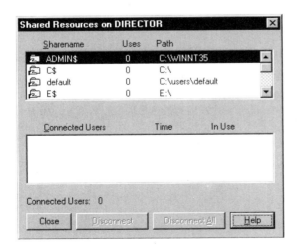

Figure 14.12 Scroll through the shared resources and see if any users are currently connected.

Advanced Network Management

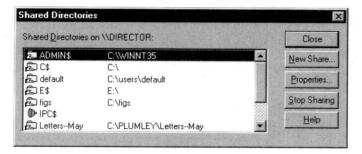

Figure 14.13 View and control shared resources on a selected computer in the Shared Directories dialog box.

Shared Directories

To view shared directories for any selected computer, follow these steps:

1. To view any connected computer's shared directories, select the computer in the Server Manager and choose **C**omputer, **S**hared Resources. The Shared Directories dialog box appears (see Figure 14.13).
2. In the Shared Directories dialog box, choose the **P**roperties button to modify the properties, such as share name and user limit, of any share.
3. Choose the **S**top Sharing button to stop sharing the selected directory; make sure no users are attached before you stop sharing.
4. Select the **N**ew Share button in the Shared Directories dialog box to create a new share on the selected computer. The New Share dialog box appears, in which you can:

    Enter a new share name and path.

    Optionally enter a comment.

    Set a user limit.

    Choose the Pe**r**missions button to limit access of certain groups and/or users.

    Figure 14.14 shows the New Share dialog box with a new share created.
5. Choose OK to close the dialog box when you're finished.

Services

You can set services—such as Alerter, Plug and Play, Remote Access Server, TCP/IP, UPS, and so on—for any selected computer. This is the same Services

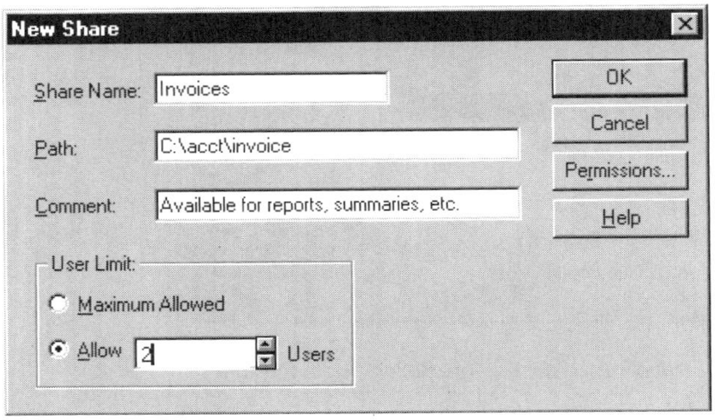

Figure 14.14 New shares enable users to access, within limits, the resource.

option found on any NT computer in the Control Panel. To set services, follow these steps:

1. In the Server Manager, select the computer and choose **C**omputer, **Se**rvices. Figure 14.15 shows the Services dialog box.
2. Scroll through the list of services and choose any of the following buttons:

    Start. Starts the selected service for this session only.

    S**to**p. Stops the services for this session only.

    Pause. Suspends the service.

    Continue. Continues a paused service.

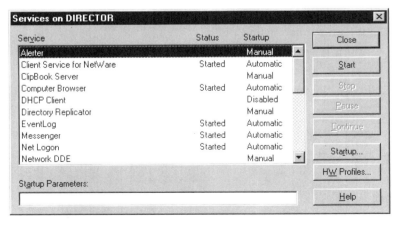

Figure 14.15 Control the services for any connected computer in the Services dialog box.

Sta**r**tup. Enables you to view and/or change a startup type: Automatic, Manual, or Disabled.

H**W** Profiles. Enables or disables the service for a specific hardware profile.

3. Choose Close when you're finished.

Sending a Message to a Computer

When you're connected to computers through the Server Manager, you can send a message to any selected computer. You might want to warn users that you're shutting down the system or tell them about a deleted share, for example.

To be able to send a message, the Messenger service must be running on both computers. The service is, by default, started automatically but you can check it in the Services dialog box (**C**omputer, **S**ervices).

To send a message, select the computer in the Server Manager to which you want to send the message. Choose **C**omputer, Send **M**essage. The Send Message dialog box appears. Enter your message, as shown in Figure 14.16, and choose OK to send it.

Directory Replication

When working on a network, users often share data files stored on the server. For shared files to remain effective and useful, all users must have updated files on which to work. Directory replication is a method of creating a duplicate of the master set of directories and files on the server for other computers on the network to use.

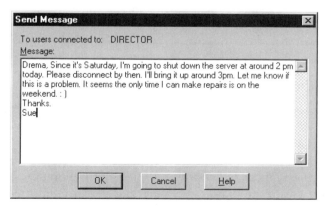

Figure 14.16 Send a message to someone connected to the server via this dialog box.

> **Note:** NT enables you to replicate not only directories but the files within those directories as well.

The server on which the master set resides is called the *export server*; all computers to which the duplicates are replicated are called import computers. Import computers must use the NT Workstation or NT Server software. The export server and the import computers are dynamically linked so that when changes are made to a directory or file on the master set, the changes are automatically reflected in the duplicates on the import computers.

In addition to ensuring that everyone is working with the same information, directory replication can also help relieve bottlenecks at the server. Suppose you have data files to which all workstations need access. If all workstations access the server at one time for these files, network traffic becomes slower and perhaps even stops periodically. However, you can replicate the directories containing the needed files to another server and direct some of the workstations to access the files from there to help balance the workload.

Requirements for Replication

Only computers running NT Server (domain controllers and/or member servers) can export directories. Import computers include computers running NT Server or NT Workstation.

> **Note:** Although a network can have multiple export servers, they usually do not export duplicate subdirectories, so as to maintain the integrity of the replicated data.

Creating the Subdirectories

The export server uses a default export path: \SYSTEMROOT\SYSTEM32\REPL\EXPORT; all subdirectories to be exported reside in this directory. The import computer uses the default import path, on which all imported subdirectories and their files are automatically placed: \SYSTEMROOT\SYSTEM32\REPL\IMPORT. The replication procedure creates the import directories automatically; you must create the export subdirectories yourself. Further, you must copy the files to be replicated into the subdirectories on the export server. You can use the Explorer on the export server to complete these tasks.

Creating Replicator Accounts

Before you can replicate directories and files, you must configure the Directory Replicator service for each participating export server, and you must create a special user account for the service. In the User Manager for Domains, create an account for the service on each export server and set the following user options:

Check the Password Never Expires option.

Enable the user to access the network during all logon hours.

Enter a password.

Assign the user to the Backup Operators group.

In the Server Manager, configure the Directory Replicator service for the export server to start up automatically and to log on under the newly created user account, by following these steps:

1. Open the Server Manager and select the export server. Choose **C**omputer, Ser**v**ices and select the Directory Replicator service in the list.
2. Choose the St**a**rtup button and in the Services dialog box; choose **A**utomatic.
3. In the Log On As area of the Services dialog box, choose **T**his Account and enter the user's name you created for the replicator service.
4. Enter the password, confirm the password, and choose OK. The Server Manager notifies you it's adding the user to the Replicator group and returns to the Server Manager window.

You also must configure the service for the import computer. In the Server Manager, select the computer that will be the import computer, then follow these steps:

1. Choose **C**omputer, Ser**v**ices, and select the Directory Replicator service in the list.
2. Choose the St**a**rtup button and in the Services dialog box; choose **A**utomatic.
3. In the Log On As area of the Services dialog box, choose **T**his Account and enter the domain name and the user's name you created for the replicator service; for example: *DOMAIN\SRepl*.

TIP: If you're in doubt about the exact account name, choose the browse button (...) and find the user account in the dialog box that appears. Choose OK.

---

4. Choose OK to return to the Server Manager.

Configuring the Export Server

You can configure the primary or backup domain controller, or a member server, as an export server for the replication service. You'll need to create the directories you want to export as subdirectories of the replication export path: *SYSTEM-ROOT*\SYSTEM32\REPL\EXPORT. You can accomplish this in the Explorer. Additionally, copy any files you want to replicate to the subdirectories you create.

To configure the export server in the Server Manager, follow these steps:

1. Open the Server Manager (Start, **P**rograms, Administrative Tools, Server Manager).
2. Select the server that will be the export server and choose **C**omputer, **P**roperties.
3. In the computer's Properties dialog box, choose the **R**eplication button. The Directory Replication dialog box appears, as shown in Figure 14.17.
4. Choose the **E**xport Directories option. In the **F**rom Path text box, the default export directory path appears.
5. Choose the **M**anage button to view and manage individual directories. The Manage Exported Directories dialog box appears (see Figure 14.18).
6. Select any subdirectory in the list and choose to Add Lock or Remove Lock; you lock the subdirectory when you do not want to replicate it.

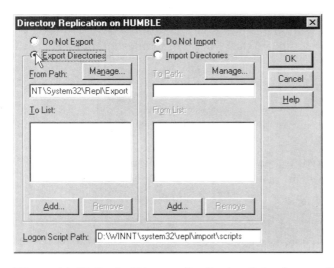

Figure 14.17 In the Directory Replication dialog box, enable the export server and set options for the process.

Advanced Network Management   **285**

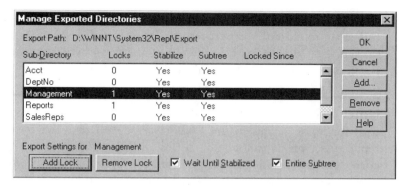

Figure 14.18 *The Manage Exported Directories dialog box displays the subdirectories in the Export directory.*

Replication on a locked subdirectory doesn't take place until you unlock the subdirectory.

7. Choose the Wait Until **S**tabilized check box. Stabilize a subdirectory to indicate the export server should wait two minutes after changes before exporting, just in case additional changes need to be recorded.

8. Choose the Entire S**u**btree check box if you want to export the subdirectory and any directories it contains; deselect the check box if you just want to replicate the first-level subdirectory.

TIP: If you choose the **A**dd button in the Manage Exported Directories dialog box, you can add subdirectories to the list; however, the Add button doesn't create subdirectories. You must create subdirectories in the Explorer.

9. Choose OK to close the Manage Exported Directories dialog box and return to the Directory Replication dialog box.

10. Below the **T**o List, choose the **A**dd button to add the computer to the list that will receive exported files. Select **A**dd a second time and enter the domain name in the text box; you must also add the domain name to the To List.

TIP: If you're replicating over a WAN, you can just add the computer names in the To List instead of the domain names and computer names.

11. Choose OK to close the Directory Replication dialog box and choose OK again to close the export server's Properties dialog box. If the REPL$ share doesn't already exist on the server, the system will start the Directory Replicator Service, if it hasn't already been started.

> **Note:** Before closing the Directory Replication dialog box, enter the path for logon scripts in the **L**ogon Script Path text box if you want to replicate scripts as well as directories and files (if the default path is not correct). Replicate logon scripts from a primary domain controller to a backup domain controller; only servers that authenticate users need to keep a copy of the logon scripts.

Configuring the Import Computer

You can configure a computer running NT Workstation or NT Server as an import computer; you can even use an export server as an import computer to create a local backup, for example. You don't need to create the subdirectories used for replication on the import computer; the Directory Replicator Service will create them for you.

To set up the import computer, follow these steps:

1. In the Server Manager, select the server or workstation that will be the import computer.
2. Choose **C**omputer, **P**roperties. The Directory Replication dialog box appears, as shown in Figure 14.19.
3. Choose the **I**mport Directories option.
4. In the To **P**ath box, check to make sure the path is correct; the default is WINNT\SYSTEM32\REPL\IMPORT.
5. In the Fr**o**m List, choose the **A**dd button to add the export server to the list from which this computer will receive exported files.
6. Choose the Mana**g**e button to review the Manage Imported Directories dialog box (see Figure 14.20).

> **TIP:** Manage locks to prevent importing subdirectories or to lock a subdirectory so it replicates to only one import computer and no other import computers.

Figure 14.19 An NT Workstation Directory Replication dialog box is different from an NT Server's Directory Replication dialog box.

7. After the first replication, you can select any directory in the Sub-**D**irectory list and choose to Lock or Remove Lock on the directory. A locked directory cannot be overwritten by a new exported, or replicated, directory.

IMPORTANT: Do not try to examine or set permissions for the import directory: SYSTEM32\REPL\IMPORT using the Explorer; you can damage or even lose the permissions set by the service if you even look at permissions in the Explorer.

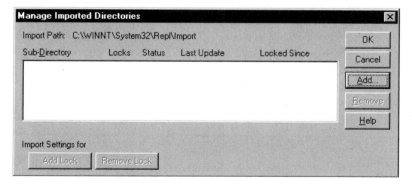

Figure 14.20 If you've never replicated to this computer, the Manage Imported Directories dialog box will be empty.

You can view the time and status of replicated directories in the Manage Imported Directories dialog box at any time. In the Sub-**D**irectory column is the name of the directory that was replicated. The Locks column indicates any locks on the directory; and if you've locked a directory, the Locked Since column lists the date and time the directory was locked. View the Last Update column for date and time of the most recent replication.

Finally, the Status column indicates the success or failure of the replication. Following are the possible entries in the Status column:

OK. Replicated subdirectory received and is identical to the exported subdirectory

No Master. Subdirectory is not receiving updates (export server locked or not running)

No Sync. Subdirectory not updated (communications failure, open files, permissions problems)

No entry (blank). Replication didn't occur for that subdirectory (improper configuration)

Diagnosing and Viewing Configuration Information

You can view information about your system—including system and environment variables, BIOS information, CPU steppings and type, memory, driver and service data, IRQs and port information, network connections and statistics, and more—using the Windows NT Diagnostics. The more you know about your system, the more likely you will be able to diagnose problems with the system. Windows NT Diagnostics can give you an overall view of the system so that you have more information with which to work.

To open the Windows NT Diagnostics dialog box, choose Start, **P**rograms, Administrative Tools, and Windows NT Diagnostics. The dialog box appears with nine tabs of information about your system. Notice you cannot change any settings in this dialog box; you can only view the data presented here.

TIP: The Windows NT Diagnostics application file is WINMSD.EXE.

Version

The Version tab gives you general information about the operating system, including the Windows NT version, your processor type, registration information, and the serial number. Within the version number, you may see a build type and number, which refer to the steps taken to produce the software—a mini version within the final version, so to speak. The registration information includes the person to whom the software is registered and your company, information you entered when installing the software.

System

The System tab offers information about your processor and BIOS, as shown in Figure 14.21. The BIOS is a set of instructions that lets the computer's hardware and operating system communicate with applications and devices. In the **BIOS** Information list box, you'll see the date and version of your system motherboard's BIOS.

If you're experiencing problems accessing devices such as higher-capacity floppy disk drives or larger hard disks, your computer's BIOS may be out of date. Normally, this information is displayed when you turn your computer on; using

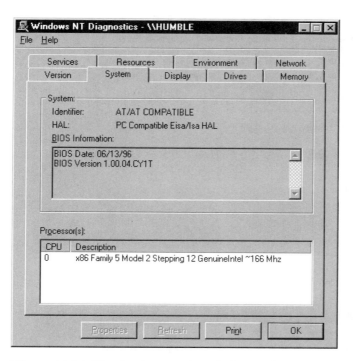

Figure 14.21 Use the System tab to find out information about your processor and BIOS.

the System tab is a handy way to view the information without rebooting the computer.

The Processors area of the System tab lists information about your CPU (Central Processing Unit). Depending on your processor and your system, the information in any of these tabs will vary.

Display

The Display tab lists information about your video driver and video card. The tab lists the BIOS date and version for your video card, resolution settings, adapter card type, video memory, and your driver vendor. Additionally, you'll find your video driver file names listed as well as the version of the video driver.

Drives

The Drives tab enables you to view your floppy drives, local hard drives, CD-ROM drives, and any mapped network drives. You can view the drives by type or by letter; Figure 14.22 shows the server's drives by type.

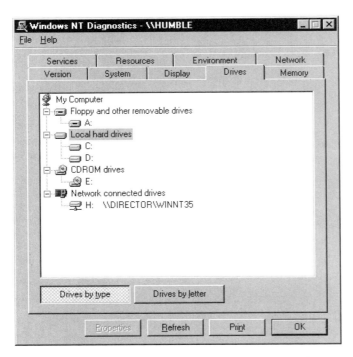

Figure 14.22 View the drives and their properties in the Drives tab.

Advanced Network Management

You must expand each drive type by double-clicking it; for example, double-click the Local Hard Drives to view the hard drives attached to the computer. Select any drive in the list and choose the **P**roperties button to view such information about the drive as volume label, serial number, size, and file system.

Memory

The Memory tab displays many types of memory. The Physical Memory area shows the total RAM in the system, the available RAM, and the amount of RAM used for file caching. All of the memory is measured in kilobytes instead of megabytes. The Kernel Memory refers to the part of the operating system that manages system memory, the file system, and disk operations, as shown in Figure 14.23.

You also might be interested in the Pagefile Space. The pagefile, also called a swap file, works as virtual memory your computer uses when NT demands more of the system memory than it can give. The pagefile.sys is a large, contiguous block of disk space that allows NT to bypass the file system and do direct hardware disk read and writes.

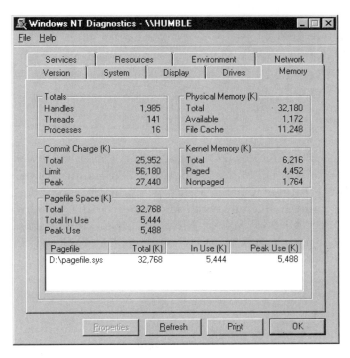

Figure 14.23 The Memory tab summarizes the system's memory usage.

NT also enables the pagefile.sys to enlarge when it reaches the specified limit. The pagefile enlarges in small amounts until it finally runs out of space; at which point you might think your server is running like cold molasses. You can keep an eye on the pagefile.sys size by watching the Commit Charge area of the Windows NT Diagnostics dialog box. The Commit Charge total size should not reach the limit. When the committed bytes exceed the commit limit, NT increases the page file size.

TIP: You can alleviate problems and get better performance out of your virtual memory system by establishing paging files on more than one local drive.

Services

The Services tab shows the current state of services and devices, both of which you can manage in the Control Panel. Services include the Directory Replicator, Event Log, Messenger, UPS, and so on. The Services tab tells you whether each service is running or stopped. You can choose to start, pause, continue, or stop these various services in the Services option in the Control Panel.

You can choose to view devices in the Services tab, as well. Devices include your CD-ROM drive, boot disk, video card, network card, and so on; the status of each installed device is listed in the Services tab. You can configure devices in the Devices option, Control Panel.

Resources

So often you'll need the IRQ or I/O port address of a device and wonder how to get it; use the Resources tab of the Windows NT Diagnostics dialog box. Figure 14.24 shows the I/O (Input/Output) Port page of the tab, listing the address, device, and type. Also in the Resources tab are buttons for IRQ (Interrupt Request Line), DMA (Direct Memory Access), Memory, and Devices. Track useful information about your tape drive, CD-ROM drive, network card, video card, floppy drives, and so on with this handy tab.

Environment

The Environment tab lists information about the server's command interpreter, which contains not only the system environment, but interprets and executes all commands and file names entered, and displays error messages. You'll also see the

Advanced Network Management

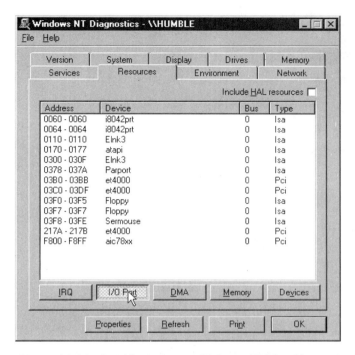

Figure 14.24 Quickly determine IRQs and I/O addresses in the Resources tab.

number of processors on the system, the operating system, and the path to the system files. Additionally, the Environment tab lists information about the processor. Figure 14.25 shows common elements in the Environment tab.

TIP: Any information in this tab that you want to change can be accessed through the System option in the Control Panel.

Network

Figure 14.26 shows the last tab of the Windows NT Diagnostics dialog box, the Network tab. In the Network tab, you'll find a summary of statistics about the network operations. The **S**tatistics page describes such information as how many bytes have been transmitted or received, how many errors occurred, and so on.

You also can view general, transports, and settings in the Network tab by choosing one of the buttons. The **G**eneral button displays a page with your access

Figure 14.25 Get a summary of the system environment in the Environment tab.

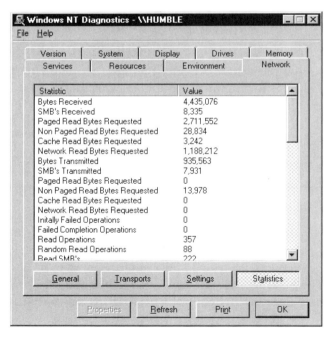

Figure 14.26 Find statistics about network operations in the Network tab.

level, workgroup or domain name, network version, number of logged-in users, the server name, and so on. The **T**ransports button displays the transport layers you're running, addresses, and other settings. If, for example, you were running a TCP/IP stack, you could look here to find out what IP addresses you were using. **S**ettings displays the current settings for such items as maximum threads, maximum locks, pipe increments, cache time out, encryption, and so on.

15 Managing Multiple Domains

Thus far, you've worked with only one domain on your network and may find that that is all you need. However, if your network starts to grow, or if you attach to another network, you may find that multiple domains are a better tool for organizing and managing the network.

You may also decide to use multiple domains as a method of preserving your NetWare 4.x hierarchy of containers and objects. If you plan to migrate from NetWare 4.x, one or two containers at a time, you should read this chapter first so you'll know how to set up your domains and trust relationships.

When working with multiple domains, the main concern is security. NT offers several security features, some you're already familiar with and others that may be new to you. This chapter explains how to set up multiple domains and how to manage security across two or more domains.

Also included in this chapter is information about how users will view the domains, how to access another domain's printers, and how to map drives for user access to other domains.

Finally, you'll learn the steps to adding computers to your domain, promoting and demoting domain controllers, and synchronizing the domain controllers in your domain.

Specifically in this chapter, you will:

- Review the workings of a single domain.
- Learn the benefits of multiple domains.
- Learn how to set up trust relationships.
- Learn how to administer users and groups in other domains.
- Learn how to access printers in other domains.
- Learn how to view resources in other domains.

- Learn how to add a computer to your domain.
- Learn how to promote and demote domain controllers.

Working in a Single Domain

A domain is an administrative unit containing network servers and workstations that share common security and common user account information. For each user on the domain, there's an account that enables him or her to log on to the network, and from the login, access any server and any resource on the domain for which her or she has rights and permissions.

Computers within a domain may be in the same office building or connected by a LAN; computers within a domain also may be in various cities, states, even continents and connected over a WAN, through dial-up networking, ISDN, fiber, satellite, or other physical connection.

Single Domain Components

Within one domain, a primary domain controller is necessary to manage interactions between users, groups, and resources. All members of the domain share a directory database that's stored on the domain controller(s) and identifies all users and groups within the domain.

There is only one primary domain controller in a domain. One domain may have additional domain controllers, however, in the form of backup domain controllers. Additionally, a domain can include multiple member servers and workstations. All computers in the domain are centrally administered and managed within the domain, and within the domain, only one user account exists for each user.

In addition to making network administration easy, users benefit from being a member of a domain. They can browse available network resources and access any resources for which they have permission.

Security Considerations

Security in a domain is based on discretionary access control. Some users can access a resource whereas other users cannot, depending on permissions and rights. User rights determine whether a user can log on only to one computer or to the entire domain, and which resources the user can access after logging in.

Organizing the users into groups makes it easier for the administrator to control access to resources. Instead of assigning rights to each user, an administrator can create a group and assign the rights to that group. Then the administrator can add specific users to the group.

Multiple Domain Considerations

When you start adding more users, servers, and resources to a network, you start having more organizational, administrative, and security problems. Questions that arise with a larger network include how will each workstation know what resources are available, by what name are the resources identified, and where are those resources actually located? Another problem is how to enable some but not all users to access some resources. NT takes care of these problems with multiple domains.

Trust Relationships

When you add a second domain to the mix, you also add the problem of how users from one domain access resources on the second domain. You could make each user a member of the second domain; assign a password, create a user account, and define rights and groups for the user in the second domain. But this causes some complications.

First, it's an administrative nightmare; trying to update and manage two sets of users would be difficult to say the least, but what happens when you add a third domain, a fourth, and so on? Second, the user now has to remember a user name and password for an additional domain; the user also must log off of one domain before logging on to another. In addition to time-consuming, this is not a very effective way for users to navigate between domains.

NT has come up with an easier answer: trust relationships. With trust relationships, NT can supply security across multiple domains. There are two types of trust relationships:

One-way trust relationship. In a one-way trust relationship, one domain trusts the users of another domain to use its resources. The *trusted* domain authenticates its users, and the users in turn access the resources on the *trusting* domain. However, users on the trusting domain cannot access the trusted domain, since this is only a one-way relationship.

Two-way trust relationship. In a two-way trust relationship, each domain trusts users accounts in the other domain, and both domains share their resources, depending on applicable rights, of course.

Naturally, the accessibility of resources on any domain is subject to permissions associated with those resources. The great thing about trust relationships is the universal access to resources; one domain user account and password is all a user needs to access resources from multiple domains.

Multiple Domain Models

When a company is small, a single domain model works well. The network has just one primary domain controller, perhaps a backup domain controller, a few member servers, and workstations for everyone who needs them. Microsoft states that 26,000 users and groups can make up a single domain; reasonably, though, that's too many elements for an administrator to handle in one domain. Instead, the users and groups can be divided into multiple domains using departments, locations, offices, jobs, or some other natural divisions as guides for the domains.

It's more efficient to set up multiple domains from an administrative point of view than to group all of your users into one domain, especially if you have a large network or a network separated by natural boundaries, such as departments or buildings. The major advantage to having multiple domains is delegating administrative duties. You can assign one person within each domain to manage that domain—create users and groups, control files and other resources within the domain, back up data, and so on.

Note: It's difficult to say you should or should not use multiple domains; you'll have to decide for yourself. If you have 10 servers, for example (used for file and print services as well as for authentication), and perhaps more than 100 users, one domain might fit your network perfectly. On the other hand, you may have 5 servers and 25 users, all separated geographically so that management by a single administrator is impossible. In this case, two or more domains would make the job workable.

In Chapter 6, "Preparing for the Migration," I discussed various domain models you could use in your network. In the multiple domain models, each domain has one primary domain controller, one or more backup domain controllers (BDC), and then various combinations of member servers and workstations.

One tried and true method of organizing multiple domains is to place the authentication server, a primary domain controller (PDC), for all domains in a domain to itself—often called the master domain. The master domain enables centralized administration for all user and group accounts. Other domains within the model, then, control the various resources within the network.

Say you have six domains in your network, for example. One domain, the master, controls all user and group accounts for the network. Two other domains control the printing services for the entire network, and yet another two domains control all files and directories. You have users attached to each domain, but all users are authenticated in the master domain and all users access one or more of the resource domains for printing and file services.

On the other hand, suppose your NetWare 4.x server is divided into six containers. Each container is organized into a set of users and groups for easy administration, organization, and practicality. You can set up six NT domains, one domain for each container. After you migrate the users and groups to their domains, you can migrate your files and directories to one master domain or divide them appropriately between all six domains. No matter what you decide, you can see that setting up multiple domains will take some planning and forethought.

Note: Each domain must have a primary domain server and should have at least one backup domain server. You can add other computers running Windows NT Server 4.0 software as member servers that supply files, or printers, or other resources within each domain. If you're using the master domain/resource domains model, member servers in each domain contain the resources but all users are authenticated from the master domain.

Logging On Multiple Domains

As you know, logon security is the first, and perhaps the greatest, means of security for a network. When a user logs on, his or her user name and password are checked against the directory database in either the computer or the domain, depending on which the user is accessing; the user enters either the domain name or the computer name in the Logon Information dialog box if he or she is using Windows NT Workstation, a Windows NT member server, or a Windows 95 computer.

The same is true if the network is set up with multiple domains. If the user is logging on to a domain, the domain controller processes the request using the Net Logon service, which initiates discovery, a secure communications channel, and pass-through authentication.

Discovery is when the Net Logon service attempts to locate a domain controller in the trusted domain. The secure communications channel is a verification of the computer accounts in preparation to pass the user identification data. Finally the pass-through authentication passes the user's identification on to the appropriate domain controller, if the computer being used for logon is not the domain controller in the domain where the user account is defined. Naturally, both domain controllers must share a trust relationship for pass-through authentication to work.

The Net Logon service uses pass-through authentication depending on the domain name the user enters. If the domain name isn't the domain to which the domain controller belongs, the domain controller checks trusted domains and passes on the user data if it locates the appropriate domain. If the user data is authenticated, the logon succeeds; if the domain controller cannot find an appropriate trusted domain or the trusted domain cannot authenticate the user's name and password, the logon fails.

Note: If you have multiple administrators, they should use two domain accounts for their local domain: one as a member of the Administrators local group, used to perform local network management tasks, and one in the Users local group, to perform the same tasks as other users. This way your network will be more secure. Members of the Administrators group can accidentally change configurations, introduce viruses, and so on; these accidents will be less likely to cause major damage if administrators log on as a user instead of as an Administrator most of the time.

Administering Multiple Domains in the User Manager

The first thing you must do to set up multiple domains is install the primary domain controller (PDC) for each domain. When installing Windows NT Server 4.0 software, you choose the type of server you want to set up: primary domain controller, backup domain controller, or member server (standalone). Since each domain must have a primary domain controller, you set up that server first. When creating the PDC, make sure you assign a unique name to the new domain. See Appendix A for information about installing Windows NT Server 4.0 and about changing domain names in the Network dialog box.

After you install the PDC, you can create client software, attach workstations, add users and groups, install printers, perhaps install a backup domain controller and a few member servers, as well. Additionally, you can create as many domains as needed for your network; you can always add more domains later, as well. Now you're ready to set up a trust relationship.

You configure trust relationships in the User Manager for Domains on the computer running NT Server; however, to set up trust relationships, the other domain involved must participate as well.

You can set up trust relationships and then manage users and groups of multiple domains in the User Manager for Domains, if you have the Administrator rights on all domains.

Setting Up Trust Relationships

You must have the cooperation of the other domain(s) in order to set up a trust relationship, no matter if the relationship is one-way or two-way. Make sure you're logged on as a member of the Administrators group; if you're not logged on as the Administrator, then make sure your name is added to the second domain's user list and is a member of the Administrators group as well. It's easier if you keep the same password for all domains.

One-Way Trust Relationship

To set up a one-way trust relationship, the trusted domain adds a domain to its trusting list; then the trusting domain adds the first domain to its trusted list.

TIP: Remember, the *trusted* domain is the one accessing resources from the *trusting* domain.

To set up a one-way trust relationship, follow these steps:

1. Open the User Manager for Domains (Start, **P**rograms, Administrative Tools, User Manager for Domains).
2. Choose **P**olicies, **T**rust Relationships. The Trust Relationships dialog box appears (see Figure 15.1).

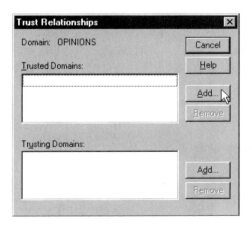

Figure 15.1 *The Trust Relationships dialog box lets you add trusting and/or trusted domains.*

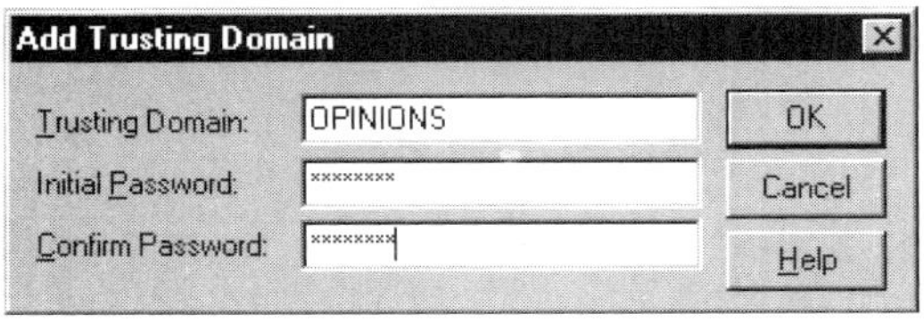

304 Chapter 15

Figure 15.2 Enter the trusting domain name and your password in this dialog box.

3. Choose the **A**dd button to the right of the T**ru**sting Domains list box and the Add Trusting Domain dialog box appears (see Figure 15.2).
4. Enter the name of the Trusting Domain and the password you will use for that domain; confirm the password and choose OK.
5. Move to the server in the second domain and open the User Manager; you should be logged in as a member of the Administrators group.
6. Choose **P**olicies, **T**rust Relationships. The Trust Relationships dialog box appears.
7. To add the trusted domain, choose the **A**dd button to the right of the **T**rusted Domains list. The Add Trusted Domain dialog box appears (see Figure 15.3).
8. Enter the name of the trusted domain and then enter your password to that domain; choose OK.

Two-Way Trust Relationship

To perform a two-way trust relationship, the first domain must add the second domain to its trusting list and add the domain to its trusted list. The second domain must also add the first to its trusting list and add the first to its trusted list. You must perform the steps in the following order for the two-way trust to work; if you don't, you'll receive an error message that says the trust relationship could not be

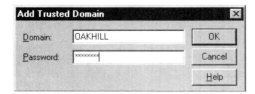

Figure 15.3 Enter the trusted domain name and your password.

verified. If that happens, remove all trust relationships and repeat the steps in the correct order.

To set up a two-way trust relationship, follow these steps:

1. On the first computer, open the User Manager for Domains (Start, **P**rograms, Administrative Tools, User Manager for Domains).

2. Choose **P**olicies, **T**rust Relationships. The Trust Relationships dialog box appears.

3. Choose the **A**dd button to the right of the Tr**u**sting Domains list box and the Add Trusting Domain dialog box appears. Enter the name of the Trusting Domain and the password you will use for that domain; confirm the password and choose OK.

4. Move to the server in the second domain and open the User Manager; choose **P**olicies, **T**rust Relationships. The Trust Relationships dialog box appears.

5. Choose the **A**dd button to the right of the Tr**u**sting Domains list box and the Add Trusting Domain dialog box appears. Enter the name of the Trusting Domain and the password you will use for that domain; confirm the password and choose OK.

6. On the same server, you can now choose the **A**dd button to the right of the **T**rusted Domains list. The Add Trusted Domain dialog box appears. Enter the name of the trusted domain and then enter your password to that domain; choose OK.

7. Move back to the first server and choose the **A**dd button to the right of the Tr**u**sting Domains list box. Enter the domain name and your password and choose OK.

Figure 15.4 shows the Trust Relationships dialog box with one trusted domain and two trusting domains. The trusted domain (OAKHILL) can access the resources from this domain (OPINIONS). OPINIONS can access the resources for both the trusting domains (BECKLEY and OAKHILL). Therefore, OAKHILL and OPINIONS have a two-way trust relationship, whereas BECKLEY and OPINIONS have only a one-way trust relationship.

TIP: It's a good idea to set the Audit policy (**P**olicies, Au**d**it) on your own domain to track events, since you're now allowing other users to access your resources. You can view the audit log in the Event Viewer. For more information, see Chapter 4, "Managing Security Policies."

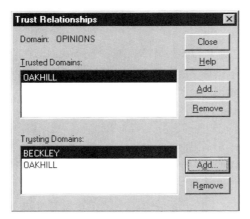

Figure 15.4 Results of a two- and a one-way trust relationship in the Trust Relationships dialog box.

Removing Trust Relationships

Removing trust relationships is also a process that you must perform in both domains. The trusted domain must remove the second domain from its list of trusting domains and the trusting domain must remove the first domain from its list of trusted domains.

To remove trust relationships, follow these steps:

1. In the User Manager for Domains on the first server, choose **P**olicies, **T**rust Relationships.
2. Select the domain you want to remove from the relationship and choose the Remove button. The User Manager displays a message dialog box, as shown in Figure 15.5.
3. Choose OK to confirm the removal of the domain.
4. Repeat steps 1 through 3 on the server in the second domain.

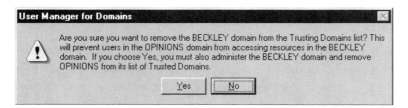

Figure 15.5 A confirmation dialog box verifies your choice to remove the domain from the trust relationship.

Managing Multiple Domains **307**

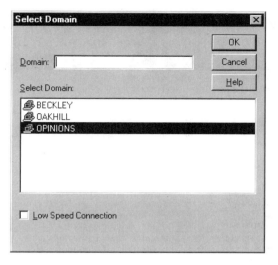

Figure 15.6 *In the Select Domain dialog box, you can select a domain or double-click a domain to display computers in the domain.*

Administering Users in Multiple Domains

In the User Manager for Domains, you can select users and groups in other domains and administer them as if they were in your domain. Additionally, you can set policies for users in other domains with which you have a trust relationship, as long as you have administrative rights in that domain.

You can display an individual computer running NT Workstation, NT Server as a member server, or a Microsoft LAN Manager server. If you select a primary or backup domain controller, the domain is displayed instead of the computer. To display a computer instead of a domain, enter double slashes and the computer name, for example, \\MANAGEMENT.

To change domains and administer users and groups in that domain, follow these steps:

1. In the User Manager for Domains, choose **U**ser, **S**elect Domain. The Select Domain dialog box appears (see Figure 15.6).
2. Choose a domain to administer, or select a specific computer.
3. Choose OK and the User Manager accesses the users and groups on the selected domain. Figure 15.7 shows the BECKLEY domain in the OPINIONS User Manager for Domains.

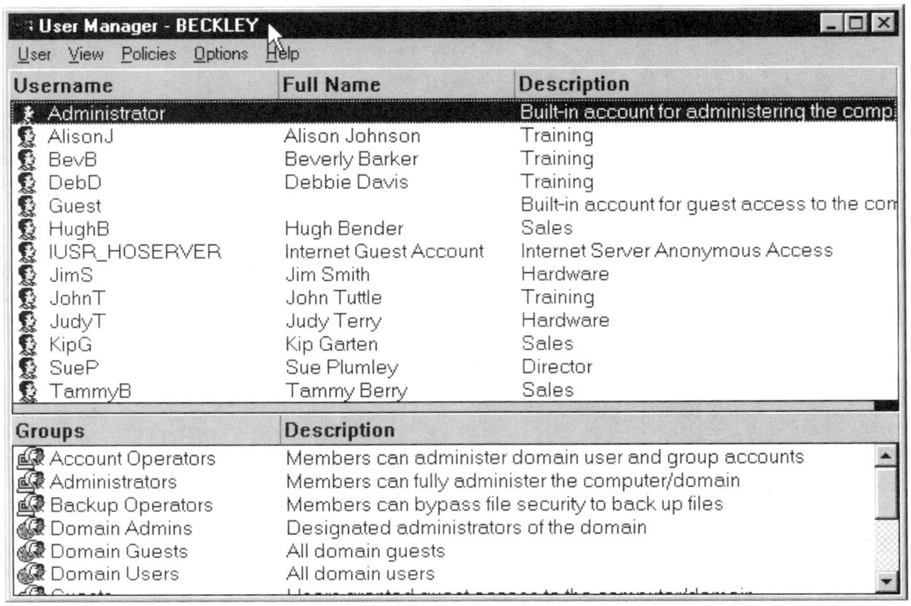

Figure 15.7 The domain name appears in the title bar of the User Manager for Domains window.

TIP: Use the Low Speed Connection option if connections to other domains seem slow to you; but be aware that using this option prevents you from seeing the users and groups. Although you can still administer local groups, you cannot administer global.

After choosing the domain, you can add, modify, remove, and otherwise manage users and groups, change account policies and user rights, and so on. See Chapters 3 and 4 for more information.

Managing the User Rights Policy

You already have a user rights policy for the groups and users on your domain, as discussed in Chapter 4. When you add new domains to your network, you may need to assign rights to the new users or groups for your domain. The user rights policy enables you to grant rights to individuals and/or groups. To manage rights for users and groups from other domains, follow these steps:

Global Groups Revisited

In Chapter 3, you learned about local and global groups, but you may not have been too concerned with the concept at that time. But now you're getting ready to work with multiple domains, and you need to understand the difference between the two. Basically, a local group is used within one domain and global groups are used when the network is set up in multiple domains.

Remember, you can put users and global groups into a local group; however, you cannot put one local group into another. Global groups are those that can only contain users, and these users can only be from the domain in which the global group was created.

The three built-in global groups include:

Domain Admins. A member of the Administrators local group can administer the domain, the primary and backup domain controllers, and all other computers running both NT Server and Workstation in the domain.

Domain Users. A member of the Users local group for the domain and of the Users local group for every NT Workstation and member server on the network have normal user access.

Domain Guests Members of the domain's built-in Guest user account have limited rights. You could move any Domain Users to the Domain Guests group if you want to limit their rights and permissions.

In addition, remember these guidelines when working with global and local groups:

- If you need a group that can contain users from multiple domains, you must use a local group. Local groups can only be used in the domain in which they're created; so, if you need to grant this local group permissions in more than one domain, you'll have to manually create the local group in every domain in which you need it.
- You can group the users of one domain into a single unit for use in other domains; this would be a global group. Global groups can be put into other domains' local groups and can be given rights and permissions directly in other domains.
- If you have a group that needs to be in more than one domain, then create two groups: a local and a global.
- User accounts should be members of global, not local groups, to enable them to access multiple domain resources. Place people with administrative privileges in the Domain Admins group instead of the Administrators; place new users in the Domain Users group instead of Users. To create global groups, open the User Manager for Domains and choose **U**ser, New **G**lobal Group. The New Global Group dialog box appears. Enter the name for the new group and assign rights as explained in Chapters 3 and 4.

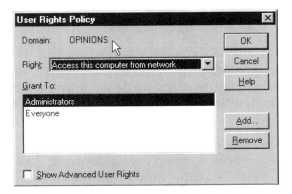

Figure 15.8 *Set rights for users and groups using resources in your domain in this dialog box.*

1. Choose **P**olicies, **U**ser Rights. The User Rights dialog box appears (see Figure 15.8).
2. In the Righ**t text box**, select the right you want to grant to the user and or group.
3. Choose the **A**dd button and the Add Users and Groups dialog box appears.
4. Choose the **L**ist Names From drop-down list box and select the domain, as shown in Figure 15.9.
5. To view the members of any group, select the group and choose the Show **U**sers button. The users are displayed at the end of the groups list in the **N**ames list box, as shown in Figure 15.10.
6. Select any names of users or groups you want to add and choose the **A**dd button. When you're done, choose OK to return to the User Rights Policy dialog box.

Using Domain Resources

Now that you can see how to secure your domain when working with multiple domains, you may be wondering how users browse the domains and access resources.

IMPORTANT: Only computers running Windows NT Workstation, Windows NT Server, or Windows 95 can browse and access the resources of domains other than the one on which they are a member. Windows for Workgroups and MS-DOS clients can only access the resources from their own domain.

Managing Multiple Domains

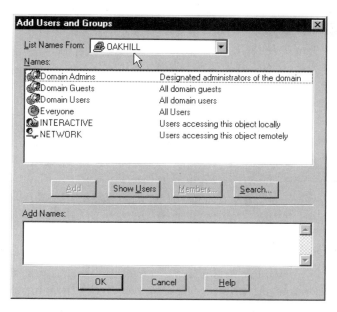

Figure 15.9 Choose a domain and then choose the groups to add.

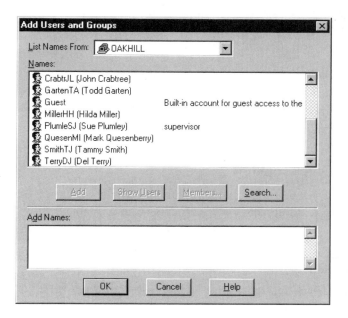

Figure 15.10 In the Add Users and Groups dialog box, choose individual users and/or groups.

312 CHAPTER 15

Figure 15.11 Users access the domains from the Network Neighborhood.

Browsing the Domains

Users browsing the network see resources grouped in domains rather than just a listing of multiple servers and printers. Viewing resources in this manner makes it easier for the users to locate the resources and identify resources.

Clients can use the Network Neighborhood to view available resources. Figure 15.11 shows the Neighborhood window with all three available domains, as well as a workgroup, for resource sharing. To view the resources on any domain, the user double-clicks the domain name, and then continues to expand from computer to folder to access files and directories.

TIP: Users can also access the domains from the Explorer window. They locate the Network Neighborhood and then double-click to expand the domains and resources.

Mapping Drives to Domains

Users can map drives to other domains similarly to the way they map drives to their own domain. Additionally, users can choose to reconnect the mapped drive automatically at logon. To map drives to another domain, follow these steps:

1. In the Network Neighborhood, choose **V**iew, **T**oolbar to display the toolbar if it is not already showing.
2. Select the Map Network Drive icon, as shown in Figure 15.12.
3. In the Map Network Drive dialog box, expand the domain to which you want to map a drive; continue to expand the drive until you find the folder you want.

Managing Multiple Domains

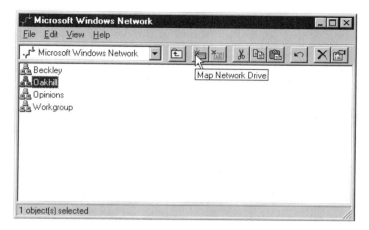

Figure 15.12 Use the Map Network Drive icon to quickly connect to another domain.

4. Select a **D**rive from the drop-down list and then select the folder in the **S**hared Directories list. The path to the folder appears in the **P**ath text box, as shown in Figure 15.13. Choose **R**econnect at Logon to connect to the selected drive each time you log on.

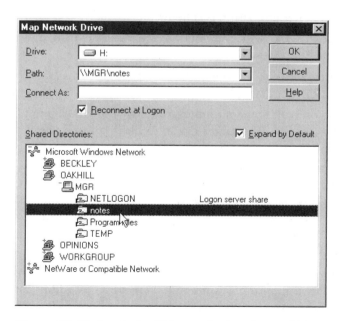

Figure 15.13 Locate the folder on the domain to which you want to map a drive in the Map Network Drive dialog box.

5. The users enter their user names in the **C**onnect As text box and choose OK. The mapped connection shows in the My Computer window and in the Explorer.

Note: The administrator can also map drives in this manner for user profiles. On a workstation, the Administrator sets up the drive mappings and any other environment settings for the user, then saves the configuration as a user profile. See Chapter 14 for more information.

Sharing Printers

Before the users can access a printer on another domain, you must add the printer as a network printer to a server in the users domain. You add a printer to the domain as you would any network printer and then administer the print queue in the same manner as well. See Chapter 5 for more information about setting up printers and managing print queues.

Briefly, to set up a printer in another domain for use in your domain, follow these steps:

1. Choose Start, **S**ettings, **P**rinters. The Printers window appears.
2. Double-click the Add Printers option and the Add Printer Wizard dialog box appears.
3. Choose the **N**etwork Printer option and choose the Next button. The Connect to Printer dialog box appears.
4. Expand the domain containing the printer by double-clicking first the domain name and then the server name. Available printers display below the server, as shown in Figure 15.14.
5. Select the printer and choose OK. Follow the directions on-screen to complete setting up the printer. Users then access the printer the same as they would any other printer on the server in their own domain.

Managing Servers and Domains

In Chapter 14, you learned about the Server Manager and how to manage your domain. As your network enlarges, you'll find there are a few additional tasks you'll need to perform. For example, when you add workstations or servers to your network, you must tell the server and the network that you've added another computer. You can accomplish this task in the Server Manager.

Managing Multiple Domains

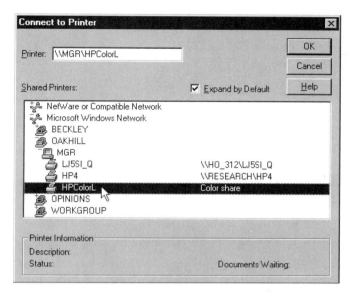

Figure 15.14 Display available domain printers in the Connect to Printer dialog box.

Another task you'll need to perform at some point is promoting a domain controller. You may, for example, have trouble with your primary domain controller and need to shut it down for servicing. Rather than shutting down the entire network, you can promote a backup domain controller to primary, and let the users continue with their work. This chapter shows you how to further manage your servers and domain.

Adding Computers to the Domain

Add a computer—a workstation, member server, or backup domain controller—to the network at any time. When you add a computer, you must identify the domain and the name of the computer to the server; and then you must set the computer to the appropriate domain and restart the computer before it becomes a member of the domain. You must be a member of the Administrators or Account Operators group to add a computer to the domain.

To add a computer to the domain, follow these steps:

1. On the primary domain controller of the domain, open the Server Manager (Start, **P**rograms, Administrative Tools, Server Manager).
2. Choose **C**omputer, **A**dd to Domain. The Add Computer To Domain dialog box appears (see Figure 15.15).

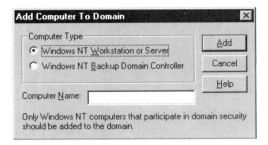

Figure 15.15 In this dialog box, identify the computer type to the server of the domain.

3. In Computer Type, choose one of the following:

    Windows NT **W**orkstation or Server. This computer can be running NT Server as a member server, NT Workstation, or Windows 95.

    Windows NT **B**ackup Domain Controller. This computer must be set up as a BDC (through installation).

4. In the Computer **N**ame text box, enter the computer's name.

5. Choose **A**dd. You can add more computers at this time or close the dialog box.

On the workstation or server you're adding to the domain, follow these steps:

1. Open the Control Panel (Start, **S**ettings, **C**ontrol Panel).
2. Double-click the Network option to display the Network dialog box.

> **Note:** If you are just installing the software to the client computer, you can enter the domain name and the computer name as you set the computer up. See Appendix A for information.

3. In the Identification tab, choose the **C**hange button. The Identification Changes dialog box appears (see Figure 15.16).
4. Choose OK. NT prompts you to restart the computer. When the login dialog box appears, the correct domain appears.

> **Note:** You can move member servers and/or workstations from one domain to another simply by removing the computer from its current domain and adding it to another domain. You cannot, however, move a backup domain controller unless you reinstall the Windows NT Server 4.0 software.

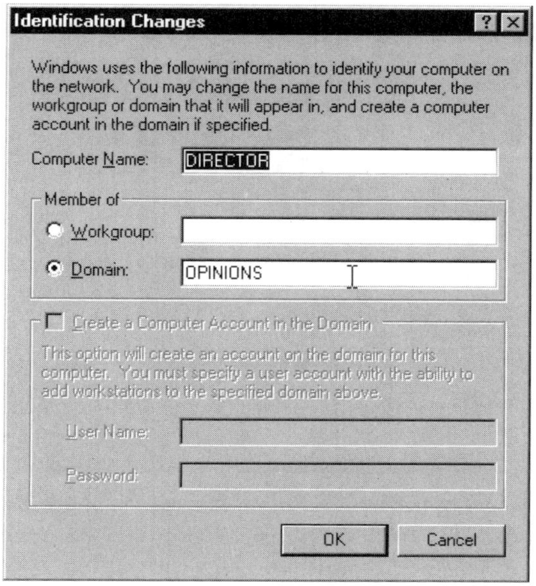

Figure 15.16 Change the domain name and the computer's name to match those entered in the Add Computer to Domain dialog box on the server.

Promoting a Domain Controller

If you have a problem with your primary domain controller, such as a crash or major hardware failure, you can assign any backup domain controller in your domain to take over as primary domain controller by promoting the server. The data on the BDC is up-to-date, due to the automatic directory replication between the two domain controllers. User and group information, rights, permissions, files, trusting domains, the BDC is a perfect replica of the PDC.

If the current PDC is still active when you promote the BDC, the current PDC is demoted to a BDC automatically. If the current PDC is not available when you promote the BDC but you return it to service later, you must demote the former PDC to a BDC else it will not run the Net Logon service or participate in authentication of user logons.

To promote a BDC to a PDC, follow these steps:

1. Open the Server Manager by choosing Start, **P**rograms, Administrative Tools, and Server Manager.
2. Choose **C**omputer, Promote to Primary Domain **C**ontroller as shown in Figure 15.17.

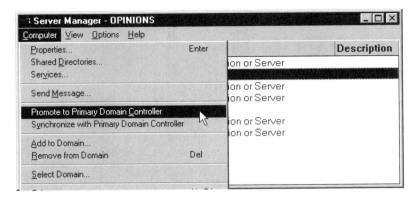

Figure 15.17 The Promote to Primary Domain Controller command promotes the BDC.

> **Note:** When you select a former PDC in the list of computer in Server Manager, the Promote to Primary Domain Controller command changes to Demote to Backup Domain Controller command.

3. The User Manager carries out the change.

Synchronizing Controllers

Usually, the system takes care of all synchronization of backup and primary domain controllers; however, if the BDC is unable to establish a connection for some reason, you can do it manually. The BDC will send an administrative alert to the PDC if it cannot, for some reason, synchronize. Make sure the Alerter service and the Messenger service are set to automatic on both the PDC and BDC.

To manually synchronize domain controllers, follow these steps:

1. Open the Server Manager by choosing Start, **P**rograms, Administrative Tools, and Server Manager, and select the BDC you want to synchronize.
2. Choose **C**omputer, **S**ynchronize with Primary Domain Controller. The User Manager takes care of the task.

If you have more than one BDC in your domain and you want to manually synchronize all of them, select the PDC in the domain and choose the **C**omputer menu. The **S**ynchronize with Primary Domain Controller command changes to Synchronize Entire Domain. Choose that command and choose OK.

PART VII

Reference

A Installing Windows NT Server and Configuring the Network

When you're ready to install the NT Server software, you'll want to make sure you have the right hardware and that it's compatible with NT. When installing the operating system, NT offers many options for setup and configuration. This appendix helps you prepare for installation and then install the NT Server software.

Preparing to Install

Before installing NT Server, make sure you have backups of any important files on the computer to which you plan to install. Check over the Hardware Compatibility List included with your NT documentation to make sure your hardware—network card, video driver, sound card, CD-ROM, and so on—is compatible with NT. For an updated version of the Hardware Compatibility List, access the World Wide Web at http://www.microsoft.com/ntserver/hcl/hclintro.htm. Additionally, make sure you have all of the device drivers and installation software for your applications, printers, modems, CD-ROMs, and any other devices you want to use on the server on diskette.

You'll need the following items to complete the installation of the operating system:

NT Server CD and three 3.5-inch setup disks

20-digit-Product ID number (printed on inside back cover of your installation documentation) or the 10-digit CD key (printed on the back of the CD case)

Computer name, workgroup or domain name, IP address (if applicable)

IRQ addresses for any hardware on the server

One 3.5-inch 1.44M floppy disk for the Emergency Repair Disk

> **Note:** I strongly recommend you create an Emergency Repair Disk. The disk is bootable and contains the necessary data to reconstruct a configuration if your NT system is no longer able to boot, or when other configuration problems occur.

Following is a description of the system requirements for running Windows NT Server 4.0, as based on an Intel processor. You also can install NT to RISC-based microprocessors; for more information, see the NT documentation.

Using an Intel processor, you'll need a 32-bit x86-based microprocessor that is 80486/25MHz or higher for NT to run successfully. Alternatively, you can use an Intel Pentium processor, which is highly recommended for efficiency and effective server operation.

You may be used to using any old low-resolution, monochrome monitor for your NetWare server. For NT, however, make sure your display is a VGA or higher resolution. I suggest staying with an S3-based video accelerator; it may not be the fastest board, but it is the most solid, and less expensive than most. NT includes a S3 video driver you can use.

Although you can run NT Server with 12M RAM, you will want at least 16M on the server and preferably 32M. Depending on your server needs—file and print server, RAS, Internet connections, and so on—you'll want to add RAM to the original 12M Microsoft suggests. You should definitely add an additional 4M RAM for ever six printers on the network, if you're using your NT server as a print server. Using the fault-tolerance driver means another 2M; add 4M RAM to support the overhead involved with RAID. I recommend 32M RAM for NT Server to run efficiently and effectively.

You'll need 123M minimum free disk space to hold the NT Server system files; don't forget to consider the disk space for applications and files. I find at least 1G and preferably 2G is most practical for a small to medium size server. You may want to use a SCSI-based hard disk, or controller; NT supports most SCSI adapters, although you should refer to the Hardware Compatibility List (HCL) before you purchase one. Using a SCSI-based system means you'll have better fault tolerance; disk mirroring and RAID work best with a SCSI disk subsystem. Additionally, NT successfully supports IDE (Integrated Device Electronics) drives.

You'll also need a 3.5-inch floppy high-density disk drive plus a CD-ROM drive. Again, check the HCL before trying to install NT. If you do not have a CD-ROM drive on the server, you can install the software over the network.

A mouse or other pointing device is strongly recommended, as with any Windows program. You'll have better luck with a PS/2-type mouse than any other.

And to use NT Server on a network, you'll need a network adapter card. NT can support one or more network adapter cards; check the HCL for compatibility.

> **Note:** You will also want to consider some sort of backup device, such as a tape drive; again, check the HCL for NT's compatibility list. Other considerations for the NT server include a CD-ROM drive, UPS, and modem.

Installing NT Server

When you install NT, you'll need a set of disks included with the NT Server package; the disks are labeled Setup Boot Disk, Setup Disk 2, and Setup Disk 3. If you do not have those disks—as when installing over the network—NT will create those disk for you before installing the program. This section guides you through NT installation.

Beginning Setup

If you do not have the three 3.5-inch floppy disks needed to start NT setup, you must create them. To create the setup disks, attach to the network and change to the directory containing the setup files. At an MS-DOS prompt or in the Run dialog box from Windows, type **winnt** if the operating system of your server is anything other than a previous version of NT; type **winnt32** if a previous version of NT is currently running. Follow the directions on-screen to create the disks, and then you can pick up with the following instructions.

If you have the three setup diskettes, follow these steps:

1. Insert the 3.5-inch floppy disk labeled Setup Boot Disk in the disk drive and turn the computer on. Setup begins automatically.
2. Read each screen and follow the directions that appear near the bottom of the screen for continuing, getting help, or exiting the program.

Some of the screens Setup displays include a Welcome to Setup screen, autodetection for hardware, license agreement (you must agree to the licensing, else you cannot install the software), display options, hard disk examination, copy files, and so on. Many screens are self-explanatory—follow the directions on-screen. The following sections describe some of the choices you must make during the installation that may not be so obvious. If you have questions about the setup at any time, press F1 for help.

Configuring a Mass Storage Device

The NT Setup program automatically scans and detects such devices as CD-ROM drives and SCSI adapters and then lists them on a screen as mass storage devices.

Don't worry if you do not see your hard disks listed; NT doesn't include them. Also, NT detects all IDE and ESDI (Enhanced Small Device Interface) drives but doesn't list them either.

You can either accept the list, by pressing Enter to continue; or you can add other devices if you have a manufacturer's disk for the device. Press **S** for Specify to install a device not listed. Naturally, you can always install additional devices after setup is complete (Start, **S**ettings, Control Panel, choose the SCSI Adapters option).

Configuring Disk Partitions

NT Setup displays a list of existing partitions and any space available for creating new partitions. Each drive and its file system is displayed in this list. You can install NT to any permanent hard disk with enough disk space (123M); however, NT must have access to the root directory of drive C (Disk 0) to be able to boot when you start your computer.

You may want to partition the NT server's disk so you can copy NetWare volumes to corresponding volumes on the NT disk.

You can install NT to a FAT file system for use with MS-DOS or Windows 95 (dual boot) or you can install NT Server to an NTFS file system. In the real world, however, I see no reason to install a dual boot to your primary domain controller, but , you may want to install dual boot to a member server. For the server, I recommend using the NTFS file system. With NTFS, NT security features are available. You may also want to dedicate the entire domain controller to NTFS instead of splitting the machine for use with another operating system, for more efficient file, print, and network administration.

NTFS or FAT?

The NTFS file system completely supports NT security; you can assign users to groups that grant them specific rights and abilities on the network and permissions to use certain files and directories. The FAT system provides much less security through NT; for example, you cannot assign NT file permissions to files on an FAT system. An NTFS system also supports larger file sizes (up to 64G) than FAT (4G maximum), per-file compression, and event tracking you can use in case of power failure.

The FAT system allows file access when your computer is running another operating system, such as MS-DOS or OS/2. On the other hand, when the computer is running another operating system, it cannot recognize the NTFS files. Similarly, NTFS cannot share data with MS-DOS on the same partition but a FAT system can.

If you want to use both MS-DOS and NT, thus using the FAT file system, install MS-DOS to the computer first. Then you can choose that drive for installing the NT system files. The default option is to preserve the current file system and all existing files on the partition; so you can simply press Enter to continue.

If you want to use the entire partition for a FAT system and the disk has not been formatted, you can format it from Setup. If you want to use the NTFS file system, you can also format the drive to NTFS from Setup. Before you format a drive, you must delete the partition. Then you create a partition, specifying the size or accepting the default, and then choose to format the drive. When preparing to format, NT Setup asks which file system you prefer. Just follow the directions on the screen.

Directory Considerations

If you're installing NT to a newly formatted drive, you can accept the default directory or enter another directory in which to install the system files. However, if you are running Windows NT version 3.1, 3.5, or 3.51, Windows 95, or MS-DOS and Windows 3.x, NT Setup detects the operating system and displays the options. You can either let Setup migrate the registry settings from the current system or you can create a dual boot. A dual boot lets you choose the operating system you want to start when you turn on the computer. If you're running Windows 95, however, you must install Windows NT in a new directory; you cannot migrate the registry files.

Setup Type

After you choose from the previously described options, NT reboots your computer and then gathers information about your computer. This part of setup is completed through the use of a set of "wizard" dialog boxes; wizards describe the process, give you choices, and let you go forward and/or backward in the process. In any wizard dialog box, choose the **N**ext button to continue or the **B**ack button to go to the previous wizard dialog box and change or check your options.

When setup displays the Setup Options dialog box, you can choose from the following types of setup:

Typical. A standard installation that installs all of the optional Windows NT Server components and configures hardware automatically. This is the easiest installation, and recommended for those who are new to NT Server.

Compact. A condensed installation that does not install optional components. Not recommended for a primary or backup domain controller.

Custom. Gives you more control over the features and configuration of the server. Recommended for experienced users only.

Licensing

After you select the setup type, NT asks for your name, organization name, licensing mode, and computer name in a series of wizard dialog boxes. You must enter the information for NT Setup to continue.

The licensing mode may confuse you. NT Server is part of the larger Microsoft BackOffice family of products which include several server types: Exchange Server, SQL Server, SNA Server and so on. Each server on the network needs a license, and each client computer that accesses the server needs a Client Access License. You most likely have only NT Server in your network so you don't have to worry about the other servers. You can choose the server license according to the following guidelines.

If you have only one server, choose the Per Server option. If your server is a dedicated Remote Access server, choose the Per Server option. Choose or convert to Per Seat mode if you have multiple servers and a lot of simultaneous workstation connections to each server.

If you're in doubt, choose the Per Server option. If you see that network traffic increases, you add more servers; and as simultaneous client connections increase, you can legally switch—one time and one way only—from Per Server mode to Per Seat mode at no additional cost for licensing.

For more information about licensing, refer to your NT Server documentation.

Server Type

When installing the server, you must choose its type from these options:

Primary Domain Controller. Choose this option for the first server in the domain. The PDC contains all user and group accounts and authenticates users as they log on. A PDC can also be a file and application server and a print server as well, depending on system resources, of course. There is only one primary domain controller per domain.

Backup Domain Controller. The BDC automatically and periodically backs up the user and group account information from the primary domain controller. You can promote the BDC if something happens to the primary domain controller. There can be multiple BDCs in a domain.

Stand-Alone Server (Member server). This server can work as a workstation and/or a resource server, such as a file and/or print server. The member server doesn't contain a user database and therefore cannot authenticate users. There can be multiple member servers in a domain.

Installing Windows NT Server and Configuring the Network   **327**

After you select the server type, enter the password for the Administrator account. The Administrator account enables the user to manage the configuration of the server, clients, and the entire network.

Enter the domain name and continue Setup by clicking the Next button.

Note: If your Pentium-based computer contains the faulty programming for performing the floating-point division, NT detects it and a screen appears next that offers the choice of letting NT turn off your computer's floating-point mode and run NT's floating-point operations instead. Choosing this option may slow the system considerably.

Optional Components

The first optional component is the emergency repair disk. You should definitely create this disk. You can use the emergency repair disk for a variety of problems, including server crashes, lost setup configuration, expired password, restoring damaged files, and so on. By the way, you should keep your emergency repair disk under lock and key; it could be a security risk in the wrong hands.

The other components you can choose to install include Microsoft Exchange, multimedia, games, and so on. Depending on your use of the server, you can choose whether you want to install these components.

Networking Components

The network connections wizard dialog box enables you to choose the type of network connection you want for the server. Choose Remote Access to the Network only if you're setting up an RAS server to use with clients using a modem to connect (see Chapter 4 for more information). For any other network connection, choose the Wired to the Network option. Choose Next.

If you want your server to be connected to the Internet as a server, you can choose that option in the next wizard dialog box. Setup's default settings are suitable in most cases without modification; however, you can modify the settings at a later time after setup. Choose Next.

Setup next displays your network adapter card. You can accept this card, choose the Find Next button to have Setup search for other adapter cards in the server, or choose the Select From List button to select the card you want to install and use the manufacturer's disk to complete the configuration.

When NT displays the Adapter Card Setup dialog box, enter the correct IRQ number, I/O base port address, and any other settings NT requests to configure the adapter card. These settings must be correct for NT to connect to the network. You can, however, modify these settings after setup using the Network option in the Control Panel. Whether or not the settings are correct, NT displays a message telling you it cannot confirm the IRQ and port address. Choose OK to continue. You'll have to confirm the choices yourself by connecting to the network.

Setup's next wizard dialog box contains the protocol options you can choose. For more information about protocols, see Chapter 2. You can choose one, two, or all three protocols to install. Following is a list of the protocols:

TCP/IP. Use TCP/IP within your own NT network or if your server is connected to many, diverse operating systems (such as UNIX, Internet, and so on). See Appendix E for TCP/IP information.

NWLink IPX/SPX Compatible. Install this protocol for use with the NetWare network, Gateway Services, and migration. IPX/SPX Compatible Transport supports routing, NetWare-aware applications, and NetWare servers.

NetBEUI. You should use this protocol if your server will communicate with other Windows computers (Windows for Workgroups, NT 3.1 and later, or even LAN Manger 2.x), for smaller LANs, and if you install the Remote Access Service.

Choose Next to continue. If NT asks about Network Services, accept the defaults and choose Next to continue. After you complete setup, you can always add or remove protocols and/or services from the server (Control Panel, Network option).

As NT installs the network components you've selected, it may prompt you for options about the hardware or configurations. Accept the defaults if in doubt; or you can enter the settings, if you prefer.

In the wizard dialog box that asks you if you want to join a workgroup or domain, choose domain. See Chapters 2 and 3 for more information about domains.

The final steps of installation include choosing the time and configuring the display. Follow the directions on-screen to complete the installation. You'll be prompted to reboot the computer. When the computer restarts, it performs some final configuration that may take a few minutes.

Starting and Shutting Down NT Server

After you turn your server on, a boot loader menu appears. If you have a dual boot, you can use the arrow keys to choose the operating system you want to start and then press Enter. Notice NT has two choices, exactly the same except for the addition of [VGA mode] to the second choice. Use the first option to start NT.

You use [VGA mode] only when you've loaded a video driver that isn't working. Choosing the [VGA mode] option from the boot loader menu starts NT with a standard, default video driver so you can see the screen and options. Open the Control Panel (Start, **S**ettings, Control Panel) and double-click the Display option to change the video driver.

A logon message appears next. Press Ctrl+Alt+Del to log on to the server. The login dialog box appears; enter the Administrator's password and press Enter. I recommend you immediately create a User account for yourself with Administrative rights and save the Administrator user for emergencies. See Chapter 3 for information about creating users.

If you want to shut down the server, follow these steps:

1. Choose Start, Sh**u**t Down. The Shut Down Windows dialog box appears.
2. Choose from one of the following options:

    Shut Down the Computer. Prepares the computer for shutdown by saving settings and data to the hard disk.

    Restart the Computer. Saves any settings to disk and restarts the computer.

    Close All Programs and Log on as a Different User. Closes all programs and disconnects the computer from the network. You can then log on as another user.

3. Choose **Y**es to shut down the computer; choose **N**o to cancel the shutdown and return to the desktop.
4. It takes a few minutes for NT to prepare the computer to shut down. Do not turn the computer off until NT displays a message saying it is safe to turn off your computer; else you might lose some data or configuration files.

Configuring Network Components after Setup

Although you set up your network components during installation, you may find you need to modify settings, add an adapter or protocol, or otherwise change options after installation. This section gives you a brief overview of the Network dialog box.

To open the Network dialog box, choose the Start button, **S**ettings, **C**ontrol Panel. In the Control Panel, double-click the Network icon. The Network dialog box appears. The following sections describe each tab in the Network dialog box.

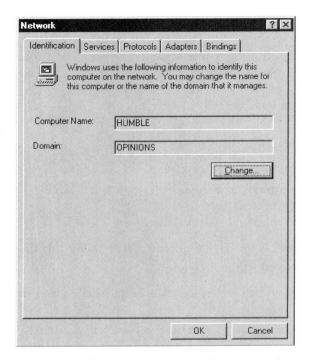

Figure A.1 *The Identification tab distinguishes the server on the network.*

Identification

The server must have a name to identify it on the network. You can change that name in the Identification tab (see Figure A.1). You also can change the name of the domain; however, changing the domain name affects all other computers on the network. If you chose a workgroup instead of domain during installation, you can change to domain using the **C**hange button, as well.

To change the computer or domain name, or to change from a workgroup to a domain, choose the **C**hange button. Enter the new name and choose OK to return to the Network dialog box. You can either choose OK to close the Network dialog box or choose another tab to configure. When you do close the dialog box, NT may prompt you to restart the computer to allow the configuration changes to take place.

Services

Use the Services tab to view the list of network services installed to the computer and to add or remove services. Network services support specific operations on the net-

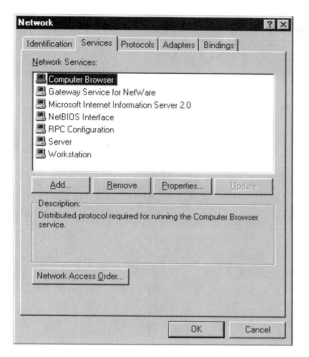

Figure A.2 *Add or remove network services that enable network procedures to take place.*

work, such as sharing files and printers, automatic backup, the Gateway Service for NetWare, and so on. Figure A.2 displays the Services tab in the Network dialog box.

To add a service, choose the **A**dd button. NT displays a list of available services; select one and choose OK. You may need either a manufacturer's disk or the NT Server CD to complete the installation of the service.

To remove a service, select the service in the list and choose the **R**emove button. Be careful when removing services; you may stop the entire system.

To view the properties of any service, select the service and choose the **P**roperties button. Some services do not display a properties dialog box. The properties enable you to configure the service, such as setting ports, addresses, and so on.

You can either choose OK to close the Network dialog box or choose another tab to configure. When you do close the dialog box, NT may prompt you to restart the computer to allow the configuration changes to take place.

Protocols

The Protocols tab (see Figure A.3) enables you to add, remove, and configure protocols. To add a protocol, choose the **A**dd button. NT displays a list of available

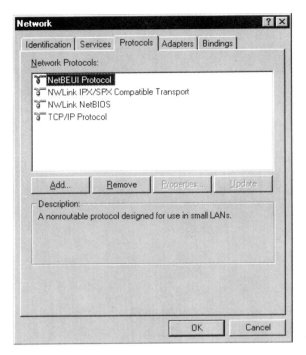

Figure A.3 *Add and configure protocols for the server.*

protocols (you also can add a protocol for which you have a manufacturer's disk). Select the protocol and choose OK.

To configure a protocol, select the protocol from the list and choose the **P**roperties button. Figure A.4 shows the NWLink IPX/SPX Properties dialog box in which you configure frame type for each adapter you have in the server.

You can either choose OK to close the Network dialog box or choose another tab to configure. When you do close the dialog box, NT may prompt you to restart the computer to allow the configuration changes to take place.

Adapters

You probably configured your network card adapter during the initial installation of NT; however, you can always add or remove an adapter, or change configuration settings in the Adapters tab of the Network dialog box (see Figure A.5).

Add or remove adapters by clicking the appropriate button in the Adapters tab. NT includes many drivers for various manufacturers and models of adapter cards; you can, alternatively, provide a manufacturer's disk to install the adapter's driver. Set IRQ and I/O port addresses for an adapter by selecting it in the Adapters list

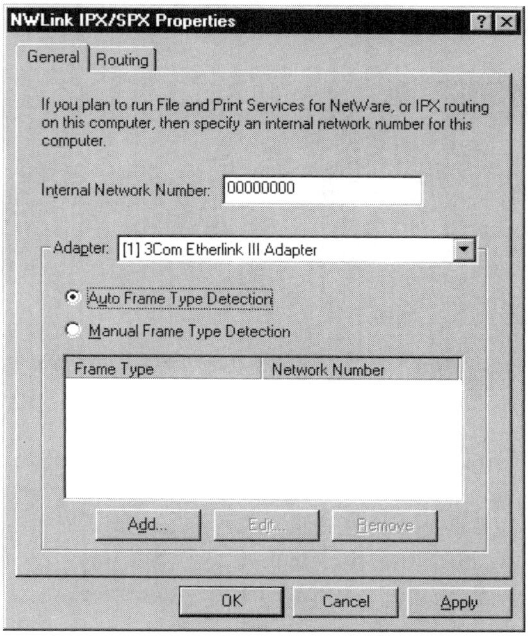

Figure A.4 Each protocol includes applicable properties you can modify.

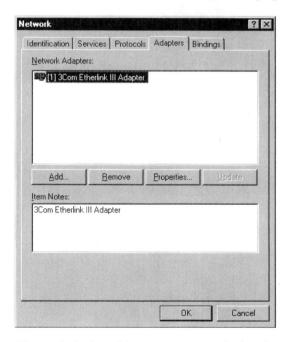

Figure A.5 An NT server can use multiple adapter cards that you can configure in the Adapters tab.

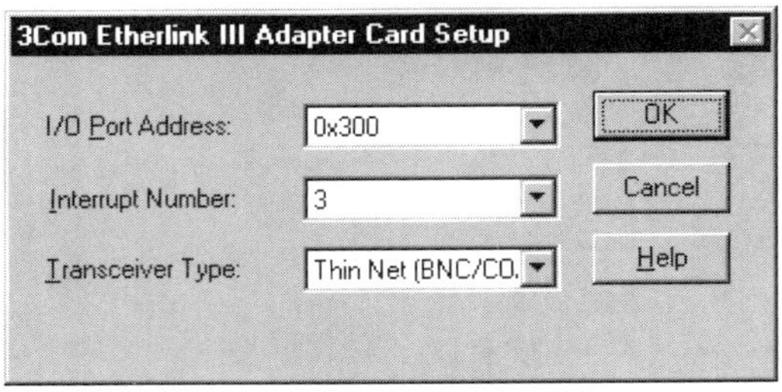

Figure A.6 Configure the adapter's properties from the Network dialog box.

and then choosing the **P**roperties button. Figure A.6 shows the Setup dialog box for a 3Com Etherlink III adapter.

You can either choose OK to close the Network dialog box or choose another tab to configure. When you do close the dialog box, NT may prompt you to restart the computer to allow the configuration changes to take place.

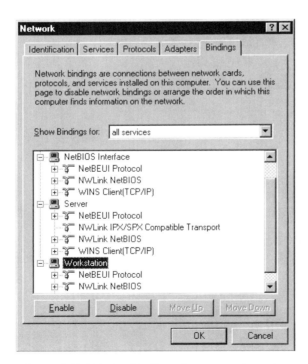

Figure A.7 Display bindings for a protocol, service, or card.

Bindings

The Bindings tab shows a list of network services, protocols, and adapter cards, and the bindings that connect them. To view the bindings for any object in the list, double-click the object and then click any plus signs preceding the object in the list (see Figure A.7).

You can also choose to enable or disable a binding by selecting it and choosing the appropriate button; however, do not change the bindings unless you understand the affects of your actions. You could disable users' access to the server.

You can either choose OK to close the Network dialog box or choose another tab to configure. When you do close the dialog box, NT may prompt you to restart the computer to allow the configuration changes to take place.

TIP: If you install a service from the Network dialog box and the service doesn't start, double-click the Services option in the Control Panel and see if the service is listed in the Services dialog box. If it is, make sure that its Status is Started and its Startup is Automatic. You can change any of the Status or Startup options by selecting the service and then choosing the **S**tart button and/or the Sta**r**tup button.

B NetWare to NT Server Terms

The following table translates some NetWare terms and concepts to NT terminology. Some translations may not be an exact interpretation; refer to the chapter referenced for exact interpretation. Or you can look up most of the following terms in the Glossary, Appendix C.

NetWare	NT	Chap. Ref.
Access Control directory rights	Change Permissions (P)	7
Access Control file rights	Change Permissions (P)	7
Account Disabled user restriction user restriction	Account Disabled	7
Admin (4.x)	Administrator	2, 3, 7
Allow User to Change Password	User Cannot Change Password	7
Archive Needed attribute	Archive	7
ATTACH	Attach As	2
Attributes	Permissions	2, 4, 7
Bindery (3.1x)	Directory Database	2
Days between Forced Changes user restriction	Maximum Password Age	7
Directory	Folder, Directory	3, 4, 7
Erase (E) directory rights	Read, Write, Execute, Delete (RWXD) permissions	7

(continues)

NETWARE	NT	CHAP. REF.
Erase (E) file rights	Read, Write, Execute, Delete (RWXD) permissions	7
Expiration Date user restriction	Expiration Date	7
Force Periodic Password Changes user restriction	Password Never Expires	7
Group accounts	Group accounts	2, 3
Hidden (H) attribute	Hidden (H)	7
Intruder Detection/Lockout user restriction	Account Lockout	7
IPX protocol	IPX/SPX-compatible protocol	2, Appendix A
LOGIN	Attach As	2
Login	Logon	2
Login Scripts	Logon Scripts/User Profiles	2, 13
MAP	Map Network Drive	2
Minimum Password Length user restriction	Minimum Password Length	7
Modify (M) directory rights	Read, Write, Execute, Delete (RWXD) permissions	7
Modify (M) file rights	Read, Write, Execute, Delete (RWXD) permissions	7
NDS (4.x)	Directory Database	2
NETADMIN (4.x)	User Manager for Domains	2, 3
NWADMIN (4.x)	User Manager for Domains	2, 3
NetWare Shell	Network Neighborhood	2
NetWare User Tools (4.x)	Network Neighborhood	2
NCP (NetWare Core Protocol)	SMB (Server Message Block)	6
Print Queue	Print Queue	2, 5
Print Server	Print Server	2, 5
Print Server Operator	Print Operator	7
PCONSOLE	Add a Printer	2, 5
QUEUE	Printers folder	2, 5

NetWare	NT	Chap. Ref.
Read (R) directory rights	Read, Execute (RX) permissions	7
Read (R) file rights	Read, Execute (RX) permissions	7
Read Only (Ro) attribute	Read Only (R)	7
Read Write (Rw) attribute	Files without the R attribute	7
Require Password user restriction	Permit Blank Password	7
Require Unique Passwords user restriction	Password Uniqueness	7
Rights	Rights	2, 4, 7
Server	Server (primary domain controller)	2, 6, 15
Supervisor (3.1x)	Administrator	2, 3, 7
Supervisory (S) directory rights	Full Control (All) permissions	7
Supervisory (S) file rights	Full Control (All) permissions	7
System (SY) attribute	System (S)	7
SYSCON	User Manager for Domains	2, 3
Time Restrictions user restriction	Logon Hours	7
User account	User account	2, 3
User Account Manager	Account Operator	7
Workgroup Manager	Account Operator	7
Write (W) directory rights	Read, Write, Execute, Delete (RWXD) permissions	7
Write (W) file rights	Read, Write, Execute, Delete (RWXD) permissions	7

C Glossary

In the glossary, terms commonly used by their abbreviations are listed with their spelled out names in parentheses; however, when terms also have commonly used abbreviations, those abbreviations are placed in parentheses after the term.

Abilities In NT, built-in devices or rights, that enable users to perform tasks.

Access permission In NT, in regards to a directory, file, or printer, regulates which users have access to the resource.

Account For administrative, security, and communication purposes, as well as for use of on-line services, a user account identifies a subscriber by name, password, server or domain, and information about the groups to which the user belongs.

Account policy A plan that controls the use of passwords, including the minimum password length, how often users can reuse old passwords, and so on. In NT, you set account policy for all user accounts in a domain.

Account Operators group In NT, this group has the abilities to manage and create accounts for users and groups via the User Manager for Domains. An Account Operator cannot, however, modify the Administrators, Servers, Account Operators, Print Operators, or Backup Operators local groups or any local groups that are members of these local groups.

Account policy A set of rules that defines whether a new user is permitted to access a system and its resources; in NT, also defines the way passwords are used in a domain or on an individual computer.

Add In NT, in directory permission that enables the user to add files to the directory; users cannot read or change the contents of current files.

Administrative alerts In NT, alerts that warn about security, access, user session, and power loss problems on the server. Alerts can be sent to any computer the administrator deems necessary.

Administrator The person responsible for setting up and managing the network.

Administrators group In NT, a group whose members have full control access of the network to its members, by default. Administrators can access workstations, files, and folders; manage and control users and groups; choose which resources to share, such as printers, CD-ROM drives, and so on. The Administrator has all rights and abilities on the NT Server and Workstation.

API (Application Programming Interface) A set of routines used by a program to request and carry out lower-level maintenance services.

ARP (Address Resolution Protocol) ARP enables a host to find the physical address of a node on the same network when it only knows the target's logical address. Part of TCP/IP.

Attach To access a server from a workstation; often to access additional servers after logging in to one server. Also, a NetWare 3.x workstation utility used to attach to an additional server after login.

Attributes Characteristics of a directory or file dictating what can and cannot be done with a file, such as read-only, write, and so on.

Auditing Tracking certain network events—such as security breaches, application errors, or system problems. Results are stored in a security log file, which can be viewed only by users with special rights and/or permissions. In NT, audit logs are viewed in the Event Viewer.

Audit policy In NT, this policy defines the type of security events that will be logged.

Authentication The process of validating a user's login information by comparing the user name and password to a list of authorized users of the network.

Backup Domain Controller (BDC) In NT, the backup domain controller contains a copy of the database and periodically and automatically updates it with the Primary Domain Controller (PDC).

Backup Operators In NT, this group has the control over the server t to perform backup and restores.

Bindery In NetWare 3.1x, the database maintained by the operating system that contains information about users, servers, and other configuration details. In NetWare 4.x, the bindery is replaced by NetWare Directory Services (NDS).

Bindery context In NetWare 4.x, a container object in which a server's bindery services is enabled.

Bindery context path In NetWare, a path statement that allows bindery context to be set in as many as 16 containers. Use the SET parameter to set bindery contexts; separate multiple contexts by semicolons. For example:

Glossary

```
SET BINDERY CONTEXT = OU=HUMBLE.O=OAKHILL;OU=
ADMINISTRATION.O=OAKHILL
```

Bindery emulation   A NetWare 4.x feature that provides backward compatibility with NetWare systems still using the bindery.

Boot loader   In NT, the boot loader defines the location of the operating system files plus other information needed to start the system. The boot loader is automatic.

Boot partition   The boot partition is the volume on which the NT operating system and support files are located; it may or may not be the same as the system partition, and may be formatted FAT or NTFS.

Browse   In NT, to view available network resources via folders, files, user accounts, groups, domains, or computers. Browsing enables the user to see what resources are available to him or her. Use Network Neighborhood or the Explorer to browse the network.

Built-in groups   In NT, the default groups provided with the software. Each group defines a collection of rights and abilities for members that provide access to commonly used network resources.

Campus Network   A network that connects local area networks (LANs). Even though a campus network may extend several miles, they do not include wide area network (WAN) services.

Change   A file or directory permission in NT that enables the user to read and add files, and change contents of current files.

Change Permissions   Standard NT permission that permits changes to the file's or directory's permissions.

Client Service for NetWare   Client software included with NT, with which you can enable workstations to directly connect to file and printer resources at a NetWare server running NetWare 2.x or later.

Container object   An NDS object that can hold, or contain, other objects, such as an Organizational Unit.

Context   The position of an object in the Directory tree (NetWare 4.x).

Creator Owner   In NT, for permissions sake, the creator of a file or directory is a member of this group.

Ctrl-Alt-Del   A three-key combination used on most IBM-compatible computers to restart or reboot the machine; however, with NT, this combination is used to display the logon dialog box.

Daemon   A networking program that runs in the background, unattended, and collects information or performs operating system administration tasks.

Dedicated Server A computer on the network that functions solely as a server by performing such tasks as storing files, printing, and managing users.

Default Gateway In TCP/IP, the intermediate network device on the local network that governs the IDs of other networks.

Default user profile Each user who logs on a computer running NT Workstation, NT Server, or Windows 95, is assigned a default user profile that defines the working environment, such as items on the desktop, colors, and other settings. As the user customizes his or her working environment, the default user profile changes to a profile specifically descriptive of the user.

Delete Standard NT permission that enables deletion of a directory or file.

Device fonts Fonts that reside in the print device or a font cartridge.

DHCP (Dynamic Host Configuration Protocol) DHCP offers automatic configuration of IP addresses and related information to clients attaching to the DHCP server.

Dial-Up Networking The client version of Windows NT RAS (Remote Access Service).

Directory In a hierarchical file system, a method of organizing and grouping files and directories on a disk. In NT, directories are also called folders; subdirectories are also called subfolders.

Directory Database A system used to track and maintain user accounts.

Directory Replication In NT, copying a master set of directories and files to another computer and maintaining the two sets so they are identical, thus alleviating bottlenecks of network traffic.

Directory Services A listing of all users and resources on the network. In NetWare, called NDS (NetWare Directory Services); in NT, called Directory Services.

DLL (Dynamic Link Library) A library feature in Windows that allows executable routines to be stored separately as files with DLL extensions. These DLL files load only when they're needed by a specific program.

DNS (Domain Name System) An e-mail addressing service that registers and queries domain names on an internetwork, such as the Internet.

DNS Name Server Contains information about a portion of the DNS database that makes computer names available across the Internet.

Domain A single computer, entire department, complete site, and so on, used for naming, grouping, and management purposes, in NT.

Domain Admins In NT, a member of the Administrators local group; the built-in Administrator user account is a member of the Domain Admins global group. An Administrator can administer the domain, the primary and backup domain controllers, and all other computers running both NT Server and Workstation in the domain.

Domain Guests group In NT, a group that contains the domain's built-in Guest user account; the rights are limited.

Domain Users In NT, a member of the Users local group for the domain and of the Users local group for every NT Workstation and member server on the network. Domain Users have normal user access.

Downloadable soft fonts Fonts installed to the computer for use with applications; when you're ready to print, the fonts are downloaded to the printer before the document can actually be printed.

Drive Mapping In NetWare or NT, assigning a drive letter to represent a complete directory path statement.

DHCP (Dynamic Host Configuration Protocol) A protocol that enables automatic configuration of TCP/IP on computers running Windows NT from a host computer.

Enterprise Describes an entire business group, organization, or corporation and all local, remote, and satellite offices associated with the group.

Enterprise server In NT, a server to which multiple primary domain controllers in a large organization will replicate.

Error.log A log that records the transfer of user and group accounts and files and directories during a migration or trial migration, in NT.

Everyone group In NT, anyone using the computer is a member of this group.

Event A significant occurrence in NT, in the system, or in an application that requires users to be notified or an entry to be added to a log. In NT, the Event Viewer enables you to review system security and application events.

Execute Standard NT permission that allows display of attributes, permissions, and owner, changing to subdirectories, and running program files.

Export server In NT, the server from which a master set of directories is exported for replication.

Fault tolerance A method of ensuring continued system operation in the event of individual failures. Backups, UPS (Uninterrupted Power Supply), disk duplexing, disk mirroring, and so on are methods of providing fault tolerance.

File Allocation Table (FAT) An operating system table that lists all disk space available on the disk in blocks. The table lists the location of each block, whether it's being used or available for use, disk damage, and so on. NetWare needs at least a portion of the disk formatted to FAT as a boot sector; NT can run on a FAT system or an NTFS file system.

File Server On a network, the computer used to store files for access by other computers.

File and Print Services for NetWare (FPNW) A separate Microsoft product that enables an NT Server computer to provide file and print services directly to NetWare client computers; using FPNW, no changes or additions to the NetWare client software are necessary.

FTP (File Transmission Protocol) One of the TCP/IP protocols used to log in to a network, list files, and transfer files. FTP supports many file types and formats, including ASCII and binary files.

Full Control Permission granted to read and change files, add files, change permissions for the directory and its contents, and take ownership of the directory and its files, as well as to print, manage print jobs in the queue, and to manage the printer in NT.

Gateway A shared communication between two networks, often between a LAN and a larger system.

Gateway Service for NetWare Included with NT, a redirector of sorts that enables a computer running NT Server to connect to NetWare servers.

Global group In NT, a group that can be used in its own domain, member servers, and workstations of the domain, and in trusting domains. A global group can be a member of a local group; but it can only contain user accounts from its own domain.

Group In NT, an account containing other accounts called members; permissions and rights are granted to a group and therefore are granted to its members.

Guest In NT Workstation and NT Server computers, a built-in account used for logons by people who don't have a user account on the computer or domain.

HCL (Hardware Compatibility List) Included with NT, a list of devices supported by NT. Download updated version from the Microsoft Web Page (microsoft.com) on the Internet.

Home directory A directory accessible to the user that contains files and programs; may be shared by multiple users.

ICMP (Internet Control Message Protocol) ICMP provides the functions used for network-layer management and control. Part of TCP/IP.

Import computer In NT, during directory replication, the servers or workstations that receive the copies of the master set of directories from the export server.

Interactive In NT, anyone using the computer locally is a member of this group.

IP (Internet Protocol) IP regulates packet forwarding by tracking Internet addresses, routing outgoing messages, and recognizing incoming messages. Part of TCP/IP.

IP address A number that identifies the node on a network and its routing information; the number is made up of the network ID and the host ID, and is represented in dotted-decimal notation, such as 124.31.2.22.

IPX (Internet Packet Exchange) Part of NetWare's protocol stack used to transfer data between the server and workstations on the network. *See* SPX (Sequenced Packet Exchange).

IPX/SPX compatible In NT, a protocol compatible with NetWare's IPX/SPX for communications between NT computers and NetWare servers.

IRQ (Interrupt Request Lines) Lines over which devices can send signals to get the attention of the processor when the device is ready to accept or send information; each device in the computer uses a different IRQ.

LHOSTS A text file that maps IP addresses to NetBIOS computer names.

List A directory permission that enables the user to list subdirectories and files in the directory and change to a subdirectory; the user cannot access new files created in the directory.

Local Group In NT, a group granted rights to just the resources on the servers of its own domain.

Login/Logon In NetWare, login, and in NT, logon. Lets a user establish a connection to the computer system by entering a user name and password.

Login scripts Files containing commands that set up users' workstation environments whenever they log in. You can use login scripts (in both NT and in NetWare) to map drives, display messages, set environment variables, and execute programs and menus.

LPD (Line Printer Daemon) In TCP/IP printing, a service that enables the print server to receive documents from line printer remote (LPR) utilities running on client systems.

Manage Documents In NT, permission granted to open the print queue and rearrange printing order, delete or pause printing, and otherwise manage the printing of the documents in the queue.

Mandatory user profile In NT, an environment profile that's downloaded each time the user logs on to a workstation; the administrator assigns a mandatory user profile to create consistent or job-specific user profiles and these profiles cannot be changed by the user.

Map *See* Drive Mapping.

Mapping file In NT, a file in which you specify the user and group account information that will transfer during the migration, including old user and group names, new user and group names, and individual passwords for users.

Master domain The domain that contains all user and group accounts; generally, in NT, resource domains control files and printers and master domains simply authenticate users.

Member servers Servers running NT Server software that do not contain the database of users, and can be used as workstations, file servers, print servers, and so on. A member server can be used as a workstation, file server, and/or print server.

Migration A movement of one operating system to another, including user and group information, resources, rights, files, directories, and so on.

Migration Tool for NetWare In NT, a tool that enables you to transfer user and group accounts, volumes, directories, and files from a NetWare server to a computer running NT Server.

Multiple master domain model An organizational method in which you use two or more single master domains to serve as user and group account domains. The trust relationships in a multiple master domain model differ from the single master domain model in that every master domain is connected to every other master domain in a two-way trust relationship; used in NT.

Named pipe An interprocess communication mechanism that enables one process to communicate with another local or remote process.

NCP (NetWare Core Protocol) In NetWare, this is the core protocol.

NetBEUI (NetBIOS Extended User Interface) A network device driver used in LAN Manager, Windows for Workgroups, Windows 95, and Windows NT to communicate with the network interface card. Usually used in small LANs of fewer than 200 clients.

NetBIOS (Network Basic Input/Output System) A protocol that manages data exchange and network access.

Network In NT, all users connected over the network are members of this group.

NDS (NetWare Directory Services) A NetWare 4.x database that maintains information and provides access to every resource on the network, including users, groups, printers, volumes, and servers.

NLM (NetWare Loadable Module) In NetWare, a program you load and unload from the server memory while the server is running. NLMs can control disk drivers, LAN drivers, management utilities and server applications modules, and name space support.

No Access   User or group does not have permission to access a file, directory, or printer; used in NT.

NTFS (New Technology File System)   In NT, the native file system that supports long file names, permissions for sharing files, a transaction log, and the FAT file system.

NetWare Link IPX/SPX Compatible Transport (NWLink)   The NWLink protocol ships with NT and is compatible with NetWare's IPX/SPX stack. NWLink supports the sockets application program interface (API).

One-way trust   In NT, a relationship between domains where one domain trusts the other domain's primary domain controller to authenticate user accounts.

Organization object   In NetWare, a container object for organizing objects in the Directory, a level below the Country object and a level above the Organizational Unit object.

Organizational Unit object   In NetWare, a container object that helps you organize objects in the Directory, a level below the Organization object.

Paging file   In NT, a file on the computer's hard disk that acts as a swap file. With NT's virtual memory, some of the program code is kept in RAM while other information is temporarily swapped into virtual memory to supply the RAM with an extra boost (also pagefile.sys).

Permission   In NT, authorizations given to certain user accounts to access files and directories.

PPP (Point-to-Point Protocol)   A protocol that provides router-to-router and host-to-network connections. Part of TCP/IP suite.

Primary Domain Controller (PDC)   A domain's master security database (which approves or rejects requests for resources on the network) is located on the primary domain controller. Also, any and all changes made to user accounts for the domain are made to the PDC, and there is only one PDC per domain.

Print   Permission granted to output to the printer in NT.

Printer   The interface between the operating system and the print device.

Print Device   The actual printer.

Printing pool   A pool consists of multiple, identical print devices associated with one printer.

Print Operators In NT, this group can log on to the server and shut down the system. A Print Operator is only given the ability to create, edit, delete, and manage printer shares.

Print Queue A list of documents in line to be printed on any network printer. In NetWare, you create a print queue with NETADMIN or PCONSOLE; in NT, you create a queue by first assigning a printer to represent the print device.

Print Server A server designated to handle all printing for the users of a network by collecting print jobs and routing them to one or more print devices attached to the print server.

Print Spooler In NT, a collection of DLLs that receive, process, schedule, and distribute documents for printing.

Protocol A set of rules for sending information over a network. NT ships with NetBEUI/NetBIOS, IPX/SPX-compatible, and TCP/IP protocols.

RAID (Redundant Array of Inexpensive Disks) A method used to standardize fault-tolerant disk systems using six levels to gauge performance, reliability, and cost; NT includes three RAID levels: 0, 1, and 5.

Read A file or directory permission that enables the user to read file contents and run applications in the directory.

Read Standard NT permission that allows display of a directory or file's contents, attributes, owner, and so on.

Redirector The redirector intercepts application requests for file- and printer-sharing services and sends them to the file server for action.

Registry Used in NT, a database of information about the computer's configuration, organized in hierarchical structure; changes you make in the Control Panel, for example, are recorded in the Registry as well as many other system configurations.

Remote administration In NT, administering one computer from another across the network; for example, when replicating directories, the administrator can set services and accounts on a remote computer that will receive the replicated directories and files while he or she is working on the server.

Replication *See* Directory replication.

Replicator group In NT, this group does not have actual users as members; instead, the only member of the Replicator group is an account used to log on to the Replicator services of the primary domain controller and the backup domain controllers of the domain.

Resource Any part of a network that can be shared with the members of the network, including files, applications, directories, CD-ROM drives, printers, modems, and so on.

Resource domains Part of a master domain model, the resource domains share their resources—such as printers and file servers—with the users and groups in the master domain. All resources are located in other domains. The resource domains establish a one-way trust with the master domain which enables the users access to the resources.

Rights Privileges granted to a user or group by the network administrator. Rights determine the operations a user can perform on the system.

Roaming user profiles In NT, a profile created by the administrator for a user, stored both on the local computer and the server; the server copy enables the user to log on to any workstation in the domain and see the working environment he or she is used to seeing.

RPC (Remote Procedure Call) A set of procedures that describe how an applications initiates a process on another network node. Additionally, RPC defines how an applications retrieves the appropriate result. Part of TCP/IP.

SCSI (Small Computer Systems Interface) An industry standard containing guidelines for connecting peripheral devices (hard drives and tape drives, for example) and their controllers to a microprocessor. SCSI interface defines both hardware and software standards for communication between a host computer and a peripheral device.

Screen fonts Those fonts you see on-screen; screen fonts are installed to the computer for use with applications and are not necessarily sent to the printer.

Security ID (SID) Used in NT, a unique name that identifies a logged-on user to the security system. SIDs can identify an individual user or a group of users.

Security log In NT, the security log records and tracks changes to the security system. You view the security log in the Event Viewer.

Security policy In NT, a security policy consists of the Account, User Rights, Audit, and Trust Relationships policies managed in the User Manager for Domains.

Server Operator group In NT, this group grants its members the rights and abilities needed to administer the primary and backup domain controllers: logging on locally to the server, shutting down the system, backing up and restoring files, locking and unlocking the server, sharing resources, and so on.

Server service In NT, a service (Services option, Control Panel) that provides remote procedure call support, and file, print, and named pipe sharing.

Service In NT, a process that performs a specific system function and often provides an application programming interface for other processes to call, such as the UPS service, Replication service, Alerter service.

Share name In NT, refers to the name used by the clients to access a shared resource on a server.

Sharing In NT, a method of designating a resource—such as a directory or printer—as available for network users to access.

Single domain Used in NT, a single domain model includes only one PDC, but may consist of a BDC, a member server, and multiple workstations.

Single master domain model Used in NT, this model consists of a master domain and one or more resource domains. The master domain contains all user and group accounts, and the resource domains share their resources—such as printers and file servers—with the users and groups in the master domain. All users log on to the master domain. All resources are located in other domains. The resource domains establish a one-way trust with the master domain, which enables the users access to the resources;.

SLIP (Serial Line Internet Protocol) A protocol that runs IP over serial, or telephone, lines using a modem. Slowly being replaced by PPP; a part of the TCP/IP suite.

SMB (Server Message Block) In Windows NT, the core protocol is the server message block protocol.

SNMP (Simple Network Management Protocol) A standard protocol used to manage and monitor nodes on a network. SNMP provides a method for setting and monitoring configuration information, adds increased security, and enables the transfer of large amounts of data at the same time. Part of TCP/IP.

Sockets Windows sockets is an interface that communicates between programs and the transport protocol, and works as a bidirectional pipe for incoming and outgoing data.

SPX (Sequenced Packet Exchange) A set of NetWare protocols implemented on top of IPX to form a transport layer interface. *See* IPX and IPX/SPX compatible.

Subdirectory A directory within another directory; also a subfolder in NT.

Subnet A part of a network that shares the network address with other parts of the network; the subnet is distinguished by a subnet number.

Subnet mask A 32-bit value that enables the recipient of IP packets to distinguish the network ID from the host ID in the IP address.

Subtree In NT directory replication, the export subdirectory and all of its subdirectories.

Swap file *See* Paging file; used in NT.

Synchronize In NT, to replicate the domain database from the primary domain controller to the backup domain controller of the domain; usually automatic, but can be invoked manually.

System log In NT, a log that contains all events tracked by the NT components, such as drivers or hardware components. You can view the system log in the Event Viewer.

Take Ownership Standard NT permission that allows changes to directory's or file's ownership.

TAPI (Telephony Application Program Interface) In NT, TAPI is used by programs to make data/fax/voice calls.

TCP/IP (Transmission Control Protocol/Internet Protocol) A set of communications protocols that encompass media access, packet transport, session communications, file transfer, electronic mail, and terminal emulation.

TCP/UDP (Transmission Control Protocol/User Datagram Protocol) TCP is a transport-level protocol, which is connection-oriented. UDP is also transport-level but connectionless, so it is bundled with TCP and often used with SNMP applications. Part of TCP/IP.

Telnet One of TCP/IP's protocols, a terminal emulation protocol that provides remote terminal-connection services.

TrueType fonts TrueType fonts ship with most Windows versions, including NT. They are device-independent, meaning the font you see on the screen can be duplicated in any print device. Additionally, TrueType fonts are stored as an outline, so they can be scaled and rotated.

Trust relationship In NT, an established link between domains that enables pass-through authentication, thus enabling users of one domain to access other domains.

Two-way trust relationship In NT, each domain trusts user accounts in the other domain to use its resources.

UNIX A 32-bit, multiuser, multitasking operating system that uses the TCP/IP set of protocols.

UPS Service In NT, a service that manages an uninterruptible power source connected to the computer; the UPS service is found in the Control Panel.

User Account A security measure used to control access to a network by identifying users by a name and password.

Users group In NT, this group has no rights on the server and no abilities either, unless you assign them.

User profile In NT, configuration information that is saved in an individual's profile to define such environmental settings as desktop arrangement, personal program groups, screen colors, screen savers, network connections, printer connections, and so on.

Virtual memory In NT, the space on your hard disk that NT uses as if it were actual memory, enabling you to run more applications at one time than your system's physical memory would allow. *See* Paging file.

Volume In NetWare, the highest level of the file server directory and file structure. In NT, a partition or collection of partitions formatted for use by the system.

WINS (Windows Internet Name Service) a utility for dynamically registering and querying NetBIOS computer names on an internetwork.

Workgroup In NT and other Windows versions, a group of users who work together and share files and databases over a LAN.

Workstation service In NT, a service (Services option, Control Panel) that enables network connections and communication.

Write Standard NT permission that permits creation of subdirectories and files, changes to file's data and attributes, display of permissions and owner.

D Common Problems and Solutions

An ounce of prevention is worth a pound of cure. You may be able to save your server from disaster by performing a few preventative measures as outlined in this introduction.

First, you can create an emergency repair disk, if you did not create one during installation of NT. The emergency repair disk contains all of the initial setup information of your system, and can help you in case of a server crash and several other problems. To create an emergency repair disk that also backs up accounts and file security, type **rdisk /s** at the command prompt (Start, **P**rograms, MS-DOS Command Prompt).

You can also use the Setup Boot Disk, the same one you used during installation, to boot NT if it's not cooperating.

As a precaution, you can save your configuration *before* you run into a problem. To do so, open the Disk Administrator (Start, **P**rograms, Administrative Tools, Disk Administrator) and choose Partition, Configuration, Save. Insert a disk to save the configuration to and choose OK. Follow directions and then choose OK when you're done. Keep the disk in a safe place in case you need to restore the configuration at some point.

In addition, create a recovery disk in case of a boot failure, as described later in the section, "Server Crashes and Boot Failure."

One of the handiest NT features is the Event Viewer. If you have any problems—security, application, printing, and so on—first view the logs in the Event Viewer (Start, **P**rograms, Administrative Tools, Event Viewer). These logs may contain important information you can use to help you solve your problem. Chapter 3 covers opening and viewing logs in the Event Viewer.

You can use the **chkdsk** command on both NTFS and FAT file systems; check disk corrects the errors if you use the **/f** switch. Run **chkdsk** from a command prompt window (Start, **P**rograms, MS-DOS command prompt). You also can run **chkdsk** from the Tools menu in the Disk Administrator or from the Properties/Tools menu in the NT Explorer.

Windows NT also includes Dr. Watson, a utility from previous Windows versions that detects, diagnoses, and logs application errors. To start Dr. Watson, type **start drwtsn32** at a command prompt.

And as always, creating backups of the server and important files and applications is a must for any network. If you have a backup domain controller on the network, then all the better for you; the backup domain controller stores copies of all user and group profiles, permissions, rights, and so on, but does not store files, directories, applications, and so on. You create a backup of an NT system as you would create a backup to a NetWare system. Choose your favorite software and tape drive, optical drive, or other storage device, and make a backup now and often in preparation for a certain disaster.

Finally, as a global reminder, make sure that in NT you're logged on as a member of the Administrators group (or other group with appropriate rights) before you panic about being denied access to a tool, program, or utility on the server or on a workstation.

Installation Problems

While installing NT, Setup reboots the computer several times. Often it takes a while to start the system again; be patient. If it seems like the system gets stuck somewhere and you don't think it will continue after it reboots itself, turn the computer off, wait 10 seconds, and then turn the computer back on. Setup should continue from where it left off. If it does not, insert the first Setup disk—the boot disk—and start the computer again. Setup may need to start over completely or it may pick up where you left off.

Floppy Disk Problems

If you have a 2.88M 3.5-inch floppy drive and use a 2.88M formatted disk for creation of the emergency repair disk during installation, you may have problems creating the disk. Use a disk formatted to 1.44M instead and the disk should work fine.

CD-ROM Recognition

If you have trouble with NT recognizing the CD-ROM device after using the third Setup floppy disk, check the Hardware Compatibility List to see if the device is listed as compatible. If your CD-ROM is not listed, you may want to install NT Server from the network instead of from CD. To do this, copy the CD to a directory on the network, access the network from the server to which you'll install NT, and enter the **winnt** command at the DOS prompt or in the Run dialog box. See Appendix A for information about installing NT.

Partitioning the Drive

When choosing to format or partition your drive before installation of NT, be careful if your hard disk contains stripe sets, volume sets, or mirrors. NT's Setup screen displays these elements as Windows NT Fault Tolerance. If you delete any of these elements, or if you delete a partition, you'll lose the data in that area.

Disk Compression

If you're having trouble installing NT, make sure the drive to which you are installing is not compressed with any compression utility other than an NTFS compression. NT cannot install to the drive if that's the case.

Server Crashes and Boot Failure

If your server crashes or refuses to boot because of something you've done to your system configuration, such as changing a video card, you can try several things to get the configuration back before you try reinstalling NT. Reinstalling almost always works; however, you may have to reconfigure users, groups, print servers, and other important settings that make the process time-consuming.

Try the following solutions when you have a server configuration problem before reinstalling:

- As your computer boots, it displays the message "Press spacebar now to Evoke the Last Known Good Configuration." Press the spacebar and choose to start the computer using the configuration that was used the last time you successfully booted the machine. From the list of choices, choose Switch to the Last Known Good Configuration. If you shut down normally after this, the configuration is saved.

- Use the emergency repair disk you created during installation. Place the disk in the floppy drive and reboot the computer and follow the directions on-screen. The repair disk has information based on your initial setup; now users, permissions, or other changes you've made to the system will be applied.

- If you changed video drivers and have a hard time seeing the screen and choices because of it, restart the system. When the computer displays the options for starting NT Server, choose the option NT Server 4.0 (VGA drivers). The system will boot with generic video drivers; go to the Control Panel and double-click the Display icon and then choose the appropriate driver.
- You can use the repair process in the Windows NT Setup program if you think the problem is corrupted files. Insert the original Setup boot disk in the floppy drive and the NT CD in the CD drive and start the computer. When the text-based screen appears asking if you want to reinstall NT Server or repair files, choose to repair files. You'll likely need the Emergency Repair Disk for this process, but you can do without it; just follow directions on-screen.

Memory Dump

You may come across a memory dump before your server crashes. A memory dump occurs when you get a fatal system error or stop error, and you'll know it because the screen turns blue. NT performs a dump of system memory to a file you can view to try to diagnose the problem. When the memory dump is complete, NT restarts the server so that downtime is less than with previous versions. NT writes the memory dump to the file MEMORY.DMP, by default, and each time an error occurs, it overwrites the file. If you want to save the file, for future reference or to show tech support personnel, then save the file under a new name after the incident. You can control how Windows NT reacts to a STOP error in the System option in the Control Panel.

Boot Failure

If the server refuses to start because the boot partition of a disk fails, there's little you can do unless you've created a recovery disk in advance. To create a recovery disk, format a floppy disk using the NT operating system; then copy the following files to the disk from the root directory of the system partition:

NTLDR

NTDETECT.COM

NTBOOTDD.SYS (only if the boot partition is on a SCSI disk and BIOS is not enabled on the controller)

BOOT.INI (with an alternated path pointing to the mirrored copy of the system partition, using ARC naming conventions)

BOOTSECT.DOS (for dual or multiple boot computers)

The ARC (Advanced RISC Computing) name is located in BOOT.INI and describes the path to the boot partition. The ARC is listed in both the [boot loader] section and the [operating systems] of the file. An example would be:

```
scsi(0)disk(2)rdisk(0)partition(1)\winnt40="Windows NT Server"
```

The name construction is as follows:

```
component(a)disk(b)rdisk(c)partition(d)
```

component identifies the hardware adapter for the device; this field could be **scsi** or **multi**. Multi indicates a disk interface other than SCSI or a SCSI interface for which the BIOS is enabled on the disk controller.

(a) indicates the ordinal number of the adapter, or its loading priority.

disk represents the hard disk on the system.

(b) for **scsi** only; the bus number for multiple-bus SCSI adapters; for multi, always 0.

rdisk is the utility to create the emergency repair disk.

(c) for **scsi** always; but for multi, the ordinal for the disk on the adapter.

partition is the partition used on the disk.

(d) is the partition ordinal; all partitions receive a number, beginning with 1, except for type 5 and type 0 partitions.

Edit BOOT.INI using the Notepad accessory (Start, **P**rograms, Accessories, NotePad). You will need to change the read-only, hidden, and system attributes of BOOT.INI first using the **attrib** command at a command prompt.

Client Software Problems

Generally, if you have trouble connecting a client to the server, check the I/O settings and the IRQ of the adapter card first. Following are a few more complicated problems you may encounter. Update the recovery disk every time your partitions change.

MS-DOS Client

One likely problem you may find when installing the MS-DOS client to a workstation that also has Windows on it is that the DOS client removes Windows from the path line in the AUTOEXEC.BAT; therefore, when the user types **win** at the C-prompt, nothing happens. After installing the client, check the path for the Windows directory and add it if necessary.

If the client has an 8088 processor, you must use the basic redirector instead of the full redirector when installing the client. And note that Setup may be extremely slow on older computers; the Setup program may pause for as long as five minutes before continuing. Don't restart the computer during this time; be patient.

The Client Setup program requires 429K of conventional memory to run; so if you're having trouble starting the Setup program, close any open programs before trying to start Setup.

If the COMMAND.COM is not in the root directory of the client computer, the Network Client won't start. You can place a SHELL command in the CONFIG.SYS to specify the location of the COMMAND.COM, and this will take care of the problem.

You may notice that the NWLink protocol used with the Microsoft Network Client only supports IPX; SPX isn't supported. This should cause you no problems, however.

Windows for Workgroups

If you have trouble installing the TCP/IP WFW client and you have an IBM or EtherLink III card, you need to obtain updated drivers to use with the client. On CompuServe, go to the Microsoft Software Library and search for the keyword WG0990 to download documentation and the updated EtherLink III software; WG0988 for the updated IBM TokenRing driver and documentation.

If you have trouble running Microsoft's TCP/IP-32 protocol—such as setup errors for creating the protocol.ini, or errors locating the win.ini—make sure you remove any other TCP/IP protocol from the WFW workstation first.

You will not be able to browse the network if you log on to a Windows for Workgroups computer whose workgroup name is the same as the name of the network domain. If the user name and password aren't valid for the domain, you can't log on to the domain; however, you can log on using a valid user name and password.

If a user is having trouble with a Windows for Workgroups password, you can delete the passwords list on the client computer (PWL file in the Windows directory) and a new list will be created the next time the user logs on.

Problems with Users and Groups

The primary problem you'll find with users and groups occurs when someone thinks he or she has rights to perform certain tasks that he or she does not. Confirming group membership and understanding the rights and abilities assigned to

Common Problems and Solutions **361**

each group will help you if you have any problems in this area. See Chapter 3, "Working with Users and Groups," for information about editing, adding, and managing users and groups. See Chapter 4, "Managing Security Policies," for help with assigning rights and permissions to users and groups. Following are a few common problems you may encounter.

Re-creating a User Account

User and group accounts each have a unique SID (Security Identifier) number assigned to them. Internal processes in NT user the account's SID instead of a group or user name. If you change your mind after deleting a user or group, you must re-create the account from scratch, assigning rights, adding groups, and so on. Just re-creating a group or user name doesn't retrieve the SID and the properties attached to that SID.

Unavailable Features in the User Manager for Domains

If your computer communicates across a connection with low transmission rates—such as a Remote Access Service connection or overseas connection—you can reduce delays in the display of accounts, groups, and so on in the User Manager for Domains by choosing Low Speed Connection in the Options menu. If you use the Low Speed Connection option, however, you'll find that some features are not available to you, including the Refresh command, Select Users command, the ability to create new or modify global groups, and so on. Change the Low Speed Connection to make these features available again.

Deleting a Group

You cannot recover a group once you've deleted it; the SID (Security Identifier) for the group is deleted as are the resource permissions associated with the group. To re-create the group, you must start from scratch. You cannot, however, delete the users in a group simply by deleting the group.

Home Directories

When assigning home directories to a user's profile (User Manager for Domains, User dialog box, Profiles button) remember you cannot use a file or directory name longer than the 8.3 DOS convention unless you're using the NTFS file system. FAT file systems restrict the file and directory names. You also cannot use the wildcard %USERNAME% when creating a home directory.

User Profiles

If you cannot see the User Profiles folder or file in the Windows 95 Explorer, make sure you've enabled user profiles first. Open the Control Panel, Passwords option, and select the User Profiles tab. Check the appropriate options and choose OK; you must restart the computer to create the user profile folder.

When copying user profiles in Windows NT, you cannot copy the NTuser.dat file using the Explorer, My Computer window, or any other tool except the System option from the Control Panel, User Profiles tab.

If you assign a roaming user profile path to a group, the profiles will keep changing unless you make the user profiles mandatory, because each time a group member logs off, his or her profile overwrites the user profile on the server.

Sharing Resources, Rights, and Permissions

If you have problems with rights and permissions, check the group memberships first. See Chapter 4 for information about rights, abilities, and permissions. Following are a few other problems you might run across.

Sharing Problems

If you choose to stop sharing a directory while users are connected to that directory, the users can lose their data. Make sure everyone is disconnected from the directory before stopping sharing.

Default Permissions

If you revoke default permissions for any directories created by NT Server and/or NT Workstation, you could create problems for the operating system. If this happens, you can try to reset the permissions, using the NT documentation as a guide to the defaults; if all else fails, you'll have to reinstall the software.

Do not open or change permissions on the SYSTEM\REPL\IMPORT directory; even opening the permissions could change or damage settings in this replication directory.

Printing Problems

Before listing specific printing problems, I'll offer a list of questions you can ask yourself in an effort to find a solution. And refer to Chapter 5, "Managing Print Services," which explains creating and configuring printers and print devices.

Is the correct printer port specified?

Is the correct printer driver installed? If the answer is yes, try deleting and re-installing the printer driver in case the file is corrupted in some way.

Have you tried printing to another printer? Perhaps the application is at fault. Can you print to the printer from another application?

Is the printer cable bad? Try using another cable.

Will the printer output when attached to another port?

Parallel Port Problems

Even though most personal computers support three parallel ports, they usually have only one installed. If you have trouble locating or connecting to LPT2 or LPT3, check installed ports first. Additionally, when configuring parallel ports, you might have to set hardware jumpers or switches or change settings in the computer's BIOS setup program. Refer to the device's documentation for instructions.

Serial Port Problems

Serial ports can be set for flow control through the Ports icon in the Control Panel. Default settings are typically 9600 baud, no parity, 8 bits, 1 stop bit, and hardware handshaking. If you change these settings and have trouble, change back to the default settings or check your print device's documentation to confirm these settings.

Unsupported Printer

If NT doesn't list a printer driver for your specific print device and you don't have a disk containing the driver, you can often use a different supported driver instead. When using an HPPCL (LaserJet)-compatible laser printer, for example, try a Hewlett-Packard LaserJet Plus driver. For a PostScript compatible printer, try the Apple LaserWriter Plus driver.

If you're using a 9-pin dot-matrix printer that's IBM-compatible, try an IBM Proprinter driver; if the printer is Epson-compatible, try the Epson FX-80 (for narrow) or FX-100 (for wide) carriage. For a 24-pin dot matrix printer, you can try the IBM Proprinter X24 for an IBM-compatible and the Epson LQ-1500 for an Epson LQ-compatible.

If you have another type printer, call the manufacturer or refer to the printer's documentation for emulation types.

Printing from DOS-Based Applications

If you're printing from a DOS-based application through the command prompt window on an NT computer and going to an NT print server, you'll have trouble if you don't first issue the NET USE command. At the command prompt (Start, MS-DOS Command Prompt), type NET USE /? to get help entering the switches and parameters that suit your situation.

Gateway Services

If you're having trouble getting the Gateway Service to start, first check your configuration of the network card. Configure the network card in the Control Panel, Network option. Following are some additional problems and solutions.

Access Denied

If you are denied access to a Windows NT Server computer while you're trying to configure it as a file or print gateway, you may not be using a NetWare user account that is a member of the NTGATEWAY group or that group may not have appropriate rights. Create the group. Using SYSCON, NETADMIN, or NWADMIN from a NetWare-attached workstation, create a user on the NetWare server that matches the user that will log on from the NT computer. Set the password for the user. Next, create a NetWare group called NTGATEWAY and place the newly created user in that group. See Chapter 9, "Using the Gateway Service for NetWare," for more information.

Gateway Service Unavailable

If the Gateway Service is unavailable in the Network dialog box, Services tab, you may not have removed the NetWare redirectors first. To remove existing NetWare redirectors, open the Network icon in the Control Panel and choose the Network Settings dialog box, Services tab; select the existing redirector—such as NetWare Services for NT from Novell—and choose the Remove button. Confirm the choice and choose OK to close the dialog box. You'll have to reboot your computer.

Service Startup Problems

If the Gateway service doesn't start, or starts and then abruptly stops, first check your adapter card configuration (Control Panel, Network option). Next, check the

Common Problems and Solutions **365**

Event Viewer. If you cannot find a problem, delete the Gateway Service from the Services tab of the Network dialog box and then reinstall it. The service may have been installed or configured incorrectly.

Can't See NetWare Server

If the frame type is incorrectly listed, you won't be able to see the NetWare server. Change the frame type in the Network dialog box (Control Panel).

If you're unsure of the frame type, open the NetWare server's AUTOEXEC.NCF file and read the network adapter's load line. Multiple frame types may be configured.

File Attribute Problems

It's important to understand that, when using the Gateway Service for NetWare, some NetWare file attributes are not supported, specifically Read Write, Shareable, Transactional, Purge, Read Audit, Write Audit, and Copy Inhibit. Only the Read Only, Archive, System, and Hidden file attributes are preserved.

Migration Problems

Most of the migration problems you may encounter are addressed in Chapter 6, "Preparing for the Migration," and Chapter 11, "Running a Migration." If you plan ahead and then perform a trial migration, you should be able to work out all of the kinks before performing the final migration. This section presents just a few problems that are not addressed in the text elsewhere.

Migration Tool Won't Start

To run the Migration Tool, the Windows NT server computer must be running the NWLink IPX/SPX Compatible Transport (Control Panel, Network option, Protocols tab). Additionally, you must have installed the Gateway Service for NetWare prior to running the Migration Tool.

Can't Select NetWare Server

If you cannot see a NetWare server when selecting servers for migration, you may not be logged on to the NetWare server as a Supervisor.

Can't Select NT Server

If you have trouble selecting the NT Server in the Migration tool window or you cannot transfer data to the NT server, check to make sure you're logged on as a member of the Administrators group.

Application Problems

Windows NT can run MS-DOS, Windows 3.x, Windows NT and Windows 95, 16-bit OS/2, and POSIX applications. Applications not designed specifically for Windows NT or Windows 95, however, need a device driver designed to run with NT. If you have applications that do not supply an NT-compatible driver, contact the manufacturer of the application to see if there is an updated driver for that program. NT prevents the application from running properly without a compatible driver. Applications supporting fax cards, scanner cards, and disk maintenance software fall into this category as well as applications that rely on their own graphics device drivers or disk device drivers.

Windows 3.x Application Problems

If you're running several Windows 3.x applications at one time and in the same memory space, one application crashing can result in all Windows 3.x applications locking up. You can avoid this problem by running a Windows 3.x-based application in its own memory space.

Running several Windows 3.x-based programs each in its own memory space will use more NT memory and may slow the system.

Windows for Workgroups Password Problem

If you have a password problem when logging on to a Workgroups client, you can delete the PWL file with your user name (found in the Windows directory) to get rid of your password list. The next time you log on, you enter a password, thus starting a new list.

Memory Allocation Error When Using the MAP Utility

If you receive a memory allocation error when using the NetWare MAP utility from an NT Command Prompt window, you can alleviate the problem by entering the following line in the CONFIG.NT: shell=%systemroot%\system32\command.com /e:4096. What you're doing is forcing the COMMAND.COM to be the command interpreter for the window for as long as it remains open and it allocates 4096 bytes to 16-bit programs you run in the window.

NetWare-Aware Application Problems

Many 16-bit Windows applications require NWIPXSPX.DLL to run. If an application cannot find the file, verify the file is on your system and then check the path to the file so the application can find it. If you cannot find the file, you can obtain one from Novell (check out its Web site on the Internet: http://www.novell.com). Place the file in the \systemroot\SYSTEM32 directory. If you modify your Windows NT Server by modifying the path or adding the file, you must log off and then log back on before the changes take effect.

AUTOEXEC.BAT and CONFIG.SYS

People often ask where are the AUTOEXEC.BAT and the CONFIG.SYS files in the Windows NT system. Briefly, here's what happens to them. NT uses the AUTOEXEC.BAT to define path and environment variables at system startup. You set environment variables in the Control Panel, System option, Environment tab. NT ignores the CONFIG.SYS.

NT uses the AUTOEXEC.NT and CONFIG.NT files to configure environment for applications. Each MS-DOS application you start in a Command Prompt window reads these two files and performs any commands in them. You can edit either of these files as you would the AUTOEXEC.BAT and the CONFIG.SYS. The files are located in the \SYSTEM32 directory.

When modifying the CONFIG.NT file, you can use several NT commands (see the On-line Command Reference in Help for more information), including COUNTRY, DEVICE, DOS, DOSONLY, ECHOCONFIG, FILES, INSTALL, LOADHIGH, and so on. If you use any commands that NT doesn't recognize, NT ignores them. To modify the AUTOEXEC.NT, you can use similar commands. Again, see the On-line Command Reference in NT for more information.

If you receive an error message concerning either the AUTOEXEC.NT or the CONFIG.NT, check the files to see if they are correct. If there is a problem with the file, or if one or both of the files have disappeared from the \SYSTEMROOT\SYSTEM32 directory, you can copy the original files from the Emergency Repair Disk to the hard drive SYSTEM32 directory.

PIFs

You can modify the PIF (program information file) file for MS-DOS applications by right-clicking the file in the Explorer (Start, **P**rograms, Windows NT Explorer) and choose the Properties command. Changing the properties creates and modifies the PIF file. If you have problems locating a PIF file for any MS-DOS application, you can use the NT-supplied PIF for most DOS-based applications. NT's PIF is named _DEFAULT.PIF and is located in the %*SystemRoot*% folder.

TSRs

NT supports TSRs (Terminate-and-Stay-Resident) programs; however, do not place TSRs in your AUTOEXEC.NT or CONFIG.NT files. Since the AUTOEXEC.NT and the CONFIG.NT files run each time you open a Command Prompt window, the TSR would also start each time you open a new window, thus you would have several copies of the TSR running at one time, and that would tax your system memory. To run a TSR, use the Run command (Start, **R**un).

Replication Problems

Some replication problems appear in the Manage Imported Directories dialog box after replication. The Status column in the dialog box may indicate the following problems:

No Master indicates that the subdirectory isn't receiving updates; the export server might not be running, or a lock might be in effect.

No Sync indicates that the updates are not up-to-date. There could be open files on the export server or the import computer; the import computer might not have access permissions; or the export server might not be performing properly.

No entry in the Status column means no replication has taken place for that specific subdirectory. Replication might not be configured correctly in the export server, the import computer, or both.

You can also view replication errors in the Event Viewer, as described in these next sections:

Access Denied

If this error appears in the Event Viewer for the Directory Replicator service, the service may not be configured to log on to the account created specifically for the service. Check the following things: in the User Manager for Domains, make sure the account has membership in the domain's Backup Operators group and that the password is typed correctly; in the Server Manager's Service dialog box, enter the password again to make sure it is entered properly and check the account the service will log on as.

Additionally, make sure the import computer has permission to read the files on the export server and that you've assigned a logon account to the Directory Replicator service on the import computer.

Exporting and Importing to All Computers

If you want to export from specific computers and import to specific computers, but the service is replicating to all computer on the domain, you must specify which computer you want to use in the replication process in the Directory Replication dialog box, To List and From List.

Lost Permissions

If you lost permissions for the import directory, you'll have to set up the import computer again in the Server Manager. Viewing and changing permissions in the Explorer for the SYSTEM32\REPL\IMPORT directory can make you lose permissions on the directory.

Domain Problems

If your network is set up as a single domain, the only problems you're likely to encounter concern organization and management. If you find you're adding multiple users and computers, and you need more and more member servers to handle printing and/or file services, you might consider dividing your network into multiple domains.

Multiple Domain Sharing

If you're having trouble seeing a printer or other resource from a trusting domain, make sure permissions are set in the domain, verify you're logged on as a member of a group that can access the resource, and, finally, check connections through the Server Manager to confirm that trust relationships are set appropriately.

Generally, when access is denied to a user or group within the domain, it has to do with logon status. The Administrator always has the right to change users, groups, resources, and so on.

Access Is Denied

If you try to access a domain in the User Manager for Domains or in the Server Manager, and NT displays a message stating that access is denied, then you possibly set your trust relationships in the wrong order. Make sure you set the trusting domain first on one domain and then on the other domain. Next, set the trusted domain, first on one domain and then on the other.

TCP/IP Configuration

To configure TCP/IP, you must be logged on as a member of the Administrators group for the server.

Be extremely careful that you use no duplicate addresses for IP addresses; duplicate addresses can cause some network computers to fail and/or disrupt network operations. Here are some other possible problems with TCP/IP configuration and use.

Client Problems with IP Addresses and Related Data

If a client has connection problems using the TCP/IP protocol, check the settings for the IP address, gateway router, and the subnet mask. If the client should be using the DHCP automatic configurations, any values entered in the Specify an IP Address area of the IP Address tab (Microsoft TCP/IP Properties dialog box) automatically override DHCP automatic settings. Make sure the user has not changed the settings in this dialog box.

DHCP Functionality

If your DHCP doesn't work—you can't open the DHCP Manager or some options are not available, for example—make sure the DHCP services are enabled. In the Control Panel, open the Services option by double-clicking it. Find the Microsoft DHCP Server and make sure it is set to automatically start. You can also stop or pause the DHCP Server in this dialog box.

WINS Problems

If you're having problems with your WINS services, check for these problems:

If the server has more than one adapter card, make sure that the binding order of the IP addresses lists the WINS server first.

Make sure the WINS server is not a DHCP client.

Make sure the computer running the WINS server is not assigned a fixed IP address.

Workstation Disk Space Problems

If a user is running out of hard disk space on his or her workstation, check the Recycle Bin. Often users delete folders and files but forget or are unaware that deleting an item sends it to the Recycle Bin, where it remains on the disk until you empty the bin.

Another space consideration for workstations is to reduce the amount of space the Recycle Bin uses. Right-click the Recycle Bin and choose **P**roperties. Move the **M**aximum Size of Recycle Bin slider to the left to reduce the percent of the space allotted for each drive.

You can search for and delete temporary files on a workstation that's running out of disk space. Search the drive for folders named Temp or Tmp and delete all temporary files. You can use the Start, **F**ind, **F**iles or Folders command for this purpose or the Explorer.

Another idea for workstations is to compress the volume, if it's formatted as NTFS. To compress a volume, select the volume in the Explorer and choose **F**ile, **P**roperties, and choose the Compress check box and OK. In the message dialog box that appears, choose to compress subfolders and choose OK again.

Finally, you can defragment the workstation disk to get a bit more disk space. In the Explorer, choose the drive and then choose **F**ile, **P**roperties, and choose the Tools tab. Choose Defragment Now and follow the instructions on the screen. If the button is not available, you'll have to add the tool from the NT CD-ROM.

The Registry

The NT Registry is a database of configuration information that replaces previous Windows versions INI, SYS, and COM files. You can change the Registry's contents using the REGEDT32 command in the Run window (Start, **R**un); but be very, very careful. One wrong move, however minor, can cause the entire system to shut down, and the only way out most likely will be to reinstall NT. The Registry does not consist of one file but of many files, located in many different folders; so backing up the Registry as you might have backed up INI files is not nearly as easy. For information about backing up the Registry, see the Windows NT Workstation Resource Kit.

If I've scared you away from the Registry, good. If not, be prepared for heartaches and headaches. I suggest leaving the Registry alone until you're absolutely positive you understand the inner workings of NT and the Registry.

E TCP/IP Issues

TCP/IP (Transmission Control Protocol/Internet Protocol) is a set, or suite, of communications protocols that include media access, packet transport, session communications, file transfer, electronic mail, and terminal emulation. TCP/IP is supported by numerous hardware and software vendors and is available on various types of computers.

You can use Microsoft TCP/IP with NT Server to perform several different tasks: communicate over the network to other servers and clients, print to UNIX printers, communicate over the Internet, and so on. This appendix presents an overview of TCP/IP and related services for Windows NT.

Note: If you'd like to learn more about TCP/IP, read Stephen A. Thomas' *Ipng and the TCP/IP Protocols* published by John Wiley & Sons. You may also want to view Thomas' book, *Building Your Intranet with Windows NT*, also published by John Wiley & Sons, for information about installing, configuring, and operating an Intranet based on Windows NT.

TCP/IP Structure

Microsoft's TCP/IP provides many of the TCP/IP protocols and services, including Transmission Control Protocol (TCP), Internet Protocol (IP), User Datagram Protocol (UDP), and so on. It also provides support for Point-to-Point Protocol (PPP) and Serial Line IP (SLIP) for access by modem to TCP/IP networks, such as the Internet. Microsoft's TCP/IP also includes basic utilities—such as finger, ftp, telnet, tftp, and so on—that enable users to connect and use resources of other

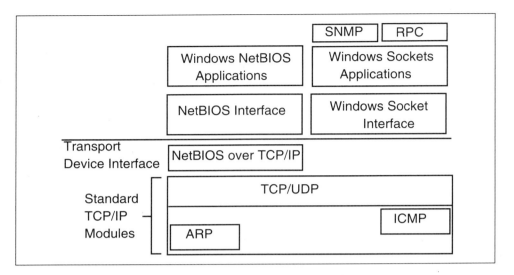

Figure E.1 *NT uses TCP/IP to enhance its networking abilities.*

hosts, such as UNIX. Figure E.1 illustrates the Microsoft TCP/IP structure as it is incorporated into the Windows NT architecture.

Additionally, Microsoft's TCP/IP supports tools and utilities for setting up Internet and intranet Web sites, including the following:

- DHCP (Dynamic Host Configuration Protocol) to automatically configure TCP/IP on clients and servers
- WINS (Windows Internet Name Service) for dynamically registering and querying computer names on an internetwork
- DNS (Domain Name System), a communications protocol for registering and querying DNS domain names on an internetwork
- TCP/IP printing for accessing printers on computers running UNIX

Microsoft's TCP/IP for NT doesn't include a complete suite of TCP/IP utilities or server services; however, many third-party vendors produce such applications and utilities that are compatible with Microsoft TCP/IP, such as HTTP, WAIS, NFS, and so on.

TIP: For more detailed information, refer to the Microsoft Windows NT Resource Kit Networking Guide.

Common TCP/IP Protocols

TCP/IP is a suite of protocols that work together to connect computers and enable communication between them. The most common of the protocols in the TCP/IP suite are TCP, UDP, IP, ARP, and ICMP. This section briefly explains those common protocols.

TCP (Transmission Control Protocol) is the part of TCP/IP that guarantees the delivery of packets and the accuracy of the data. TCP secures proper sequencing of the data, which also requires additional network traffic.

UDP (User Datagram Protocol) works hand in hand with TCP to exchange data without any guarantees of delivery or correct sequencing. UDP doesn't require the additional network traffic or time that TCP does so it can be more efficient, even if it is less secure; therefore, UDP depends on TCP and other higher-level protocols to provide consistency and accuracy.

IP (Internet Protocol), like UDP, transfers data without a guarantee, and relies on higher-level protocols for the data's sequencing. Its purpose is it's quick and inexpensive (in system resources).

ARP (Address Resolution Protocol) is a maintenance protocol that requests an IP address from the network, and then sends the reply packet containing the address and stores the address in the ARP cache for subsequent use.

ICMP (Internet Control Message Protocol) is a maintenance protocol that enables two systems to share status and error data; ICMP works with the IP network. The ping utility, which checks an IP system to see if the network is functional, uses the ICMP echo request and reply packets.

TCP/IP Utilities

You can use Microsoft's TCP/IP within an enterprise network, incorporating many clients and networks to provide connectivity and server support. Among the Microsoft networks, TCP/IP is compatible with Windows NT Workstation and Server, Windows 95, Windows for Workgroups, and Microsoft LAN Manager. Various utilities are supported for each network type, as described in Table E.1; see Appendix C for definitions of the following utilities.

Using TCP/IP, Windows NT also can communicate with many non-Microsoft systems, including Internet hosts, Macintosh systems, IBM mainframes, UNIX systems, and others.

Table E.1 TCP/IP Connectivity

Operating System	Supported Utilities
Windows NT Workstation	WAN, TCP/IP printing, FTP, Telnet, DHCP, WINS, DNS client software, Windows Sockets, and extended LMHOSTS file
Windows NT Server	WAN, TCP/IP printing, FTP, Telnet, DHCP and DHCP Server, WINS and WINS Server, DNS client software, Windows Sockets, extended LMHOSTS file, and Internet Information Server
Windows 95	WAN, DHCP, WINS, DNS client software, extended LMHOSTS file, and Windows Sockets
Windows for Workgroups using TCP/IP-32	Windows NT, LAN Manager, DHCP, WINS

Installing and Configuring TCP/IP

To use TCP/IP for the Internet, communicating with other operating systems, or for network communications, you must configure an IP address, a subnet mask, and a default gateway. You can manually configure the addresses.

Each device attached to a TCP/IP network has a unique IP address; one IP address is assigned to each network adapter in the computer. An IP address is represented in dotted-decimal notation, for example: 122.59.2.25. The IP address contains a network ID and a host ID; each is a unique address that identifies which packets the computer receives.

Subnet masks distinguish the network ID and the host ID portions of the IP address. A subnet mask is created by assigning 1s to network ID bits and 0s to host ID bits, which are then converted to dotted-decimal notation. A subnet mask might look like this: 255.255.255.0. All computers on a logical network must use the same subnet mask and network ID.

IP routing connects the devices from one network to another and enables the IP packets to transfer. Generally, a default gateway router, a computer connected to the local subnet and to other networks, is used for IP routing. The default gateway is also written in dotted-decimal notation: 198.33.34.1, for example.

TCP/IP Issues

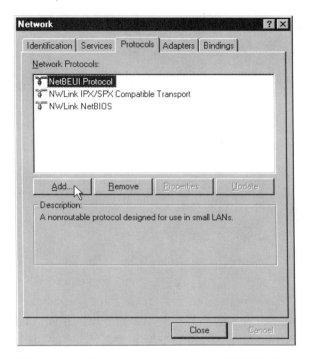

Figure E.2 *Use the protocols tab to add TCP/IP.*

Adding TCP/IP

You can install TCP/IP protocol in NT during installation or after setup is complete. See Appendix A for information about installing NT. To add TCP/IP, follow these steps:

1. Choose Start, **S**ettings, **C**ontrol Panel.
2. In the Control Panel, double-click the Network icon. The Network dialog box appears.
3. Choose the Protocols tab (see Figure E.2).
4. To add TCP/IP protocol, choose the **A**dd button. The Select Network Protocol dialog box appears (see Figure E.3).
5. Choose the TCP/IP Protocol in the list of **N**etwork Protocols and choose OK. NT may prompt you for the Windows NT CD-ROM so it can copy files. When copying is complete, NT returns to the Network dialog box.

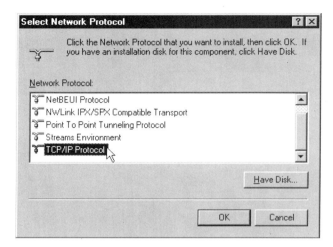

Figure E.3 *Add the TCP/IP protocol to the list of Network Protocols.*

Configuring TCP/IP

To configure TCP/IP, you'll need to know the IP address, subnet mask, and the default gateway of your network. To configure the protocol, follow these steps:

1. In the Network dialog box, Protocols tab, select the protocol in the **Ne**twork Protocols list and choose the **P**roperties button. The Microsoft TCP/IP Properties dialog box appears.
2. In the IP Address tab (see Figure E.4), select the adapter you're configuring with TCP/IP.
3. In the **S**pecify an IP address area of the tab, enter the **IP** Address, S**u**bnet Mask, and the Default **G**ateway.
4. You can choose the A**d**vanced button to configure additional gateways, addresses, and subnets, and other settings as described in Table E.2. Figure E.5 shows the Advanced IP Addressing dialog box.
5. Choose OK to close the Microsoft TCP/IP Properties dialog box, and OK again to close the Network dialog box. You'll be prompted to restart the computer for the configuration changes to take place.

DHCP Configuration

A DHCP server provides automatic TCP/IP configuration, prevents address conflicts, and makes centralized management of address allocation easier for the ad-

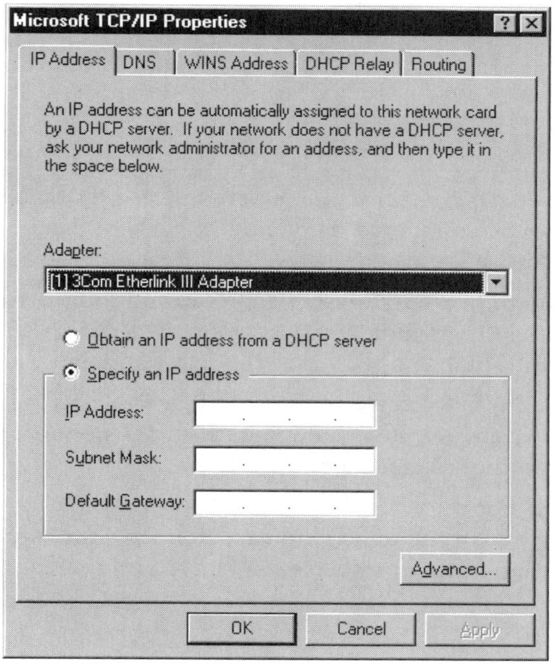

Figure E.4 Use the IP Address tab to enter the data needed to configure TCP/IP.

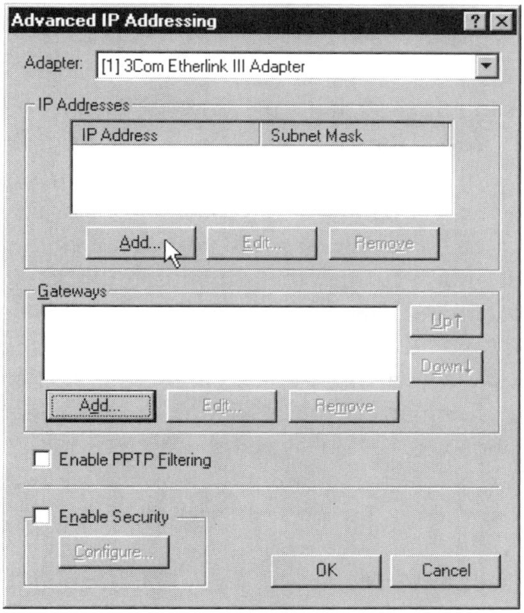

Figure E.5 Configure advanced options for the IP addressing.

Table E.2 Advanced IP Addressing Options

Option	Description
Ada**p**ter	A server can contain multiple network adapter cards and each one can be configured differently; select the adapter card you want to configure.
IP Ad**dr**esses Area	**A**dd up to five additional IP addresses and subnet masks for any selected adapter; **E**dit any selected item in the IP Address or Subnet Mask list; or **R**emove the selected item.
Gateways area	**A**dd up to five gateway routers; **E**dit any selected gateway; or **R**e**m**ove any selected gateway in the list. Choose **U**p or **D**own to move the selected gateway in the list.
Enable PPTP **F**iltering	Enables Point-to-Point Tunneling Protocol filtering so users can access corporate networks securely over the Internet (when enabled, no other protocols can be used on the selected adapter, only PPTP).
E**n**able Security	TCP/IP security lets you control network traffic, typically for Internet servers.
Configure	Use to add, remove, and permit TCP ports, UDP ports, and IP protocols.

ministrator of the intranet. You can configure a Windows NT Server 4.0 to act as a DHCP server. As a DHCP server, the computer would automatically configure client computers using the TCP/IP protocol. By choosing to enable the DHCP server, you enable the server to configure the protocol automatically. The server "leases" the configuration to each client for a specified amount of time and automatically updates any address or data changes the administrator makes to the protocol. (You must manually configure a server for DHCP; you cannot use DHCP configuration when installing as a DHCP server.)

To add the DHCP service to your NT Server, choose the **A**dd button in the Services tab of the Network dialog box. In the Network Services list, choose Microsoft DHCP Server and choose OK. You'll need the Windows NT CD-ROM; or you can enter a path to the NT files, if they're stored on the network. Next, install TCP/IP manually as described in the previous section. When you restart the computer, the DHCP data will be ready to use.

You use the DHCP Manager (Start, **P**rograms, Administrative Tools) to add the DHCP server to the DHCP scope, to define properties of the scope, and to configure DHCP option types and values of the lease duration. Configure DHCP in the DHCP Relay tab of the Microsoft TCP/IP Properties dialog box. For more information about setting up a DHCP server, refer to NT Server on-line help and the *Microsoft Windows NT Resource Kit Network Guide.* For more information about how to use the DHCP Manager, see on-line help in the DHCP Manager.

Note: A client Windows NT Workstation or Server computer can make use of the DHCP automatic configuration by opening the Network dialog box and choosing the Protocols tab. Select the TCP/IP protocol, choose the **P**roperties button, and in the IP Address tab of the Microsoft TCP/IP Properties dialog box, select the option: **O**btain an IP Address From a DHCP Server. Other clients—Windows 95 and Windows for Workgroups 3.11—can also take advantage of the DHCP automatic configuration; see the documentation of the operating system.

WINS Configuration

WINS (Windows Internet Name Service) is a replicated, dynamic database that registers and queries NetBIOS computer names in a routed network environment. The more complex a network is, the more you'll need a WINS service for name resolution. WINS enables users to quickly and easily locate systems on remote networks; additionally, the WINS service updates changes to IP addresses through DHCP addressing automatically.

Consider these facts before installing the WINS service:

- Do not assign a fixed IP address to a WINS server.
- Do not make a WINS server a DHCP client.

To install a WINS server, open the Network dialog box and choose the Services tab. Choose the **A**dd button, and from the list of network services, choose Windows Internet Name Service, and choose OK. Insert the Windows NT CD-ROM or enter a path to the NT files and choose Continue.

After installation of the WINS files, you must configure TCP/IP as described in the previous section; use the WINS Address tab of the Microsoft TCP/IP Properties dialog box to enable DNS and configure LMHOSTS. See Figure E.6. After you restart the computer, the WINS software will be ready to use.

Use the WINS Manager to administer WINS. Access the WINS Manager through Start, **P**rograms, Administrative Tools, and then choose WINS Manager.

Note: You can start and stop the WINS Server service by opening the Services option in the Control Panel and selecting the Windows Internet Name Service in the list and choosing Start, Stop, Pause, or Continue.

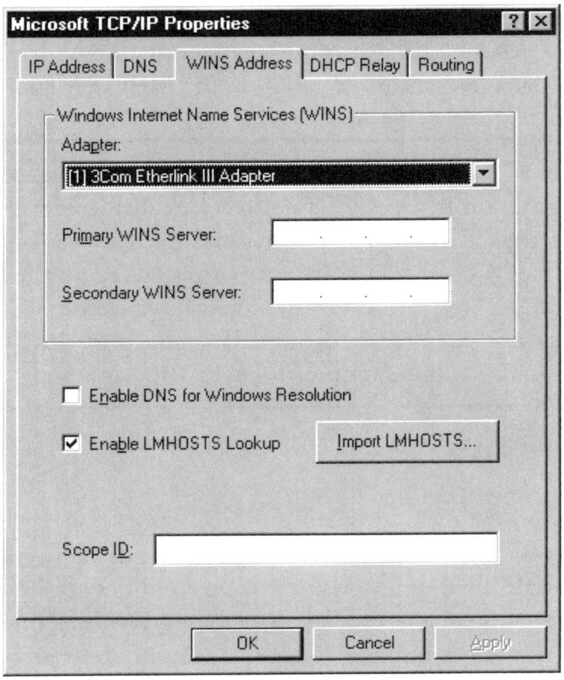

Figure E.6 Configure the WINS address and LMHOSTS.

Domain Name System (DNS) Server

The DNS server is a database that identifies hosts information and resolves names to IP address mapping queries from clients or from DNS name servers. The Windows NT DNS name server can use WINS for host name resolution, thus allowing more efficient name resolution.

If you have a small and/or single network, you do not really need a DNS server; your Internet Service Provider maintains a DNS server, and you can use the DNS client software to query its DNS server instead. If, on the other hand, you want to access DNS from your LAN, you'll need to provide your own DNS server. A DNS server system is large and involved. You'll most likely want to use two computers—a primary and a secondary name server—with replicated data to the secondary server for backup purposes.

Note: The DNS naming system can be compared to a filing cabinet. Each domain is a drawer in the cabinet; and subdomains compare to file folders within the domain drawer. When writing out the domain name, periods are used to separate

TCP/IP Issues **383**

each part of the name; for example, the DNS domain name *humble.com* defines *humble* as a subdomain of the parent *com* domain. You're probably familiar with the seven organizational domain name abbreviations: com (commercial), edu (educational), gov (government), org (noncommercial), net (networking), mil (military), and int (international).

To add the DNS server service, open the Network dialog box (Control Panel, Network icon) and choose the Services tab. Choose **A**dd and select the Microsoft DNS Server; choose OK. You'll need your NT CD-ROM or a path to the NT files. Restart the computer to enable the DNS server software. Configure the DNS host and other settings in the DNS tab of the Microsoft TCP/IP Properties dialog box (see Figure E.7).

You can use the DNS Manager (Start, **P**rograms, Administrative Tools) to administer the name servers. For more information about DNS, use on-line help. NT supplies a complete help file specifically for Microsoft TCP/IP; to get help, choose Start, **H**elp, and in the Index tab, type **dns**. In the list of help topics that

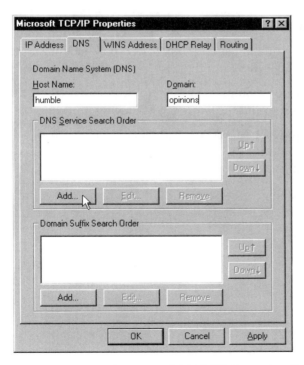

Figure E.7 *Use the Microsoft TCP/IP Properties dialog box to configure the DNS host.*

appears, double-click "DNS Servers, installing and configuring." NT displays the specialized TCP/IP help contents screen.

TCP/IP Utilities and Services

TCP/IP utilities provide diagnostic tools for connecting to other systems, for network administration, and for troubleshooting the network. You use TCP/IP utilities at an MS-DOS command prompt (Start, **P**rograms, Command Prompt); some applications are configured with the Control Panel. It is important to note that NT's TCP/IP utilities are not full-blown applications; many are only basic, even simple, tools that may or may not serve your needs. Following is a brief description of TCP/IP utilities and services available with Windows NT Server:

> The **Telnet** client application is a tool you can use to connect to a remote host, along the lines of a basic terminal application.
>
> The **Finger** client is a way to query a remote system for information in the form of text. Use Finger to identify users.
>
> **RCP** (remote copy) is a command for exchanging files with a remote host or copying files from one host to another using a trust between systems.
>
> **FTP**, a simple command line utility in NT, lets you establish a connection, log in as a user, and transfer files from the host.
>
> **Gopher server** is a distributed menu system that can provide a menu of files, links to other menus, or links to other servers' menus.
>
> **SNMP** (Simple Network Management Protocol) provides basic administrative information about a device so you can monitor the system; you must install the SNMP service from the Network dialog box to take advantage of this utility.

Index

A

abilities, 64, 65
  built-in, 67–68
    Add workstation to domain, 67
    Assign user rights, 67
    Create common groups, 68
    Create/manage local groups, 67
    Create/manage user accounts, 67
    Create/manage global groups, 67
    Format server's hard disk, 68
    Lock the server, 67
    Override the lock of the server, 68
    Share/stop sharing printers, 68
    Share/stop sharing directories, 68
  and local groups, 55–57
  what they are, 65
access
  denied
    to a domain, 370
    replication problem, 368–369
    to NT Server computer, 364
  Full Control access, 108, 110–111
  network, 32–36, 235
    time restriction, 130
  No Access file attribute, 137
  printers, 92, 93–94
  resources, 33–35
  right, 66

Account Information dialog box, 50–51
Account Operators group
  abilities, 134
  description, 55
  rights, 134
account policies, 71–72
  options, 72
  set defaults, 127–128
account restrictions transferred
  by user account, 129–130
  for entire domain, 130–132
  rights not transferred, 132
accounts
  determine information, 50–51
  replicator, 283
  restrictions, 129–132
    not transferred, 132
  and security, 30–31
  transferring, 185–190
adapters
  add/configure, 11, 332–334
  compatibility, 259
  remove, 332
  SCSI, 254–255, 259
adding users, 53–54
Add Name Space utility, 27
Address Resolution Protocol (ARP), 375
Add Users and Groups dialog box, 58–59, 60–61, 68–70

ADMIN, 31, 132–133
ADMIN$, 275
administrative account, 132–135
Administrative Wizards, 4–5
Administrator, 30–31, 42
    mapping drives, 314
    multiple, 302
    security, 147
Administrators group
    comparison, 132–133
    to create printer, 94
    description, 55
    file ownership, 87–88, 136
    and print queue, 108
    rights and abilities, 64
    shared directories, 79
    sharing printers, 79
alerts, 276–277
API (Application Program Interface), 28–29
AppleShare, 262
AppleTalk, 93, 262
Application Program Interface (API), 28–29
applications
    check after migration, 251
    common questions, 18–19
    and migration, 124
    NetWare support for, 148
    problems, 366–368
    supported by NT, 18
architecture, 23
ARP (Address Resolution Protocol), 375
ATTACH utility, 33
attributes, 31, 218. *See also* permissions
    common questions, 14
    not supported, 139
    NetWare to NT, 139, 147,
    and NTFS, 136
    problems, 365
audit policies, 72–73
    tip, 305
    types of events, 73
auditing security events, 88–90, 173
AUTOEXEC.BAT, 367

B

backing up
    before migration, 124–125
    bindery database, 124–125
    files, 257–260
    NDS database, 125
backup domain controllers. *See* BDC
Backup Operators, 55
basic operating system, 21–22
BDC (backup domain controllers), 26, 117, 326
    retaining NDS structure, 181
bindery database, 25, 150–151
    backing up, 124–125
    context, 150–152
bindings, 335
bitmapped fonts, 112
boot
    boot failure, 358–359
    remoteboot, 28
browsing, 312

C

CD-ROM
    problem, 356–357
    sharing, 79
chkdsk command, 355–356
client/server vs. peer-to-peer, 64
    question, 15
clients, 221
    after migration, 249–251
    common questions, 5–6
    copy installation files, 223–225
    DOS client
        creating, 225–229
        installing, 229–230, 359–360
    and Gateway Service, 146–147
    software overview, 221–225
    software problems, 359–360
    start Network Client Administrator, 222–223
    what is supported, 19
    Windows 95, 235–236

configuring, 237–240
    connect to network, 240–242
    creating, 236–237
    Windows NT workstation, 242–243
        configuring network, 243–245
        connect to network, 246
    Windows for Workgroups
        accessing network, 235
        creating, 231–232
        installing, 232–234
comparisons
    administrative account, 132–135
    concepts, 21–38
    user account, 127–132
compatibility, 259
    HCL, 93, 116, 123
    Macintosh, 262
concepts comparison, 21
    accessing the network, 32–36
    network components, 24–29
    NT overview, 22–24
    operating systems, 21–22
    printing, 36–38
    security, 29–32
CONFIG.SYS, 367
configuration information, 288
    Display, 290
    Drives, 290–291
    Environment, 292–293
    Memory, 291–292
    Network, 293–295
    Resources, 292
    Services, 292
    System, 289
    Version, 288–289
containers
    and bindery context, 150–152
    and migration, 15, 212
    NDS, 125
controllers. See domain controllers
Control Panel, 251–253
compression, 7–8, 357
core protocols, 144

Creator Owner group, 57, 87

D

database, 25
data transfer and Gateway, 152
deleting users, 53, 54
DET (Directory Entry Table), 27
device fonts, 111
devices
    setting up, 253
    tape, 256
DHCP, 378, 380–381
    problems, 370
Diagnostics, 288
    Display, 290
    Drive, 290–291
    Environment, 292–293
    Memory, 291–292
    Network, 293–295
    to open, 288
    Resources, 292
    Services, 292
    System, 289–290
    Version, 288–289
    WINMSD.EXE, 288
Dialin, 52–53
DIR command, 137
directories, 63. See also directory replication
    auditing, 88–89
    backing up, 124
    and compression, 7–8
    home directory, 49, 361
    and NT Explorer, 76
    permissions, 83, 84–87, 135–136
        setting, 85–87
        standard, 84
    rights, 137–139
    share name, 75
    sharing, 74, 75, 77–78
    to stop sharing, 78–79
    transfer problems, 212
    view shared directories, 279
    viewing transfers, 217–219

directory database, 25
Directory Entry Table (DET), 27
directory replication, 281–288
    configure export server, 284–286
    configure import computer, 286–288
    requirements for, 282–283
directory services, 24–25
discovery, 301
disk compression, 357
Display Adapters, 259
documents, 108–111
    defaults, 109
DNS (Domain Name System), 382–384
Domain Admins group, 57
    sharing printers, 79
domain controllers, 26, 117
    BDC, 26, 117, 318, 326
        promoting, 317–318
    to create a printer, 94
    PDC, 15–16, 26, 117, 181, 326
    synchronizing, 318
Domain Guests group, 57
Domain Name System (DNS) server, 382–384
domains, 26, 43. *See also* trust relationships; User Manager for Domains
    adding computers, 315–316
    advantages of, 25
    to assign rights, 65
    browsing, 312
    choosing, 117–121
    common questions, 6–7
    controllers, 15–16, 26, 117
        promoting, 317–318
        synchronizing, 318
    mapping drives, 312–314
    multiple domains, 297
        administering, 302–310
        logging on, 301–302
        mapping drives, 312–314
        master domain, 119, 120, 191
        models, 118–121, 300–301
        multiple master, 120
        printer, sharing, 314

promote a BDC, 317–318
    resources, 310
    retaining NDS structure, 181
    servers and domains, 314–318
    single master, 119
    user rights policy, 308, 310
name, position of, 44
problems, 369–370
rights transferred, 130–132
resource domain, 120
single domain, 298–299
    components, 298
    model, 118
    security, 298–299
what is a domain, 6
Domain Users group, 57, 216–217
DOS, 18–19
    and migration, 5
downloadable soft fonts, 111
drives
    mapping, 35–36, 250–251
        to domains, 312–314
    partitioning, 357
    designate and view, 79
Dr. Watson utility, 356

E

editing users, 44–53
    account information, 50–51
    to change name, 46
    Dialin, 52–53
    groups, 46
    hours, 49–50
    Logon To, 50
    several at one time, 44
    profile, 47–49
    User Properties, 45
emergency repair disk, 355
Error.log, 202, 209
    printing, 202
    viewing, 201, 210
Event Viewer
    and Gateway Service, 153

helps solve problems, 355
view security log, 74
Everyone group, 56
and NetWare 3.1x, 31, 43
Explorer. *See* NT Explorer
export server, 284–286

F

FAT (File Allocation Table), 27, 324
long file names, 7
and permissions, 83–84, 135
and security, 29
and trustee rights, 116
and %USERNAME%, 49
File Allocation Table. *See* FAT
File Manager in Windows 3.1, 18
file names
check for duplicates, 121
long file-names, 7, 27, 76
share names, 75
File and Print Services for NetWare. *See* FPNW
files
attributes, 139, 147, 218
auditing, 88–90
backup, 124, 257, 260
common questions, 7–8
installation files, 223–225
Migration Tool, 192–195
options, 192–195
ownership, 87–88
permissions, 83, 84–87, 135–136
list of, 147–148
setting, 85–87
standard, 84
restore, 124, 257, 260
rights, 136–137
sharing, 74
transferring, 192, 194–195
problems, 212
view transfers, 217–219
File Scan, 121, 137
File Server Console Operator, 134–135

file system, 27
and permissions, 83–84
Finger, 384
floppy drives
problems, 356
sharing, 79
folder, 29, 63. *See also* directories
to create/delete, 76
default user profile, 264–266
hidden, 266
sharing, 34
fonts, 111–112
question, 12
form, 106
FPNW (File and Print Services for NetWare)
account restrictions, 132
login scripts, 122, 197, 249–250
FTP, 384
Full Control access
and print queue, 108
and print server, 110–111

G

Gateway Service for NetWare, 116–117
bindery context, 150–152
can't see server, 365
and clients, 146–147
common questions, 8–9
configuring, 161–167
eliminate need for, 147
enabling, 161–163
installing, 155–161
add Gateway Service, 157–158
create NetWare user, 158–159
create NT user, 156–157
completing installation, 159–161
remove redirectors, 156
when to install, 8
and Migration Tool, 140
NetWare 3.1x, 150
NetWare 4.x, 150–151
and NT Workstation, 92
options, 159–161

Gateway Service for NetWare (*continued*)
 permissions, 163–167
 printers, installing, 167–175
 printing, 149–150
 problems, 152–153, 364–365
  access denied, 364
  can't see server, 365
  password, 152
  file attribute, 365
  server, 153
  service unavailable, 364
  slows data transfer, 152
  starting, 152–153, 364–365
 security, 147–149
 understanding, 143–145
  core protocols, 144
  redirector, 144
  sharing, 144–145
 why use it, 145–146
Gopher server, 384
groups
 abilities, 55
 adding, 46, 59–62
 assigning rights, 68–70
 built-in groups, 54, 309
 common questions, 17–18
 deleting, 62, 361
 description, 54–55
 editing, 62
 global, 56, 57, 309
  built in, 309
  number of, 54
  when to use, 56
 guidelines, 309
 local groups, 55–57
  number of, 54
  when to use, 56
 managing, 54, 57–59
 names, 189–190
 predefined, 30–31, 42–43
 problems, 360–362
 rights, 55
 security, 31

 selecting options, 184–191
 special groups, 56–57
 trial migration, 211–212
 transferring, 184
 view transfers, 216
Groups Memberships dialog box, 46
Guest, 30–31, 42, 56

H

HAL (Hardware Abstraction Layer), 23
hardware
 common questions, 9
 and user profiles, 266–267
 HAL, 23
 HCL, 93, 116, 123
 requirements, 16, 115–116
Hardware Abstraction Layer. *See* HAL
Hardware Compatibility List. *See* HCL
HCL (Hardware Compatibility List), 93, 116
 prepare for migration, 123
 for updated HCL, 259
 UPS and serial cable, 257
High Performance File System (HPFS), 27
home directories, 49, 361
HOSERVER, 34
 window, 35
hours, logon, 49–50
HPFS (High Performance File System), 27

I

ICMP (Internet Control Message Protocol), 375
identification, 330
import computer, 286–287
installation
 files, copying, 223–225
 problems, 356–357
installing
 Gateway Service, 155–161
 installation problems, 356–357
 printers, 167–175
 RAS, 52

Interactive group, 56
Internet
   connecting to, 11
   and RAS, 52
Internet Control Message Protocol (ICMP), 375
Internet Packet Exchange/Sequenced Packet Exchange. *See* IPX/SPX
Internet Protocol (IP), 375
Internet User, 30–31, 42
IP (Internet Protocol), 375
IPC$, 274
IPX/SPX, 28–29, 116–117, 328
   to install, 146
IRQ level, 94
IS (Information System), 119

K

keyboards, 259

L

license, 326
   copies of software, 222
   dedicated print server, 12
line printer daemon (LPD), 95
Local Group Properties dialog box, 57–58
log
   activate security log, 88
   log spooling, 108
   migration log files, 213–214
   record migration, 196–197
   trial migration, 201–210
      Error.log, 202, 209
      LogFile.log, 202, 203–208
      LogView utility, 201–202
      printing logs, 202
      Summary.log, 202, 209–210
      view log files, 201, 210
   view security log, 74
LogFile.log, 202, 203–208
   group information, 204
   printing log, 202
   Supervisor defaults, 204
   transfer options, 204
   viewing, 201, 210
logging on, 33
   Logon Hours, 49–50, 130
   Logon To, 50
   multiple domains, 301–302
login scripts, 249–250
   do not transfer, 9–10, 250
   and FPNW, 122, 197, 249–250
   vs. user profiles, 265
LOGIN utility, 33
Logon Hours dialog box, 49–50
logon scripts, 48–49, 249–250
   to create, 48
      %HOMEDRIVE%, 48
      %HOMEPATH%, 48
      %OS%, 48
      %PROCESSOR_ARCHITECTURE%, 48
      %PROCESSOR_LEVEL%, 48
      %USERDOMAIN%, 48
      %USERNAME%, 48
   NT logon script path, 250
LOGVIEW.EXE, 180
LOGVIEW.HLP, 180
LogView utility, 201–202
   Help, 202
   printing logs, 202
   searching logs, 202
   viewing logs, 201
loose ends, 249
LPD (line printer daemon), 95

M

Macintosh, 6, 260–262
   and NT Workstation, 92
   the Set button, 46
MAIL directory, 207
Map Network Drive dialog box, 36
mapping drives, 35–36, 250
mappings file, 185

MAP utility, 35–36
member server, 17, 26, 326
  assigning rights, 68
  to create printer, 94
  Power Users group, 57
memory, 291–292
  allocation error, 366–367
  dump, 358
messages, 281
Messenger Service, 94
Microsoft
  Gateway Service, 143
  upgrade workstations, 121–122
migration. *See also* preparations; trial migration
  common questions, 10
  starting, 180–183, 213
  time it takes, 212
Migration Tool, 179–197
  check list, 179–180
  and Gateway Service, 140
  and NDS, 125
  options
    file, 192–195
    users/groups, 184–191
  and Print Queue Operator, 135
  recording migration, 196–197
  starting, 180–183, 213
  trial migration, 199
    log files, 202
    Logging options, 200
    problem solving, 210
  won't start, 365
MS-DOS
  access NT printers, 92
  create client, 225–229
  domain resources, 310
  install client, 229–230
  logon scripts, 49
  problems, 359–360
  and profiles, 47
  startup disk, 225–228
  workstations, 122
MY Computer window, 36, 37, 122

N

names
  duplicate names, 121, 212
  group names, 189–190
  share name for printer, 103
  user names, 185, 189
NCP (NetWare core protocol), 144
NDIR command, 137
NDIS (Network Driver Interface Specification), 29
NDS (NetWare Directory Services), 25, 150–151
  backing up, 125
  and NT Migration Tool, 125
  retaining structure, 4, 181
NETADMIN, 38, 158–159
NetBEUI (NetBIOS Extended User Interface), 28–29, 328
NetBIOS (Network Basic Input/Output System), 28–29, 116–117
NetBIOS Extended User Interface. *See* NetBEUI
Net Logon service, 301–302
NET$OBJ.OLD, 125
NET$PROP.OLD, 125
NET$VAL.OLD, 125
NETLOGON$, 275
NETUSER utility, 33
NetWare. *See also* comparisons
  account restrictions, 128–132
  applications, 148
  features not in NT, 121
  terms/concepts, 337–339
  TTS, 27
  utilities, 148
  version issues, 150–152, 212
NetWare 3.1x
  bindery, 25, 150–151
    backing up, 124–125
  description, 21–22
  Everyone group, 31
  File Server Console Operator, 134–135

Gateway, 150
percent of market, 143
rights, 31
Supervisor, 31, 42, 127, 132–133
NetWare 4.x, 212. *See also* NDS
   ADMIN, 31, 132–133
   backing up NDS database, 125
   and bindery services, 150–152
   description, 22
   duplicate names, 212
   and Gateway, 150, 159
   percent of market, 143
   prepare for migration, 125
   retaining NDS structure, 181
   rights, 31
   and trial migration, 200
NETWARE.DRV, 148–149
NetWare Client Administrator utility, 28
NetWare core protocol (NCP), 144
NetWare Directory Services. *See* NDS
NetWare DOS Requester, 34
NetWare Loadable Modules. *See* NLMs
NetWare printers, 167–175
NetWare shell (NETX), 33–34
NetWare User Tools for Windows 3.1, 34
network
   accessing, 32–36
   components, 24–29, 329–335
   redirector, 144
   statistics, 293–295
   time restrictions, 130
Network Basic Input/Output System. *See* NetBIOS
Network Client Administrator, 28, 44
   create client software, 221–222
   starting, 222–223
network components, 24–29, 329–335
   adapters, 332–334
   bindings, 335
   identification, 330
   protocols, 331–332
   services, 330–331
Network dialog box, 329–335

adapters, 332–334
bindings, 335
identification, 330
protocols, 331–332
services, 330–331
Network Driver Interface specification (NDIS), 29
Network group, 56–57
Network Neighborhood, 34–35
   browsing, 312
   connect workstation, 246
   drive mapping, 36
   manage print server, 110–111
   view shared drives, 75
NETX (NetWare shell), 33–34
New Local Group dialog box, 60, 62
New Technology File System. *See* NTFS
NLMs (NetWare Loadable Modules), 29
   application considerations, 124
   verify drivers, 123
No Access file attribute, 137
Novell, 143
   data protection, 22
   to run utilities, 148–149
NT CD-ROM, 223–225, 380, 383
   device drivers, 259
NT Diagnostics. *See* Diagnostics
NT Explorer, 32, 74–75
   mapping drives, 250
   to open, 74
   set permissions, 32, 83, 85–87
      import directory, 287
   share resources, 77–78, 79
   stop sharing directory, 78–79
   tasks you can perform, 76
   view transfers, 217–218
NTFS (New Technology File System), 27, 324
   advantage of, 7, 27
   Macintosh, 262
   permissions, 83–84, 135–136
   and security, 29
   sharing a directory, 75
   spool folder, 107

NTFS (*continued*)
   and trustee rights, 116
NTGATEWAY, 147, 150, 153, 159
NT Server, 22. *See also* server
   can't select, 365
   features not available, 121
   hardware requirements, 115–116
   installing, 321, 323–328
      preparations, 321–323
   overview, 22–24
   sharing resources, 77–78
   shut down, 328–329
   starting, 328–329
   utilities, 376
NT Server CD-ROM, 157
NT Workstation, 5–6, 23, 242–246
   assigning rights, 68
   common questions, 19–20
   configuring network, 243–245
   connecting, 246
   copying tools, 242
   to create printer, 94
   DHCP configuration, 381
   and Gateway, 92, 147
   and Macintosh services, 92
   print server, 91–92
   to run User Manager for Domains, 44
   User Manager, 42, 44
   utilities, 376
NWADMIN, 38, 158–159
NWCALLS.DLL, 149
NWCONV.EXE, 180
NWCONV.HLP, 180
NWIPXSPX.DLL, 148
NWLink, 29, 116–117, 140, 144
   automatically installed, 156
   confirm installation, 158
NWNETAPI.DLL, 149

O

operating system, 21–22
OS/2
   HPFS, 27
   and profiles, 47
overview of NT, 22–24
ownership, 87–88, 173

P

parallel ports, 363
passwords
   changing, 130
   default option, 186
   and Gateway, 152
   incorrect attempts, 131–132
   options, 188–189
   problem, 366
   required, 131
   restriction, options, 71–72
   SETPASS command, 152
   sniffers, 260
   time limit, 129–130, 131
   transferring accounts, 185
   uniqueness, 131
PCONSOLE, 38
PDC (primary domain controller), 15–16, 26, 117, 326
   multiple domains, 302
   retaining NDS structure, 181
peer-to-peer vs. client/server, 64
   question, 15
peripherals
   configuring, 251–257
      control panel, 251–253
      SCSI Adapters, 254–255
      services, 255–256
      set up devices, 253
      tape devices, 256
      UPS, 256–257
   preparing for migration, 123
permissions, 64, 83–90. *See also* sharing resources
   and attributes, 54, 218
   auditing, 88–90, 173
   default, 362

directory, 84–87, 135–136, 137–139
    Add (WX), 85
    Add and Read (RWX)(RX), 85
    Change (RWXD)(RWXD), 85
    Full Control (all)(all), 85
    List (RX), 85
    No Access, 85
    Read (RX)(RX), 85
and FAT, 116
files, 84–85, 135–137, 147–148
    Change (RWXD), 85
    Full Control (all), 85
    No Access, 85
    Read, 85
file systems, 83–84
Gateway Service, 161, 163–167
guidelines, 83
and import directory, 287
lost, 369
ownership, 87–88, 173
printers, 103–104
    NetWare, 173–175
problems, 362
and security, 31–32
set printer permissions, 80–83
setting permissions, 85–87
    Gateway, 163–167
standard permissions, 84
    Change Permissions (P), 84
    Delete, 84
    Execute (X), 84
    Read (R), 84
    Take Ownership (O), 84
    Write (W), 84
PIFs (program information file), 367–368
pointing devices, 259
ports, 94, 101–102, 106, 107
    problems, 363
Power Users group, 57
    to create printer, 94
Preparations, for migration, 115
    applications, 124
    backing up, 124–125

choosing domains, 117–121
Gateway Service, 116–117
NetWare 4.x, 125
peripherals, 123
protocols, 116–117
server hardware, 115–116
workstations, 121–123
primary domain controller. *See* PDC
PRINT$, 275
print devices, 91, 92–93
    multiple printers, 37
    settings, 104
printers, 91
    access to, 93–94
    add NetWare printer, 149
    additional, 98
    change settings, 98
    configuring, 99–105
        Device settings, 104
        General tab, 100–101
        Ports tab, 101–102
        Scheduling tab, 102–103
        Security tab, 103–104
        Sharing tab, 103
    to control, 109
    creating, 94–98
    and Gateway Service, 167–175
    install NetWare printers, 167–172
    set defaults, 109
    setting permissions, 80–83
        NetWare printer, 173–175
    sharing, 79–80
        multiple domains, 314
        NetWare printer, 172–173
    unsupported, 363
Printers folder, 80, 99
printing, 91. *See also* printers
    common questions, 12–13
    document defaults, 109
    fonts, 111–112
    from DOS-based applications, 364
    and the Gateway, 149–150
    log files, 202

printing (*continued*)
    NetWare and NT, 36–38
    planning, 92–94
    problems, 362–364
Print Operators group, 64
    to create printer, 94
    description, 55
    and print queue, 108
    rights, 64
    sharing printers, 79
print queue, 91, 108–111
    to control the printer, 109
    how they work, 37–38
    to open, 108
    set document defaults, 109
Print Queue Operator, 38, 135
print server, 91
    advantages of, 91–92
    choosing, 93
    configuring properties, 106–108
        Advanced tab, 107–108
        Forms tab, 106
        Ports tab, 107
    and Full Control access, 110–111
Print Server Operator, 135
Print wizard, 94, 95
problems. *See* troubleshooting
processor, 259
profiles, 47–48, 263
    copying, 267–268, 362
    creating, 266–267
    default folder, 264–266
    managing, 264–269
    mandatory, 268–269, 362
    and MS-DOS, 47
    and OS/2, 47
    problems, 362
    roaming, 266–269
    and UNIX, 47
    vs. login scripts, 265
    and Windows 95, 47
program information file (PIFs), 367–368
properties, 277–278
protocols, 28–29. *See also* TCP/IP
    add, 331–332
    common questions, 11, 13
    configure, 332
    core protocols, 144
    default protocol, 28
    NCP, 144
    preparing for migration, 116–117
    and print device, 93, 95
    and RAS, 52
    SMB, 144
PSERVER.EXE, 36
PSERVER.NLM, 36

Q

questions commonly asked, 3–4
    administration, 4–5
    applications, 18–19
    client software, 5–6
    domains, 6–7
    flies/file systems, 7–8
    Gateway Services, 8–9
    groups, 17–18
    hardware, 9
    login scripts, 9–10
    migrating, 10
    NDS, 4
    networking, 11
    printing, 12–13
    protocols, 13
    Registry, 13
    replication, 13–14
    security, 14
    server, 14–17
    users and groups, 17–18
    utilities, 18–19
    workstations, 19–20
queue. *See* print queue
QUEUES directory, 38

R

RAS (Remote Access Service), 52–53
raster fonts, 112

RCONSOLE, 44
RCP, 384
recording the migration, 196–197. *See also* log
redirectors, 144
    removing, 146, 153, 156
Reduced Instruction Set Computing. *See* RISC
Registry, 13, 371–372
Release Notes readme file, 259
Remote Access Service. *See* RAS
remoteboot feature, 28
replication, 13–14, 281–282
    access denied, 368–369
    configure
        export server, 284–286
        import computer, 286
    problems, 368–369
    replicator accounts, 283
    requirements, 282
    status column, 288
Replicator group, 56
REPL$, 275
resources
    accessing, 33–35
    resource usage, 272–273
    sharing, 74–78, 79–83
        and Gateway, 144–145
        viewing, 275–276
    stop sharing, 78–79
    view, 33, 275–276, 277–281
restoring files, 124, 257–260
rights, 55, 64
    Account Operators group, 134
    advanced rights, 65
    assigning, 68–70
    common questions, 14
    description of, 65–67
        Access this computer from the network, 66
        Add workstations to the domain, 67
        Back up files and directories, 66
        Change the system time, 66
        Force shutdown from a remote system, 66
        Load and unload device drivers, 66
        Log on locally, 66
        Manage auditing and security log, 66
        Restore files and directories, 66
        Shut down the system, 66
        Take ownership of files, 66
    directory, 137–139
    files, 136–137
    NetWare account restrictions, 129–132
    not transferred, 132
    transferred
        for entire domain, 130–132
        by user account, 129–130
    trustee rights, 116, 153
RISC-based microprocessor, 22, 115–116
roaming profiles, 266–269
running a migration, 199
    the migration, 212–219
    trial migration, 199–210
        problem-solving, 210–212

S

SAM (Security Accounts Manager database), 25
screen fonts, 111
SCSI Adapters, 254–255
    check the HCL, 9
    compatibility, 259
security, 29–32, 63. *See also* abilities; passwords; permissions; rights
    to activate security log, 88
    audit policies, 72–74
    auditing security events, 88–90
    common questions, 14
    domains, 298–299
    and FAT, 29
    and Gateway Service, 147–148
    logging on, 301–302
    and printer, 103–104
    set audit policies, 72–73
    SID, 53
    user accounts, 30–31
    view security log, 74
Security Accounts Manager database (SAM), 25
serial ports, 363

server. *See also* NT server; Server Manager
    common questions, 14–17
    crashes, 357–358
    managing, 314
    member server, 17, 26
    trouble connecting, 211
Server Manager, 263, 269–271
    add computers to domain, 315–316
    add a share, 79
    alerts, 276–277
    designating shares, 79
    to open, 79
    and selected computers, 277–281
        properties, 277–278
        services, 279–281
        shared directories, 279
    connections, 272–273
    designating shares, 79
    exiting, 271–272
    to open, 79
    resources
        in use, 276
        selected computers, 277–281
        shared, 275–276
        usage, 272–273
    send a message, 281
    services, 279–281
    special shares, 274–275
    starting, 271–272
    user sessions, 273–274
    viewing
        connections, 272–273
        properties, 277–278
        resources, 276
        resource usage, 272–273
        shared directories, 279
        shared resources, 275–276
        user sessions, 273–274
server message block (SMB) protocol, 144
Server Operators group
    abilities, 134–135
    to create printer, 94
    description, 55
    and print queue, 108
    rights, 134–135
    and the Server Manager, 79
    shared directories, 79
    sharing printers, 79
Server properties, 106–108
server type, 326–327
services
    change, 256
    check status, 255
    set, 279–281
    see current state of, 292
    view list of, 330–331
sessions, 273–274
SESSION utility, 33
share name
    for a printer, 103
    when sharing directory, 75
sharing resources, 74
    and Gateway, 144–145
    guidelines, 75–76
    printer, 79–83
        and Gateway Service, 172–175
        configuring, 103
    problems, 362
    on the server, 77–78
    stop sharing, 78–79
    viewing, 275–276
SID (security identifier), 53
SMB (server message block) protocol, 144
sniffers, 260
SNMP, 384
software
    common questions, 5–6
    license for, 222
    overview, 221–225
    and peripheral, 123
special shares, 274–275
spooling
    collection of DLLs, 13
    to log spooling, 108
    and NTFS drive, 107
    options, 103
starting
    Gateway Service, 152–153, 364–365

Migration Tool, 180–183, 213
Network Client Administrator, 222–223
NT Server, 328–329
Server Manager, 271–272
subdirectory, 63
  replication, 282
  sharing, 74
  using NT Explorer, 76
subfolder, 63. *See also* subdirectory
Summary.log, 202, 209–210
  printing, 202
  viewing, 201, 210
Supervisor, 31, 42
  comparisons, 132–133
  defaults, 190–191
  and LogFile.log, 204
SYS:PUBLIC, 34
SYS:SYSTEM, 38
SYSCON, 134, 158–159
system errors, 211
System group, 57
SYSTEM32 folder, 180

T

tape backups, sharing, 79
tape devices, 256
TCP (Transmission Control Protocol), 375
TCP/IP (Transmission Control Protocol/
    Internet Protocol), 28–29, 93
  configuring, 376, 378
  DHCP, 378, 380–381
  installing, 376–378
  and print devices, 95
  problems, 370–371
  structure, 373–376
  utilities and service, 384
TCP/IP Printing service, 95
Telnet, 384
terms/concepts, 337–339
testing. *See* trial migration; troubleshooting
Transaction Tracking System (TTS), 27
Transmission Control Program (TCP), 375

Transmission Control Protocol/Internet
    Protocol. *See* TCP/IP
trial migration, 199–212
  log files, 202
    Error.log, 202, 208
    LogFile.log, 202, 203–208
    printing logs, 202
    Summary.log, 202, 208–209
    view logs, 201, 210
  LogView utility, 201–202
  and NetWare 4.x, 200
  problem solving, 210–211
    connecting servers, 211
    file/directory transfer, 212
    NetWare versions, 212
    system errors, 211
    with users/groups, 211–212
  running, 200
  why run one, 199–200
troubleshooting, 355–356
  applications, 366–368
    AUTOEXEC.BAT, 367
    CONFIG.SYS, 367
    memory allocation error, 366–367
    NWIPXSPX.DLL not found, 367
    password problem, 366
    PIFs, 367–368
    TSRs, 368
    Windows 3.x, 366
  boot failure, 358–359
  client software, 359
    MS-DOS client, 359–360
    Windows for Workgroups, 360
  default permissions, 362
  domain problems, 369–370
    access denied, 370
    multiple domain sharing, 369
  Dr. Watson utility, 356
  emergency repair disk, 355
  experience, 11
  default permissions, 362
  Gateway Service, 152–153
    access denied, 364
    can't see server, 365

troubleshooting (*continued*)
   file attribute, 365
   service unavailable, 364
   startup, 364–365
   installation, 356–357
      CD-ROM recognition, 356–357
      disk compression, 357
      floppy disk, 356
      partitioning drive, 357
   memory dump, 358
   migration, 365–366
      select NetWare server, 365
      select NT server, 366
      Migration Tool won't start, 365
   printing, 362–364
      from DOS-based applications, 364
      parallel port, 363
      serial port, 363
      unsupported printer, 363
   registry, 371–372
   replication, 368–369
      access denied, 368–369
      export/import, 369
      lost permissions, 369
   server crashes, 357–358
   sharing, 362
   TCP/IP configuration, 370–371
      connection, 370
      DHCP doesn't work, 370
      WINS, 370–371
   trial migration, 210–212
      connecting servers, 211
      directory transfer, 212
      file transfer, 212
      system errors, 211
      users/groups, 211–212
   UPS not functioning, 255
   users and groups, 360–362
      deleting a group, 361
      home directories, 361
      low transmission rates, 361
      profiles, 361, 362
      re-creating account, 361
      workstation disk space, 371
TrueType fonts, 12, 112
trustee rights, 116, 153
trustee relationships, 27, 299–300
   in multiple master model, 120
   one-way, 27, 299, 303–304
   removing, 306
   setting up, 302–305
   two-way, 27, 299, 304–305
TSRs (Terminate-and-Stay-Resident), 368
TTS (Transaction Tracking System), 27

U

UDP (User Datagram Protocol), 375
UNIX
   and print devices, 37, 95
   and profiles, 47
UPS, 256–257
   not functioning, 255
   options, 258–259
User Account Manager, 134
user accounts
   built-in, 30–31
   NetWare/NT comparisons, 127–132
      account restrictions, 129
   re-creating, 361
   restrictions, 127–129
   rights transferred, 129–132
   rights not transferred, 132
   and security, 30–31
User Datagram Protocol (UDP), 375
User Environment Profile dialog box, 47
User Manager, 42, 44
   when to use, 65
User Manager for Domains, 30, 41–44. *See also* domains
   to activate security log, 88
   and NDS containers, 125
   and NT Workstation, 44
   to open, 42
   and rights, 65–67, 68–70
   set audit policies, 72–73
   unavailable features, 361

window, 30
user profiles. *See* profiles
User Properties dialog box, 44–46
   Account Disabled, 45
   Account Locked Out, 45
   Description, 45
   Full Name, 45
   Password, 45
   Username, 45
user rights policy, 308, 310
   dialog box, 68–70, 310
user rights policy, 308
users
   adding, 53–54
   assigning rights, 68–70
   common questions, 17–18
   create NetWare user, 158–159
   create NT user, 156–157
   deleting, 53, 54
   editing, 44–53
   naming, 53, 185
      options, 189
   options, 184–191
      default, 188
   problems with, 360–361
   selected computers, 277–281
   transferring, 184
   trial migration, 211–212
   view transfers, 214–215
Users Group, 56
   rights and abilities, 64
utilities
   common questions, 18–19
   NetWare support, 148

V

vector fonts, 112
Virtual Loadable Module (VLM), 34
VLM (Virtual Loadable Module), 34
volumes
   destination, 193
   limiting space, 121

W

WAN, and domain model, 120
Windows 95, 235
   configuring, 237–249
   connecting, 240–242
   create startup disk, 236–237
   getting a client, 5–6
   user profiles, 270
   utilities, 376
   workstations, 122
Windows for Workgroups
   create client, 231–235
   domain resources, 310
   and Gateway Service, 146
   how it works in a domain, 11
   problems, 360
   startup disk, 222
   utilities, 376
   workstations, 122
Windows NT Diagnostics. *See* Diagnostics
Windows NT Network Neighborhood. *See*
   Network Neighborhood
Windows NT Server. *See* NT Server
Windows NT Workstation. *See* NT Workstation
WINMSD.EXE, 288
WINS, 381
   problems, 370–371
Wizards, 4–5
Workgroup Manager, 134
workgroups, 11
   workgroups vs. domain, 20, 43
workstations, 28
   common questions, 19–20
   core protocols, 144
   preparing for migration, 121–123
   problems, 371